AF477283

The Chapters:

Chapter 1: Introduction: Embracing the AI Revolution

Chapter 2: AI and the Future of Education

Chapter 3: AI and the Future of Work

Chapter 4: AI and Its Impact on Education

Chapter 5: AI in the Workforce: Job Displacement and Creation

Chapter 6: AI and Education: Reinventing the Learning Experience

Chapter 7: AI and the Future of Work: Embracing the Shift

Chapter 8: AI in Law Enforcement: Balancing Security and Privacy

Chapter 9: The Environment - AI's Role in Combating Climate Change

Chapter 10: AI and Human Rights: Safeguarding Our Freedoms

Chapter 11: AI and Social Media: Influencing the Digital Conversation

Chapter 12: Preparing for the AI Revolution

Chapter 13: AI and Gaming: The New Frontier

Chapter 14: Education Revolutionized

Chapter 15: A New Era of Gaming and Entertainment

Chapter 16: The Future of AI and Its Impact on Society

Chapter 17: AI and the Evolution of Human-Machine Interaction

Chapter 18: Politics and AI: Shifting Power Dynamics

Chapter 19: AI and Creativity: Art, Music, and Literature

Chapter 20: AI in Sports: Changing the Game

Chapter 21:AI and Transportation: The Road Ahead

Chapter 22 AI and Privacy: The New Frontier

Chapter 23 AI and Security: Safeguarding Our Digital World

Chapter 24 AI and the Future of Finance: Banking, Investing, and Beyond

Chapter 25 AI and Agriculture: Feeding the Future

Chapter 26: AI and Space Exploration: Unlocking the Cosmos

Chapter 27: The Effect of Artificial Intelligence on Business

Chapter 28: The Future of Business

Chapter 29: AI and Spirituality: Can Machines Understand the Divine?

Chapter 30: AI and spirituality

Chapter 31: AI and Human Identity: Redefining Ourselves

Chapter 32 AI and the Media: Fact, Fiction, and the Search for Truth

Chapter 33: AI and the Future of Governance: Reinventing Democracy

Chapter 34: The Impact of AI on Business and Society

Chapter 35: AI and its potential implications for the legal system

Chapter 36: The Impact of AI on Society

Chapter 37: AI and Hardware: The Evolution of Computing

Chapter 38 Cybersecurity: Threats and Solutions

Chapter 39: robotics and their integration with AI

Chapter 40: AI and Retail

Chapter 41: AI and the travel industry

Chapter 42 AI and the Afterlife: Digital Immortality

Chapter 43: AI and Urban Planning: Designing the Cities of Tomorrow

Chapter 44 AI and Wearable Technology: Enhancing the Human Experience

Chapter 45: The integration of AI in our homes

Chapter 46 AI and Food: Crafting the Future of Cuisine

Chapter 47 AI and the Environment: Monitoring and Protecting Our Planet

Chapter 48 AI and Human Rights: Safeguarding Our Freedoms

Chapter 49 AI and Social Media: Influencing the Digital Conversation

Chapter 50 AI and Aging: Enhancing Quality of Life

Chapter 51 AI and Hobbies: Personalizing Our Passions

Chapter 52 AI and Language: Preserving and Revitalizing Cultural Heritage

Chapter 53: Embracing an AI-Driven Future

Chapter 54: Conclusion: Preparing for an AI-Infused World

Authors notes.

This book started as a discussion or to be honest many discussions on a daily basis. People I meet in my work as a professional speaker, mentor and business coach wanted to know more, and the overall question was how will this affect me, my work and our younger generations.

The answer is not one answer, it's many, which is why I wrote this book separated in chapters that address one angle each.
It's not intended that you read it back to back even if you might find it very interesting to do so, instead I believe that most of you will go through the index and choose the areas and topics that interest you. To get a better understanding about how a particular area, profession, or generation might be impacted.

We have seen an explosion in the media the last couple of months with articles about AI. Some focus on the dystopia, end of the world scenario, and some about the technology and the many opinions about it around the world. But we can also read about the amazement of the capabilities, mostly as a grassroot movement where people share how and what they use the different AI solutions for. But most people tend to read the writer's story without looking into it on their own and create their own understanding and opinion, it's a common mistake that I have seen that we humans do, but that is an entirely separate book. In short, we have been told to listen to authorities from the very first day in our life and to not question. In one way the media is considered an authority position, what is written must be true.

The last few years we have seen that that is not always the case and people start to realize that they need to create their own understanding of things based on their own research and opinion rather than being spoon-fed someone else's opinion and research only.

But learning is time and energy consuming, which is why most don't feel they have the time nor energy to do so. This is not strange, as in this particular case it is new tech, and we are used to new tech being complicated and difficult to understand.

The reality is that the concept of artificial intelligence is complicated, and we are just in the very beginning of it all. Compared to when a baby is born and breathes air for the first time. That event is a true amazement, and so is the birth of accessible AI solutions.

Because that is what it is, AI has been around for a while, but it's not been accessible to you in the way we now see with 100+ new AI empowered solutions being launched every day, and in a couple of weeks we will see 1000+ AI empowered solutions being launched per day.

Because we will not be working with one AI, we will be combining AI solutions into our very own virtual assistant that knows about all those 100 or 1000 new tools every day and will combine the use of them in the best way to reach the goal you have pointed out.
Forbes wrote back in 2018, AI is not a technology. It's a goal. Have we reached that goal, not, yet I would say, but we are for sure on a good path.

But AI is not one thing, it's a method, or it's a way of working by training a neural network with data, the “better” quality of the data the better understanding will the AI have.

The book will not step so much into the technology of AI and how it works as I don't want to bore you with that in this early stage, I want to enlighten you and make you create your own informed decision about the opportunities and challenges.

Don't jump to the end just yet, but when you are done, be sure to check out the free giveaway in the end of the book.

Chapter 1: Introduction: Embracing the AI Revolution

Welcome to "AI and Us: A Journey into the Future," a comprehensive exploration of the ever-evolving world of artificial intelligence and its profound impact on every aspect of our lives. As we stand on the precipice of a new era, it is crucial to understand the significance of AI, how it is shaping our world, and what lies ahead.

The rapid advancement of AI technology has led to a revolution that touches all aspects of our lives, from education and healthcare to politics and entertainment. This book aims to provide an accessible and engaging overview of AI's current state and its potential effects on our future. We will delve into various facets of AI, exploring the opportunities and challenges it presents, while also considering the ethical and societal implications that arise from its widespread adoption.

Throughout this journey, we will examine the ways in which AI is transforming industries and reshaping our everyday experiences. We will take a closer look at how AI might impact our jobs, relationships, and even our understanding of what it means to be human. By offering insights into the potential consequences of AI's ever-growing presence in our lives, this book aims to empower you with the knowledge necessary to navigate and embrace the AI-driven world that lies ahead.

As we embark on this exploration, we invite you to engage with the thought-provoking ideas and intriguing possibilities presented within these pages. Together, let us uncover the potential of AI and its role in shaping our collective future.

Artificial intelligence has come a long way since its inception. To appreciate the magnitude of its impact on our lives, let's take a brief look at the history of AI and the key milestones that have shaped its development:

1. 1950s: The term "Artificial Intelligence" was coined by John McCarthy, an American computer scientist, and the field of AI research was officially born. During this period, early AI pioneers like McCarthy, Marvin Minsky, and Alan Turing laid the groundwork for AI research and development.
2. 1960s-1970s: Early AI systems were created, including the General Problem Solver, which aimed to solve a wide range of problems using symbolic reasoning, and SHRDLU, a natural language understanding system.
3. 1980s: The rise of expert systems, which were designed to mimic human decision-making in specific domains, such as medical diagnosis or financial planning.

4. 1990s: The development of machine learning, a subfield of AI that focuses on creating algorithms capable of learning from data. This period saw the emergence of significant advances in areas such as neural networks, reinforcement learning, and genetic algorithms.
5. 2000s: The rise of big data and the increased availability of computing power led to significant advancements in machine learning techniques, particularly in the area of deep learning.
6. 2010s: AI began to make its way into mainstream applications, with companies like Google, Amazon, and Facebook investing heavily in AI research and development. During this period, AI technologies such as image recognition, natural language processing, and speech recognition improved dramatically, leading to widespread adoption in various industries.

This rapid progression of AI technology has created a global landscape where AI is no longer confined to research labs and academic institutions but is now an integral part of our daily lives. From virtual assistants like Siri and Alexa to the algorithms that power search engines and social media platforms, AI's presence is pervasive and continually expanding.

As we delve deeper into the world of AI, it is essential to understand the various types of AI that exist today. While there are numerous ways to categorize AI systems, one common approach is to classify them based on their capabilities:

1. Narrow AI (also known as Weak AI): These AI systems are designed to perform specific tasks, such as image recognition, language translation, or playing a game like chess. Narrow AI systems excel in their designated tasks but are limited in their ability to handle tasks outside of their expertise.
2. General AI (also known as Strong AI): This type of AI refers to hypothetical systems that possess the cognitive abilities of a human being, enabling them to learn, reason, and adapt to a wide range of tasks. General AI has yet to be achieved and remains a topic of ongoing research and debate among AI experts.
3. Superintelligent AI: This is an AI system that surpasses human intelligence in virtually every domain. While superintelligent AI is still a theoretical concept, its potential emergence raises numerous ethical and existential questions about the future relationship between humans and machines.

As we examine the impact of AI on various aspects of our lives, it is crucial to recognize that the vast majority of AI systems currently in use fall under the category of Narrow AI. However, ongoing research in AI and machine learning continues to push the boundaries of what AI systems are capable of, inching us closer to the possibility of more advanced forms of AI in the future.

As AI continues to evolve and permeate various aspects of our lives, it brings with it a host of ethical and societal implications that warrant careful consideration. Some of the key concerns surrounding the widespread adoption of AI include:

1. Bias and discrimination: AI systems are trained on vast amounts of data, which may contain inherent biases. If these biases are not identified and mitigated, AI algorithms may perpetuate or even exacerbate existing inequalities in areas such as hiring, lending, and law enforcement.
2. Privacy and surveillance: AI-powered facial recognition and data analysis tools have raised concerns about individual privacy and the potential for mass surveillance by governments and corporations.
3. Job displacement: As AI systems become increasingly adept at performing tasks previously reserved for humans, concerns about job displacement and the future of work have become more pressing.
4. AI and warfare: The development of AI-powered weapons and autonomous military systems raises questions about the ethics of AI in warfare and the potential for an AI-driven arms race.
5. AI governance: The rapid advancement of AI technologies has outpaced the development of regulations and oversight mechanisms, creating challenges in ensuring that AI systems are developed and deployed responsibly.

Addressing these ethical and societal concerns will be an integral part of our exploration into the world of AI, as we strive to understand not only the potential benefits of AI adoption but also the challenges and responsibilities it brings with it.

As AI continues to advance and become more integrated into our lives, it is natural to wonder about the broader implications of this technology for the future of humanity. Some of the key questions that arise in this context include:

1. Will AI lead to a fundamental redefinition of what it means to be human? As AI systems become increasingly capable of tasks that were once considered uniquely human, such as creativity and empathy, it may challenge our understanding of what sets us apart from machines.
2. How will AI impact our sense of identity and self-worth? In a world where machines can perform tasks more efficiently and accurately than humans, individuals may struggle to find meaning and purpose in their work and lives.
3. How will AI reshape human relationships and social interactions? As AI systems become more sophisticated and capable of forming relationships with humans, it raises questions about the nature of these interactions and the potential impact on human-to-human relationships.

4. Can we ensure that AI aligns with human values and priorities? As AI systems become more powerful, ensuring that they act in accordance with our values and intentions becomes increasingly important to prevent unintended consequences.

Exploring these questions and grappling with their implications will be a vital part of our journey through the world of AI, as we seek to understand the potential consequences of AI's ever-growing presence in our lives and the broader implications for humanity's future.

The rise of AI has implications not only for individuals and industries but also for the global landscape as a whole. As countries around the world race to harness the power of AI, we must consider the impact of AI on geopolitics, international relations, and global cooperation. Some key areas to explore include:

1. AI and the global economy: As AI technologies continue to transform industries and drive economic growth, they may also contribute to disparities between countries that possess advanced AI capabilities and those that do not.
2. AI and national security: The potential for AI-powered cyber warfare, surveillance, and autonomous weapons has raised concerns about the implications of AI for national security and global stability.
3. AI and global governance: The rapid pace of AI development and adoption has outstripped the ability of existing regulatory frameworks to keep up, raising questions about how best to govern AI on an international level.
4. AI and international collaboration: The development of AI technologies presents opportunities for collaboration among nations, fostering the sharing of knowledge and resources to tackle global challenges.

In the coming chapters, we will delve deeper into these topics, examining the ways in which AI is shaping the global landscape and the potential consequences of its continued growth and adoption.

As AI becomes increasingly integrated into various aspects of our lives, cultivating a basic understanding of AI and its underlying principles is essential for individuals, regardless of their background or expertise. AI literacy and education will play a crucial role in preparing us for the future, as we navigate the challenges and opportunities presented by AI. Some key points to consider include:

1. Demystifying AI: Dispelling common misconceptions and providing accurate information about AI is necessary to foster informed public discourse and facilitate responsible decision-making.
2. Encouraging interdisciplinary learning: Developing a well-rounded understanding of AI requires knowledge from various disciplines, such as computer science, mathematics, ethics, and social sciences.
3. Cultivating critical thinking and problem-solving skills: As AI systems increasingly take over routine tasks, individuals will need to develop higher-order thinking skills to adapt and thrive in an AI-driven world.
4. Lifelong learning and adaptability: Given the rapidly evolving nature of AI, individuals must commit to continuous learning and adaptability to stay current and competitive in the job market.

In this book, we aim to contribute to the goal of promoting AI literacy and education by providing an accessible and engaging overview of AI, its potential impacts, and the challenges and opportunities it presents.

Conclusion:

As we stand on the threshold of a new era defined by the rapid advancement and widespread adoption of artificial intelligence, it is imperative that we understand the implications of this powerful technology for our lives, our societies, and our future. In this book, we will embark on a journey to explore the fascinating world of AI and its potential effects on various aspects of our existence, from education and jobs to relationships and what it means to be human.

We will delve into the opportunities and challenges that AI presents, examining its transformative impact on industries and our daily experiences. By engaging with thought-provoking ideas and intriguing possibilities, we aim to empower you with the knowledge necessary to navigate and embrace the AI-driven world that lies ahead.

As we set out on this exploration, we invite you to join us in contemplating the potential of AI and its role in shaping our collective future. Together, let us uncover the myriad ways in which AI will continue to redefine our lives and the world around us.

In this introductory chapter, we have laid the groundwork for our exploration of the world of artificial intelligence and its far-reaching implications. We've touched upon the history and evolution of AI, the ethical and societal challenges it presents, and the importance of AI literacy and education in preparing for the future.

Summary of what you should remember from this chapter:

1. AI has evolved rapidly since its inception in the 1950s, and its impact on our lives is growing exponentially.
2. AI systems can be categorized based on their capabilities, with most current AI systems falling under the category of Narrow AI.
3. AI brings numerous ethical and societal implications, such as bias, privacy concerns, job displacement, and its role in warfare.
4. The future of humanity and the global landscape will be significantly influenced by the continued development and adoption of AI.
5. AI literacy and education are crucial in helping individuals adapt and thrive in an AI-driven world.

Suggestions that will be of interest for you to consider based on this chapter topic:

1. Learn more about the history of AI and its key milestones to gain a deeper appreciation of its development.
2. Explore real-world examples of AI applications and consider their potential implications in your own life.
3. Engage in discussions about the ethical and societal implications of AI, and consider ways in which these challenges can be addressed.
4. Reflect on the potential impact of AI on your own career and personal life, and consider the skills and knowledge you may need to adapt to an AI-driven future.

As we proceed through the subsequent chapters, we will delve deeper into the various aspects of AI's impact on our world, providing you with a comprehensive and engaging exploration of this fascinating technology and its transformative potential.

Chapter 2: AI and the Future of Education

Education has always been a cornerstone of human progress, enabling individuals to develop the knowledge and skills necessary to adapt and thrive in an ever-changing world. As AI continues to advance and permeate various aspects of our lives, it is also poised to transform the educational landscape in ways that were once unimaginable. We will explore the potential impact of AI on the future of education, examining how it may reshape teaching and learning processes, the roles of educators and students, and the overall structure of educational systems.

From personalized learning and adaptive teaching methods to the use of AI-driven analytics and virtual learning environments, we will uncover the myriad ways in which AI is poised to revolutionize education, creating new opportunities for students and educators alike. We will also address the challenges and ethical considerations that accompany the integration of AI into the educational sphere, ensuring that we approach this transformation with a balanced and responsible perspective.

Personalized Learning and Adaptive Teaching

One of the most significant ways in which AI has the potential to transform education is through the development of personalized learning and adaptive teaching methods. Traditional educational systems often rely on a one-size-fits-all approach, which may not cater to the unique needs, abilities, and learning styles of individual students. AI-driven technologies can help address this issue by enabling the creation of tailored learning experiences that adapt to each student's strengths, weaknesses, and interests.

Some key aspects of personalized learning and adaptive teaching that AI can facilitate include:

1. Customized learning paths: AI algorithms can analyze students' performance data to identify their areas of strength and weakness, allowing for the creation of customized learning paths that target their specific needs.
2. Real-time feedback and assessment: AI-driven systems can provide students with instant feedback on their work, enabling them to learn from their mistakes and adjust their learning strategies accordingly.
3. Adaptive learning materials: AI can help create learning materials that adapt to each student's level of understanding, ensuring that they are appropriately challenged and engaged throughout the learning process.

4. Learning analytics: AI-driven analytics can help educators gain insights into students' learning patterns, enabling them to identify potential issues and intervene proactively to support students' learning.

These AI-driven personalized learning and adaptive teaching methods have the potential to revolutionize education by providing students with a more individualized, engaging, and effective learning experience.

AI-Driven Analytics and Data-Driven Decision Making

The power of AI-driven analytics can extend beyond personalized learning and adaptive teaching, offering valuable insights that can inform decision-making processes at various levels of the educational system. By leveraging the massive amounts of data generated through students' interactions with learning materials, educators, and peers, AI algorithms can provide actionable insights that help shape education policy, curriculum development, and resource allocation.

Some key benefits of AI-driven analytics and data-driven decision making in education include:

1. Identifying trends and patterns: AI algorithms can analyze vast amounts of data to uncover trends and patterns in students' learning, helping educators and policymakers make informed decisions about curriculum design, teaching methods, and resource allocation.
2. Early intervention and support: AI-driven analytics can help identify students who may be at risk of falling behind or disengaging from their studies, enabling educators to provide targeted support and intervention to help them stay on track.
3. Evaluating the effectiveness of educational initiatives: By analyzing data on student outcomes and performance, AI can help determine the effectiveness of various educational initiatives, guiding decisions about which programs and interventions should be continued or expanded.
4. Resource optimization: AI algorithms can help identify areas where resources are being underutilized or where additional resources may be needed, allowing educational institutions to allocate resources more efficiently and effectively.

By harnessing the power of AI-driven analytics, educators and policymakers can make data-driven decisions that contribute to the improvement of educational systems and the overall learning experience for students.

Virtual Learning Environments and Online Education

The advent of the internet has already significantly expanded access to education, and AI has the potential to further revolutionize online learning and virtual learning environments. By combining AI technologies with online education platforms, we can create immersive, interactive, and personalized learning experiences that cater to a diverse range of students.

Some notable applications of AI in virtual learning environments and online education include:

1. Intelligent tutoring systems: AI-driven tutoring systems can provide personalized instruction and support to students, simulating the one-on-one interaction they would receive from a human tutor.
2. Virtual reality and immersive learning: AI can be integrated with virtual reality (VR) and augmented reality (AR) technologies to create immersive learning experiences, allowing students to explore and engage with educational content in new and exciting ways.
3. Language learning and translation tools: AI-powered language learning and translation tools can help bridge language barriers and facilitate communication between students and educators from different linguistic backgrounds.
4. Online collaboration and peer-to-peer learning: AI algorithms can help facilitate collaboration and peer-to-peer learning among students in online environments, fostering the development of critical thinking and problem-solving skills.

By leveraging AI in virtual learning environments and online education, we can make education more accessible, engaging, and effective for students around the world, regardless of their geographical location, socioeconomic background, or learning needs.

The Changing Roles of Educators and Students

As AI technologies continue to reshape the educational landscape, the roles of educators and students will also need to evolve to keep pace with these changes. The integration of AI into the classroom may shift the focus of educators from content delivery to facilitation and mentorship, while students will be encouraged to take a more active role in their learning and develop essential skills for an AI-driven world.

Some key changes in the roles of educators and students that may result from the integration of AI in education include:

1. Educators as facilitators and mentors: With AI systems handling some aspects of content delivery and assessment, educators can focus more on providing individualized support, mentorship, and guidance to students.
2. Emphasis on soft skills and critical thinking: As AI takes over routine tasks, educators will need to place greater emphasis on teaching soft skills such as creativity, empathy, and collaboration, as well as fostering critical thinking and problem-solving abilities.
3. Lifelong learning for educators: In order to stay relevant and effective in an AI-driven educational landscape, educators must commit to continuous learning and professional development to keep up with advances in AI technologies and pedagogical approaches.
4. Active learning and student empowerment: AI-driven personalized learning experiences can help promote active learning and empower students to take greater ownership of their educational journey.

The evolving roles of educators and students in an AI-driven educational landscape will require a shift in mindset and the development of new skills and competencies, ensuring that both teachers and learners are prepared to thrive in the rapidly changing world of AI.

Challenges and Ethical Considerations

While AI has the potential to significantly enhance and transform education, it also presents a range of challenges and ethical considerations that must be addressed to ensure its responsible and equitable integration into the educational sphere. Some of these challenges and ethical considerations include:

1. Data privacy and security: The extensive use of student data in AI-driven education systems raises concerns about data privacy and security. Safeguarding students' personal information and ensuring compliance with data protection regulations is essential to maintain trust and protect students' rights.
2. Algorithmic bias and fairness: AI algorithms can inadvertently perpetuate existing biases and inequalities if they are trained on biased data or designed without careful consideration of fairness. Ensuring that AI-driven educational tools are equitable and unbiased is crucial for promoting inclusivity and fairness in education.
3. Access and the digital divide: The widespread adoption of AI in education may exacerbate existing digital divides if access to AI-driven educational resources is not equitable. Ensuring that all students have access to the benefits of AI in education is essential to prevent further widening of educational disparities.
4. Teacher-student relationship: The integration of AI in education may impact the teacher-student relationship, with potential consequences for students' social and emotional development. Maintaining meaningful human connections in the classroom is vital for the holistic development of students.

Addressing these challenges and ethical considerations is crucial to ensure that the benefits of AI in education are realized responsibly, equitably, and for the betterment of all students.

Conclusion:

Throughout this chapter, we have explored the myriad ways in which artificial intelligence has the potential to revolutionize education. From personalized learning and adaptive teaching methods to the use of AI-driven analytics and virtual learning environments, AI offers a wealth of opportunities to reshape the educational landscape and create more effective, engaging, and inclusive learning experiences for students.

At the same time, we have also addressed the challenges and ethical considerations that accompany the integration of AI into education, emphasizing the importance of approaching this transformation with a balanced and responsible perspective. By doing so, we can harness the power of AI to create a brighter future for education, ensuring that all students have the opportunity to thrive in an increasingly AI-driven world.

As we continue our exploration of AI's impact on various aspects of our lives, we will delve into the ways in which this transformative technology is changing the world of work, reshaping industries, and influencing the global job market. In the next chapter, we will examine the implications of AI for the future of work and employment, considering both the opportunities and challenges that AI presents in this context.

Outro:

We have delved into the fascinating world of AI in education, examining its potential to revolutionize teaching and learning processes, and considering its impact on educators, students, and educational systems as a whole. As we move forward into an increasingly AI-driven future, it is essential that we continue to explore, understand, and address the myriad ways in which AI will shape our lives and the world around us.

Summary of what you should remember from this chapter:

1. AI has the potential to transform education through personalized learning, adaptive teaching methods, AI-driven analytics, and virtual learning environments.
2. The integration of AI in education will lead to changes in the roles of educators and students, emphasizing the importance of soft skills, critical thinking, and active learning.
3. Challenges and ethical considerations, such as data privacy, algorithmic bias, access, and the digital divide, must be addressed to ensure responsible and equitable integration of AI in education.

Suggestions that will be of interest for you to consider based on this chapter topic:

1. Explore the potential benefits and limitations of using AI-driven educational tools in your own teaching or learning context.
2. Investigate the ethical implications of AI in education and consider how to address these concerns in your own educational practices.
3. Engage in discussions and professional development opportunities related to AI in education, staying informed about the latest trends, technologies, and research in this rapidly evolving field.

Chapter 3: AI and the Future of Work

Introduction:

As artificial intelligence continues to advance and permeate various aspects of our lives, its impact on the world of work is becoming increasingly evident. From automating routine tasks to reshaping entire industries, AI has the potential to transform the way we work, the jobs we do, and the skills we need to succeed in the labor market. We will explore the implications of AI for the future of work and employment, considering both the opportunities and challenges that this transformative technology presents.

We will delve into the following topics:

1. Automation and its impact on jobs and industries
2. The changing nature of work in an AI-driven world
3. The need for upskilling and reskilling to stay relevant in the labor market
4. The role of AI in human resources and talent management
5. The ethical considerations and potential inequalities arising from AI in the workplace

By examining these aspects of AI and the future of work, we aim to provide a comprehensive overview of the ways in which this groundbreaking technology is shaping our professional lives and the global economy, as well as the steps we must take to adapt and thrive in this rapidly changing landscape.

Automation and its Impact on Jobs and Industries

One of the most significant and widely discussed implications of AI in the world of work is the potential for automation to replace or displace human labor across a wide range of industries. As AI systems become increasingly capable of performing complex tasks with greater speed, accuracy, and efficiency, the potential for job displacement and the transformation of entire industries has become a pressing concern.

The impact of automation on jobs and industries can be broadly categorized as follows:

1. Job replacement: Some jobs, particularly those involving routine, repetitive tasks, may be entirely replaced by AI and automation technologies. Examples of such jobs include data entry clerks, assembly line workers, and telemarketers.
2. Job displacement: In some cases, AI may not entirely replace a job, but rather displace or change the nature of the work involved. This could involve a shift in the tasks and responsibilities of a job, with some tasks being automated while others still requiring human intervention.
3. Job augmentation: AI can also be used to augment human labor, enhancing productivity and efficiency by automating specific tasks while allowing workers to focus on higher-value tasks that require human skills and expertise.
4. Job creation: The development and implementation of AI technologies may also give rise to new jobs and industries that did not exist before, such as AI engineers, data scientists, and ethical AI consultants.

While the exact impact of AI and automation on jobs and industries remains uncertain, it is clear that these technologies will play a significant role in shaping the future of work. It is essential for individuals, organizations, and governments to adapt to these changes and prepare for the opportunities and challenges that lie ahead.

The Changing Nature of Work in an AI-Driven World

As AI continues to advance and permeate various aspects of the workplace, the nature of work itself is undergoing significant transformation. The integration of AI and automation technologies into the workplace is not only changing the tasks we perform and the skills we need to succeed but also influencing the ways in which we collaborate, communicate, and make decisions. Some of the key changes in the nature of work in an AI-driven world include:

1. Increased emphasis on soft skills: As AI systems become more capable of performing routine and analytical tasks, the demand for soft skills such as creativity, empathy, and critical thinking is likely to increase. Workers will need to develop these skills in order to complement AI technologies and stay relevant in the labor market.
2. Shift towards remote and flexible work: The adoption of AI and other digital technologies has made it easier for employees to work remotely and adopt more flexible working arrangements. This trend is expected to continue as AI further enables distributed and asynchronous collaboration.
3. Focus on lifelong learning and continuous upskilling: In order to stay relevant in an AI-driven labor market, workers will need to embrace lifelong learning and continuously develop new skills and competencies. This may involve a greater emphasis on reskilling and upskilling initiatives, both within organizations and in broader society.

4. Greater collaboration between humans and machines: As AI systems become more integrated into the workplace, workers will increasingly collaborate with AI technologies to perform tasks, make decisions, and solve problems. This will require a shift in mindset and the development of new skills and competencies to work effectively alongside AI.

By understanding and adapting to these changes in the nature of work, individuals and organizations can ensure that they are well-positioned to thrive in an increasingly AI-driven world.

The Need for Upskilling and Reskilling to Stay Relevant in the Labor Market

As the integration of AI into the workplace continues to accelerate, it is becoming increasingly important for workers to develop new skills and competencies to stay relevant in the labor market. Upskilling and reskilling initiatives are essential for preparing individuals for the changing nature of work and ensuring that they are equipped to succeed in an AI-driven world.

Some key aspects of upskilling and reskilling in the context of AI and the future of work include:

1. Identifying in-demand skills: As AI reshapes industries and job roles, it is crucial to identify the skills that will be most in-demand in the future labor market. This may include a combination of technical skills related to AI and data analysis, as well as soft skills such as creativity, critical thinking, and emotional intelligence.
2. Providing accessible and flexible learning opportunities: Ensuring that individuals have access to a range of learning opportunities is essential for promoting upskilling and reskilling. This may involve offering online courses, micro-credentials, and other flexible learning options that cater to the diverse needs and preferences of learners.
3. Fostering a culture of lifelong learning: Encouraging a mindset of continuous learning and self-improvement is critical for preparing individuals for the rapidly changing world of work. This may involve promoting a growth mindset, providing ongoing feedback and support, and celebrating learning achievements within organizations and broader society.
4. Collaborative efforts between stakeholders: Upskilling and reskilling initiatives require the collaboration of various stakeholders, including employers, educational institutions, and governments. By working together to develop and implement effective upskilling and reskilling strategies, these stakeholders can ensure that individuals are prepared for the future of work.

Through effective upskilling and reskilling initiatives, individuals can develop the skills and competencies needed to thrive in an AI-driven labor market, ensuring that they are well-equipped to navigate the opportunities and challenges that lie ahead.

The Role of AI in Human Resources and Talent Management

As AI continues to influence various aspects of the workplace, its impact on human resources and talent management is becoming increasingly apparent. The integration of AI technologies into HR processes and systems offers a range of opportunities for enhancing efficiency, personalization, and decision-making, as well as addressing some of the challenges associated with traditional HR practices.

Some of the key ways in which AI is transforming human resources and talent management include:

1. Recruitment and candidate screening: AI-powered tools can streamline the recruitment process by automating tasks such as candidate sourcing, resume screening, and interview scheduling. These tools can also help to reduce unconscious bias and improve diversity by using data-driven algorithms to identify candidates based on objective criteria, rather than subjective factors.
2. Talent analytics and workforce planning: AI-driven analytics can provide HR professionals with valuable insights into workforce trends and patterns, enabling more informed decision-making in areas such as workforce planning, skills development, and employee retention. These insights can help organizations to optimize their talent strategies and ensure that they are well-equipped to meet future challenges and opportunities.
3. Personalized learning and development: AI-driven learning platforms can support personalized learning and development by adapting content and recommendations based on individual employees' needs, preferences, and performance data. This can lead to more effective and engaging learning experiences, as well as improved skill development and retention.
4. Employee engagement and well-being: AI-powered tools can also play a role in enhancing employee engagement and well-being by providing insights into factors that contribute to employee satisfaction, productivity, and mental health. This can help HR professionals to identify areas for improvement and implement targeted interventions to support employee well-being and performance.

By harnessing the power of AI in human resources and talent management, organizations can enhance their ability to attract, develop, and retain the talent needed to succeed in an increasingly AI-driven world.

Ethical Considerations and Potential Inequalities Arising from AI in the Workplace

As AI continues to transform the world of work, it is essential to address the ethical considerations and potential inequalities that may arise from the integration of these technologies into the workplace. By understanding and addressing these issues, we can ensure that AI is harnessed in a responsible and equitable manner that benefits all members of society.

Some of the key ethical considerations and potential inequalities related to AI in the workplace include:

1. Bias and discrimination: AI systems can inadvertently perpetuate and exacerbate existing biases and inequalities, particularly if they are trained on biased data or designed with biased assumptions. This can lead to unfair and discriminatory outcomes in areas such as recruitment, performance evaluation, and promotion decisions.
2. Privacy and surveillance: The use of AI and data-driven technologies in the workplace can raise concerns about employee privacy and surveillance, particularly if these technologies are used to monitor employee behavior, communications, and performance in invasive or intrusive ways.
3. Job displacement and inequality: The potential for AI to displace jobs and create new forms of inequality is a significant concern, particularly if certain groups or communities are disproportionately affected by job displacement or lack access to the skills and resources needed to adapt to the changing labor market.
4. Power dynamics and worker autonomy: The integration of AI into the workplace can also raise concerns about power dynamics and worker autonomy, particularly if AI-driven decision-making systems are used to replace or undermine human judgment and agency in ways that disempower workers and concentrate decision-making power in the hands of a few.

By acknowledging and addressing these ethical considerations and potential inequalities, we can work towards a more responsible and equitable integration of AI into the workplace, ensuring that the benefits of these technologies are shared broadly and that their potential harms are minimized.

Conclusion:

Artificial intelligence is undoubtedly transforming the world of work in profound ways, presenting both opportunities and challenges for individuals, organizations, and society as a whole. As we continue to integrate AI and automation technologies into the workplace, it is crucial to consider the various implications of these changes, including job displacement, the shifting nature of work, upskilling and reskilling needs, and ethical considerations.

By understanding and addressing these issues, we can work towards a future where AI is harnessed responsibly and equitably to enhance human potential, promote economic growth, and improve the overall quality of work and life. This will require collaboration between various stakeholders, including individuals, employers, educational institutions, and governments, to develop and implement effective strategies for adapting to the rapidly changing world of work.

In conclusion, the future of work in an AI-driven world is uncertain, but by acknowledging the challenges, embracing opportunities, and taking proactive steps to address the issues that arise, we can navigate this transformative era and build a brighter future for all.

Outro:

As we conclude our exploration of AI and its impact on the future of work, it is essential to remember that the choices we make today will shape the world we live in tomorrow. By proactively addressing the challenges and embracing the opportunities that AI presents, we can work together to build a more inclusive, equitable, and prosperous future for everyone.

In the upcoming chapters, we will continue to delve into various aspects of AI and its influence on different areas of life, such as education, healthcare, transportation, and more. Keep reading to gain a deeper understanding of the far-reaching implications of artificial intelligence and how it will continue to shape our world in the years to come.

Summary of what you should remember from this chapter:

1. AI is transforming the world of work, creating both opportunities and challenges in areas such as job displacement, skill development, and the changing nature of work.
2. The integration of AI into the workplace can lead to job displacement, but it can also create new job opportunities, particularly in areas related to AI, data analysis, and soft skills.
3. The nature of work is changing, with a greater emphasis on soft skills, remote work, lifelong learning, and collaboration between humans and machines.
4. Upskilling and reskilling initiatives are essential for preparing individuals for the changing labor market and ensuring they remain relevant in an AI-driven world.
5. AI is transforming human resources and talent management, with applications in recruitment, talent analytics, personalized learning, and employee engagement.

6. Ethical considerations and potential inequalities related to AI in the workplace include bias, discrimination, privacy concerns, job displacement, and power dynamics.
7. Addressing the challenges and embracing the opportunities presented by AI in the workplace will require collaboration between stakeholders, including individuals, employers, educational institutions, and governments.

Suggestions that will be of interest for you to consider based on this chapter topic:

1. Assess your own skill set and identify areas where you may need to develop new skills or enhance existing ones in order to remain relevant in an AI-driven labor market.
2. Explore opportunities for lifelong learning and upskilling, such as online courses, certifications, and workshops, to prepare yourself for the changing world of work.
3. Stay informed about the latest developments in AI and their impact on the workplace, and consider how these trends might affect your industry and career path.
4. Encourage a culture of continuous learning and innovation within your organization, and advocate for responsible and ethical use of AI in the workplace.
5. If you are an employer or HR professional, explore ways to integrate AI technologies into your talent management processes in order to enhance efficiency, personalization, and decision-making.

Chapter 4: AI and Its Impact on Education

Introduction:

Education is an essential pillar of society, shaping future generations and providing the skills and knowledge needed for individuals to thrive. As AI-driven technologies continue to advance, their impact on education is becoming increasingly significant. We will explore the ways AI is transforming education, the challenges and opportunities it presents, and the implications for students, educators, and institutions.

AI in the Classroom: Personalized Learning and Enhanced Teaching

AI-driven technologies have the potential to transform the classroom experience by enabling personalized learning and enhancing teaching methods. Some of the key ways AI is being used in the classroom include:

1. Personalized learning paths: AI algorithms can analyze students' learning patterns, strengths, and weaknesses to develop customized learning paths that cater to individual needs. This enables students to learn at their own pace and focus on areas where they may need additional support.
2. Adaptive assessments: AI-driven assessment tools can adjust the difficulty of questions in real-time based on students' performance, providing a more accurate and personalized measure of their understanding and progress.
3. Intelligent tutoring systems: AI-driven tutoring systems can provide students with instant feedback, hints, and explanations, allowing them to learn from their mistakes and improve their understanding of the subject matter.
4. Enhanced teaching tools: AI-powered tools can help teachers analyze student performance data, identify areas where students may be struggling, and suggest targeted interventions to support student learning.

By leveraging AI-driven technologies in the classroom, educators can provide a more personalized, engaging, and effective learning experience for students, helping them to achieve their full potential.

AI and Educational Administration: Streamlining Processes and Improving Efficiency

AI-driven technologies can also help to streamline administrative processes and improve efficiency within educational institutions. Some of the ways AI is being used in educational administration include:

1. Automating administrative tasks: AI algorithms can be used to automate routine administrative tasks, such as scheduling, attendance tracking, and report generation, freeing up time for educators and administrators to focus on more critical aspects of their work.
2. Predictive analytics: AI-driven predictive analytics tools can help educational institutions identify trends, forecast future outcomes, and make data-driven decisions. For example, predictive analytics can be used to identify students at risk of falling behind or dropping out and enable targeted interventions to support their success.
3. Chatbots and virtual assistants: AI-driven chatbots and virtual assistants can provide students, parents, and staff with instant access to information and support, reducing the burden on administrative staff and improving overall communication within the institution.
4. Resource optimization: AI algorithms can analyze data on student performance, resource utilization, and other factors to optimize resource allocation, ensuring that educational institutions can provide the best possible support for their students while operating within budget constraints.

By leveraging AI-driven technologies in educational administration, institutions can improve efficiency, reduce costs, and make more informed, data-driven decisions that support student success.

AI in Educational Content Creation and Curation

AI-driven technologies are also playing an increasingly important role in the creation and curation of educational content. Some of the ways AI is being used in this area include:

1. Personalized content recommendations: AI algorithms can analyze students' learning preferences, interests, and performance data to recommend relevant and engaging educational content, helping to keep students motivated and on track in their learning journey.
2. Content generation: AI-powered natural language processing and generation technologies can be used to create adaptive, personalized learning materials, such as quizzes, flashcards, and summaries, tailored to individual students' needs and preferences.
3. Automatic content translation and adaptation: AI-driven translation tools can automatically translate and adapt educational content for different languages and cultural contexts, making it more accessible to a diverse range of students.
4. Content curation and organization: AI algorithms can be used to analyze and categorize large volumes of educational content, making it easier for educators and students to find relevant resources and navigate complex learning environments.

By leveraging AI-driven technologies in educational content creation and curation, educators and institutions can provide students with more personalized, engaging, and accessible learning experiences that cater to their unique needs and preferences.

Challenges and Ethical Considerations in AI-driven Education

While AI-driven technologies offer numerous benefits for education, they also present challenges and ethical considerations that must be carefully addressed. Some of the key issues in AI-driven education include:

1. Privacy and data security: The use of AI-driven technologies in education often involves the collection, storage, and analysis of large amounts of student data, raising concerns about privacy and data security. Ensuring that student data is protected and used responsibly is essential to maintaining trust in AI-driven education systems.
2. Equity and access: The adoption of AI-driven technologies in education has the potential to exacerbate existing inequalities if access to these technologies is not equitably distributed. Ensuring that all students, regardless of socioeconomic status or geographic location, have access to AI-driven educational resources is critical to promoting equity and inclusion in education.
3. Bias and fairness: AI algorithms can inadvertently perpetuate or amplify biases present in the data they are trained on, leading to biased outcomes in educational contexts. Ensuring that AI-driven educational tools are designed and deployed in a way that is fair and unbiased is crucial to preventing discrimination and promoting equity in education.
4. The role of human educators: The increasing use of AI-driven technologies in education raises questions about the role of human educators in the learning process. Balancing the benefits of AI-driven tools with the need for human guidance, interaction, and empathy is essential to ensuring that AI-driven education remains student-centered and holistic.

Addressing these challenges and ethical considerations is crucial to ensuring that AI-driven technologies are used responsibly and effectively in education, and that their benefits are realized for all students.

Preparing Students and Educators for an AI-driven Future:

As AI-driven technologies continue to advance and reshape the educational landscape, it is essential for students and educators to be prepared for the changing nature of learning and work. Some key strategies for preparing students and educators for an AI-driven future include:

1. Developing digital literacy and computational thinking skills: Ensuring that students develop the digital literacy and computational thinking skills needed to navigate and succeed in an AI-driven world is crucial. This includes not only technical skills, such as coding and data analysis but also critical thinking, problem-solving, and creativity.
2. Fostering AI awareness and understanding: Educators should be well-versed in the capabilities and limitations of AI-driven technologies and be able to effectively integrate them into their teaching practice. Providing professional development opportunities for educators to learn about AI and its implications for education is essential.
3. Emphasizing human-centric skills: As AI-driven technologies take on more tasks previously performed by humans, the importance of uniquely human skills, such as empathy, collaboration, and communication, will increase. Ensuring that students develop these human-centric skills will be crucial for their success in the future workforce.
4. Encouraging lifelong learning: As the pace of technological change continues to accelerate, the need for lifelong learning and adaptability will become increasingly important. Fostering a growth mindset and encouraging students to embrace continuous learning will help them to thrive in an AI-driven future.

By equipping students and educators with the skills, knowledge, and mindset needed to navigate an AI-driven world, we can ensure that they are prepared to succeed and contribute positively to society in the face of rapid technological change.

Conclusion:

AI-driven technologies are reshaping the world of education in numerous ways, from personalizing learning experiences to streamlining administrative processes and revolutionizing the creation and curation of educational content. As these technologies continue to advance and become more integrated into the educational landscape, they offer the potential to improve access, equity, and quality in education while also presenting challenges and ethical considerations that must be carefully addressed.

Preparing students and educators for an AI-driven future involves fostering digital literacy, computational thinking, and human-centric skills, as well as promoting awareness and understanding of AI technologies and their implications for education. By embracing the opportunities and addressing the challenges presented by AI-driven technologies, we can work towards a future in which all students have access to high-quality, personalized, and engaging educational experiences that empower them to succeed in an increasingly AI-driven world.

Outro:

We have explored the numerous ways in which AI-driven technologies are transforming the world of education, as well as the challenges and ethical considerations that must be addressed in order to ensure that these technologies are used responsibly and effectively. As we continue to navigate the ever-evolving landscape of AI-driven education, it is crucial that we remain focused on the needs of students and educators, working together to create a future in which all learners have the opportunity to thrive.

Summary of what you should remember from this chapter:

- AI-driven technologies are reshaping education by personalizing learning experiences, streamlining administrative processes, and revolutionizing content creation and curation.
- Challenges and ethical considerations in AI-driven education include privacy and data security, equity and access, bias and fairness, and the role of human educators.
- Preparing students and educators for an AI-driven future involves developing digital literacy, computational thinking, and human-centric skills, as well as fostering AI awareness and understanding.
- Embracing the opportunities and addressing the challenges presented by AI-driven technologies can help ensure that all students have access to high-quality, personalized, and engaging educational experiences.

Suggestions that will be of interest for you to consider based on this chapter topic:

- Research and explore various AI-driven educational tools and platforms that can be used in your classroom or learning environment.
- Participate in professional development opportunities related to AI and education to stay informed about the latest trends and developments in the field.
- Foster open discussions with colleagues, students, and parents about the implications of AI-driven technologies for education and how best to integrate them into your learning environment.

- Reflect on your own teaching practice and consider how AI-driven technologies can be used to enhance student learning, while also preserving the essential human aspects of education.

Chapter 5: AI in the Workforce: Job Displacement and Creation

Introduction:

The rise of artificial intelligence and its integration into various industries has led to a significant shift in the workforce. AI's capabilities to automate tasks, analyze vast amounts of data, and learn from experience have given rise to concerns about job displacement, but at the same time, AI has also created new job opportunities. This chapter will examine the impact of AI on the workforce, exploring both the challenges and opportunities presented by AI-driven technologies in the context of job displacement and creation. We will discuss the industries most affected by AI, the types of jobs most at risk, and the new job opportunities that are emerging as a result of AI-driven innovation. Finally, we will explore strategies for preparing the workforce for an AI-driven future and ensuring that the benefits and opportunities created by AI are equitably distributed across society.

Industries Most Affected by AI

AI-driven technologies have the potential to significantly impact a wide range of industries. Some of the industries most affected by AI include:

1. Manufacturing: AI-powered robots and automation systems are increasingly being used in manufacturing processes, leading to increased efficiency and productivity. Tasks such as assembly, quality control, and packaging can be performed by AI-driven systems, reducing the need for human labor in these areas.
2. Transportation: Autonomous vehicles, from self-driving cars to drones, are revolutionizing the transportation industry. AI-driven systems are being used to optimize routes, manage traffic flow, and improve overall transportation efficiency, leading to a shift in the demand for human drivers and transportation professionals.
3. Retail and customer service: AI-driven technologies such as chatbots, recommendation engines, and computer vision systems are transforming the way businesses interact with customers, streamlining sales processes and improving customer service. This has implications for jobs in retail and customer service, as AI-driven systems take on tasks traditionally performed by human workers.
4. Finance and insurance: AI-powered algorithms are being used to analyze financial data, detect fraud, and make investment decisions. This has implications for jobs in finance and insurance, as AI-driven systems take on tasks such as financial analysis, underwriting, and claims processing.
5. Healthcare: AI-driven systems are being used to analyze medical data, assist in diagnosis, and develop personalized treatment plans. This has implications for jobs in healthcare, as

AI-driven technologies augment the capabilities of healthcare professionals and shift the demand for certain roles.

While these industries are most affected by AI, it is important to note that the impact of AI-driven technologies is not limited to these sectors. AI has the potential to impact a wide range of industries, and its effects will likely be felt across the entire workforce.

Types of Jobs Most at Risk

The impact of AI on jobs varies depending on the nature of the tasks involved in a particular occupation. Jobs that involve routine, repetitive tasks or tasks that can be easily codified are more susceptible to automation and displacement by AI-driven technologies. Some types of jobs most at risk include:

1. Low-skilled, manual labor jobs: Jobs that involve routine, manual tasks, such as assembly line workers, warehouse workers, and custodial staff, are more likely to be affected by AI-driven automation.
2. Data entry and administrative jobs: Jobs that involve repetitive tasks such as data entry, filing, and scheduling are more likely to be automated by AI-driven systems, as these tasks can be easily codified and performed by algorithms.
3. Customer service and sales jobs: AI-powered chatbots and recommendation engines are increasingly being used to handle customer inquiries and sales processes, reducing the need for human customer service and sales representatives.
4. Transportation jobs: With the rise of autonomous vehicles, jobs that involve driving, such as truck drivers, taxi drivers, and delivery drivers, may be at risk of displacement by AI-driven systems.
5. Jobs in finance and insurance: As AI-powered algorithms take on tasks such as financial analysis, underwriting, and claims processing, jobs in finance and insurance may be at risk.

It is important to note that while these types of jobs are most at risk, AI-driven technologies are also creating new job opportunities and transforming the nature of work across a wide range of industries. In many cases, AI-driven systems are augmenting human capabilities rather than replacing them entirely, leading to a shift in the demand for certain skills and roles rather than outright job displacement.

New Job Opportunities Created by AI

While AI-driven technologies have the potential to displace certain jobs, they are also creating new job opportunities in various industries. Some of these new job opportunities include:

1. AI and machine learning specialists: As AI-driven technologies become more prevalent, there is an increased demand for specialists in AI and machine learning to develop, implement, and maintain these systems.
2. Data scientists and analysts: The rise of AI-driven systems has led to an explosion in the amount of data generated and collected, creating a need for skilled data scientists and analysts to process, analyze, and make sense of this data.
3. Human-AI interaction designers: As AI-driven systems become more integrated into our daily lives, there is a need for designers who specialize in creating seamless and intuitive interactions between humans and AI-driven technologies.
4. AI ethicists and policy experts: As AI-driven technologies raise new ethical, legal, and social challenges, there is a growing need for experts who can navigate these complex issues and develop policies and guidelines to ensure the responsible use of AI.
5. Jobs in AI-driven industries: AI-driven technologies are also creating new job opportunities within the industries they are transforming. For example, the rise of autonomous vehicles has led to the development of new roles in vehicle design, software development, and infrastructure planning.

It is important for individuals, businesses, and governments to recognize and prepare for the new job opportunities created by AI-driven technologies. This involves fostering a workforce that is adaptable and equipped with the skills needed to thrive in an AI-driven future.

Preparing the Workforce for an AI-Driven Future

In order to thrive in an AI-driven future, it is essential to prepare the workforce for the changes and opportunities that AI-driven technologies will bring. This involves several key strategies, including:

1. Lifelong learning and upskilling: Encouraging and supporting continuous learning and skill development is crucial for adapting to the changing job landscape. This includes investing in education and training programs that focus on the skills needed for the jobs of the future, such as data analysis, coding, and AI-related skills.
2. Fostering adaptability and resilience: Cultivating a mindset of adaptability and resilience will help individuals navigate the changes brought about by AI-driven technologies. This involves

embracing change, learning from setbacks, and being open to new opportunities and challenges.

3. Emphasizing soft skills and human-centric abilities: While technical skills are important, soft skills such as critical thinking, problem-solving, communication, and creativity will continue to be valuable in an AI-driven world. These human-centric abilities can help differentiate humans from AI-driven systems and ensure that humans remain indispensable in the workforce.
4. Developing targeted policies and support systems: Governments and organizations can play a crucial role in preparing the workforce for an AI-driven future by developing targeted policies and support systems. This includes investing in education and training programs, creating job transition support systems, and fostering a culture of innovation and entrepreneurship.
5. Encouraging collaboration between humans and AI-driven systems: Emphasizing the complementary nature of humans and AI-driven technologies can help create a more synergistic and productive workforce. This involves recognizing the unique strengths of both humans and AI-driven systems and fostering environments in which they can work together effectively.

By implementing these strategies, individuals, businesses, and governments can ensure that the workforce is well-prepared for the challenges and opportunities presented by AI-driven technologies.

The Role of Businesses in Adapting to AI-Driven Workforce Changes

Businesses play a significant role in shaping the workforce of the future and adapting to the changes brought about by AI-driven technologies. In order to successfully navigate these changes, businesses should consider the following strategies:

1. Embracing AI-driven technologies: Businesses should actively explore and adopt AI-driven technologies that can enhance their operations, improve efficiency, and drive innovation. This includes evaluating existing processes and identifying areas where AI-driven systems can be integrated effectively.
2. Investing in employee development: Businesses should invest in the ongoing development of their employees, focusing on upskilling and reskilling initiatives that align with the needs of an AI-driven future. This includes offering training programs in AI-related skills, data analysis, and other relevant areas.
3. Fostering a culture of innovation and adaptability: In order to stay competitive in an AI-driven world, businesses should cultivate a culture that embraces change, encourages innovation, and promotes adaptability. This includes providing employees with the resources and support needed to experiment with new ideas and technologies.

4. Collaborating with educational institutions and government agencies: Businesses can work together with educational institutions and government agencies to develop targeted training programs, share resources, and exchange knowledge about the latest AI-driven technologies and their impact on the workforce.
5. Prioritizing ethical considerations and social responsibility: As businesses adopt AI-driven technologies, they should also prioritize ethical considerations and ensure that their use of these technologies aligns with their corporate social responsibility goals. This includes considering the potential impact of AI-driven systems on job displacement and ensuring that ethical guidelines are in place to guide their development and deployment.

By taking a proactive approach and implementing these strategies, businesses can better prepare for the workforce changes brought about by AI-driven technologies and create a more resilient and adaptable organization.

Government Policies and Support for Workforce Transition

As AI-driven technologies continue to reshape the workforce, governments play a vital role in facilitating a smooth transition for workers and businesses. Some key policies and support measures that governments can implement include:

1. Investing in education and training: Governments should prioritize investments in education and training programs that focus on the skills required for the jobs of the future. This includes providing funding for AI-related courses, data science programs, and other fields that are relevant in an AI-driven world.
2. Establishing job transition support systems: To help workers displaced by AI-driven technologies, governments can establish job transition support systems that provide resources such as retraining programs, financial assistance, and job placement services. These systems can help individuals transition to new job opportunities more seamlessly.
3. Encouraging collaboration between businesses, educational institutions, and government agencies: Governments can play a pivotal role in fostering collaboration between businesses, educational institutions, and government agencies to develop targeted training programs, share resources, and exchange knowledge about AI-driven technologies and their impact on the workforce.
4. Incentivizing businesses to invest in employee development: Governments can offer tax incentives and other financial benefits to businesses that invest in employee development, particularly in areas related to AI, data science, and other emerging technologies.
5. Implementing forward-looking regulations and guidelines: Governments should develop and implement regulations and guidelines that promote the responsible use of AI-driven technologies and protect the rights and interests of workers. This includes addressing issues related to data privacy, algorithmic bias, and ethical considerations in AI development.

By implementing these policies and support measures, governments can help to ensure that the workforce is better prepared for the changes brought about by AI-driven technologies and facilitate a smoother transition for workers and businesses.

Conclusion:

The widespread adoption of AI-driven technologies has the potential to significantly reshape the workforce, with both job displacement and creation occurring across various industries. While some jobs may become obsolete, new opportunities will also arise, driven by the unique capabilities and efficiencies that AI-driven systems can offer.

It is essential for individuals, businesses, and governments to proactively prepare for these changes in order to successfully navigate the workforce transition. This includes investing in education and training programs, fostering adaptability and resilience, emphasizing soft skills and human-centric abilities, and developing targeted policies and support systems.

By working together and implementing these strategies, we can ensure that the workforce is well-prepared for the challenges and opportunities presented by AI-driven technologies, and that we can continue to thrive in an increasingly AI-driven world.

Outro:

We have explored the potential impact of AI-driven technologies on the workforce, discussing both the risks and opportunities that these technologies present. We have also examined the importance of preparing the workforce for an AI-driven future and discussed strategies for individuals, businesses, and governments to implement in order to successfully navigate the transition.

As we move forward, it is essential to continue to monitor and assess the impact of AI-driven technologies on the workforce and to adapt our strategies and policies accordingly. By doing so, we can ensure that we are well-equipped to face the challenges and opportunities that lie ahead and can create a future in which humans and AI-driven systems work together in harmony.

Summary of what you should remember from this chapter:

1. AI-driven technologies have the potential to both displace and create jobs across various industries. While some jobs may become obsolete, new opportunities will also arise.
2. Soft skills and human-centric abilities, such as creativity, empathy, and critical thinking, will become increasingly important as AI-driven technologies are integrated into the workforce.
3. Individuals should focus on developing transferable skills, embracing lifelong learning, and fostering adaptability and resilience to prepare for the AI-driven future.
4. Businesses should invest in employee development, adopt AI-driven technologies, and foster a culture of innovation and adaptability to stay competitive.
5. Governments play a crucial role in facilitating a smooth workforce transition by investing in education, implementing job transition support systems, and developing forward-looking regulations and guidelines.
6. Collaboration between individuals, businesses, educational institutions, and governments is essential to successfully navigate the workforce changes brought about by AI-driven technologies.

Suggestions that will be of interest for you to consider based on this chapter topic:

1. Keep up-to-date with the latest developments in AI-driven technologies and their impact on the workforce. Staying informed will help you better understand the evolving job market and identify new opportunities.
2. Take advantage of online resources and courses to develop your skills in AI-related fields, data science, and other relevant areas. Many universities and organizations offer free or low-cost resources to help you learn and grow.
3. Network with professionals in your industry and attend conferences or events related to AI and workforce development. These opportunities can help you gain insights into the latest trends and connect with others who share your interests.
4. If you are an employer, consider conducting regular assessments of your organization's AI readiness and workforce needs. This can help you identify gaps in skills and knowledge and develop targeted training programs to address them.
5. Engage in conversations with policymakers and community leaders about the impact of AI on the workforce and the importance of implementing policies and support systems to facilitate a smooth transition. Your input and perspective can help shape the future of work in an AI-driven world.

Chapter 6: AI and Education: Reinventing the Learning Experience

Introduction:

The integration of artificial intelligence into the education sector has the potential to revolutionize how we approach teaching and learning. AI-driven technologies can provide personalized learning experiences, improve access to educational resources, and transform the way we assess student progress. We will delve into the ways AI is changing the educational landscape and explore the benefits and challenges that these changes present. We will also discuss strategies for educators, students, and policymakers to harness the power of AI in education and ensure that it serves as a tool for positive change.

Personalized Learning Experiences

One of the most promising aspects of AI in education is its ability to provide personalized learning experiences for students. By leveraging AI algorithms and analyzing large amounts of data, educational software can adapt to the unique needs and learning styles of individual students. This personalization can take various forms, including:

1. Adaptive learning pathways: AI-driven educational software can analyze a student's performance, learning preferences, and other factors to create customized learning pathways. These pathways can adjust the difficulty level, pace, and content presentation to optimize the learning experience for each student.
2. Intelligent tutoring systems: These AI-driven systems can simulate the experience of one-on-one tutoring by providing personalized feedback, hints, and explanations based on the student's performance and understanding of the material.
3. Recommendations for additional resources: AI algorithms can analyze a student's performance and learning preferences to recommend additional resources, such as videos, articles, or exercises, that can help reinforce the learning process.

By providing personalized learning experiences, AI-driven technologies have the potential to improve student engagement, motivation, and overall learning outcomes.

Improving Access to Educational Resources

Another significant advantage of AI in education is its ability to improve access to high-quality educational resources for students around the world. This is particularly important for students in underprivileged or remote areas, who may not have access to the same level of resources as their peers in more affluent areas. AI-driven technologies can help bridge this gap in various ways:

1. Online learning platforms: AI-powered online learning platforms can provide access to a wide range of courses and educational materials, making high-quality education more accessible to students, regardless of their geographical location.
2. Language translation: AI-driven language translation tools can help break down language barriers and make educational content more accessible to students who speak different languages. These tools can automatically translate course materials, textbooks, and other resources into various languages, helping students around the world access valuable educational content.
3. Virtual classrooms: AI-driven virtual classrooms can connect students with teachers, tutors, and peers from around the world, fostering collaboration and enabling access to educational opportunities that may not be available in their local communities.

By leveraging AI technologies, we can work towards creating a more inclusive and equitable educational landscape, where all students have the opportunity to access high-quality resources and learning experiences.

Transforming Assessment and Feedback

AI-driven technologies also have the potential to revolutionize the way we assess student progress and provide feedback. Traditional assessment methods, such as standardized tests and written assignments, can be time-consuming for both students and educators and may not always provide a comprehensive view of a student's understanding and skills. AI can help address these challenges in several ways:

1. Automated grading: AI algorithms can be used to grade multiple-choice tests, written assignments, and even more complex tasks, such as programming assignments or essays. This can save educators time and provide students with faster feedback on their work.
2. Continuous assessment: AI-driven educational software can continuously assess student performance and understanding as they engage with the material, allowing for real-time adjustments to the learning experience and providing more detailed feedback on their progress.

3. Formative assessment tools: AI-driven formative assessment tools can provide educators with valuable insights into student understanding and skill development, helping them identify areas where students may need additional support or resources.

By leveraging AI technologies in assessment and feedback, we can create more efficient, personalized, and meaningful learning experiences for students and better support their academic growth and development.

Challenges and Ethical Considerations

While AI-driven technologies offer significant potential benefits for the education sector, they also raise several challenges and ethical considerations that must be addressed:

1. Data privacy and security: The use of AI in education often involves collecting, storing, and analyzing large amounts of student data. Ensuring the privacy and security of this data is critical, as data breaches or misuse can have serious consequences for students and their families.
2. Algorithmic bias: AI algorithms can inadvertently perpetuate or exacerbate existing biases if they are trained on biased data or designed without considering the potential impact on different student populations. This can lead to unfair treatment of certain students or perpetuation of educational inequities.
3. Teacher-student relationship: While AI-driven technologies can enhance the learning experience, they should not be seen as a replacement for human teachers. Maintaining the critical role of teachers in guiding, mentoring, and supporting students is essential for a well-rounded education.
4. Digital divide: The widespread adoption of AI-driven technologies in education can exacerbate the digital divide, leaving students in underprivileged or remote areas without access to the latest tools and resources. Efforts must be made to ensure that AI-driven technologies are accessible and affordable to all students, regardless of their socioeconomic background.

By addressing these challenges and ethical considerations, we can work towards harnessing the power of AI in education while minimizing potential negative impacts.

Strategies for Harnessing the Power of AI in Education

To maximize the benefits of AI-driven technologies in the education sector, several strategies can be employed by educators, students, and policymakers:

1. Collaboration between educators and AI developers: Ensuring that AI-driven technologies are designed with input from educators can help create tools that are more effective, relevant, and beneficial for students and teachers alike.
2. Professional development for educators: Providing training and resources for educators to learn how to effectively incorporate AI-driven technologies into their teaching practices is essential for ensuring that these tools are used to their full potential.
3. Curriculum integration: Integrating AI-driven technologies into the curriculum can help students develop essential skills for the future, such as critical thinking, problem-solving, and digital literacy.
4. Promoting digital equity: Efforts should be made to ensure that all students have access to AI-driven technologies and the internet, regardless of their socioeconomic background or geographic location.
5. Ethical guidelines and regulations: Developing ethical guidelines and regulations for the use of AI in education can help mitigate potential risks, such as data privacy concerns and algorithmic bias.

By implementing these strategies, we can work towards creating an educational landscape that harnesses the power of AI for positive change while addressing potential challenges and ethical considerations.

Conclusion:

The integration of AI into the education sector has the potential to bring about transformative change, enhancing the learning experience and making high-quality education more accessible to students around the world. By leveraging AI-driven technologies, we can create more personalized, efficient, and engaging learning experiences, improve access to educational resources, and revolutionize assessment and feedback.

However, it is essential to be mindful of the challenges and ethical considerations that accompany the widespread adoption of AI in education. By addressing issues such as data privacy, algorithmic bias, and the digital divide, we can harness the power of AI for the betterment of education while minimizing potential negative impacts.

As we move forward, collaboration between educators, students, AI developers, and policymakers will be crucial in ensuring that AI-driven technologies are used effectively and ethically to enhance the educational landscape and empower students to thrive in the rapidly changing world.

Outro:

We have explored the various ways in which AI is transforming the field of education, from personalized learning experiences to innovative assessment methods. We have also discussed the challenges and ethical considerations that must be addressed to ensure the responsible and equitable use of AI-driven technologies in education.

As we progress through the book, we will continue to delve into the impact of AI on various aspects of our lives, examining both the opportunities and the challenges that this powerful technology presents. In the following chapter, we will turn our attention to the world of work, exploring how AI is reshaping the job market and the ways in which we approach our careers. Stay tuned as we embark on this fascinating journey into the future of work in the age of AI.

Summary of what you should remember from this chapter:

1. AI has the potential to revolutionize education by creating more personalized, efficient, and engaging learning experiences.
2. AI-driven technologies can improve access to educational resources, support teacher-student relationships, and transform assessment and feedback.
3. Challenges and ethical considerations, such as data privacy, algorithmic bias, and the digital divide, must be addressed to harness the power of AI in education responsibly and equitably.
4. Collaboration between educators, students, AI developers, and policymakers is essential to maximize the benefits of AI-driven technologies in the education sector.

Suggestions that will be of interest for you to consider based on this chapter topic:

1. Investigate the AI-driven technologies currently being used in your local schools or educational institutions. How are they being implemented, and what are the perceived benefits and challenges?
2. If you are an educator, consider exploring professional development opportunities focused on AI and its applications in education. This will allow you to stay informed about the latest trends and best practices for integrating AI-driven technologies into your teaching.
3. If you are a student or parent, research the AI-driven tools and resources available to supplement traditional learning methods. Experiment with various tools to determine which best suit your individual learning style and educational goals.

4. Engage in conversations with educators, policymakers, and technology developers about the ethical considerations and potential impacts of AI in education. Promote responsible and equitable adoption of AI-driven technologies within your community.
5. Stay informed about the latest developments in AI and education by following relevant news, research, and industry trends. This will enable you to be better prepared for the rapidly changing educational landscape shaped by AI.

Chapter 7: AI and the Future of Work: Embracing the Shift

Introduction:

Artificial intelligence has become a driving force behind the transformation of numerous industries, and the job market is no exception. The rise of AI and automation is changing the way we work, creating new opportunities while rendering some traditional jobs obsolete. As we navigate this transition, it is crucial to understand the impact of AI on the workforce and prepare for the changes that lie ahead.

We will explore the ways in which AI is reshaping the job market and the implications this has for workers, employers, and society as a whole. We will discuss the opportunities and challenges presented by AI-driven technologies in the workplace, the skills that will be in demand as the job market evolves, and strategies for adapting to the future of work in the age of AI.

The Impact of AI on Jobs and Employment

The rise of AI and automation is bringing about significant changes in the job market. These changes can be broadly categorized into three areas: job displacement, job transformation, and job creation.

1. Job displacement: Some jobs, particularly those involving repetitive tasks or manual labor, are at risk of being automated and rendered obsolete. Workers in industries such as manufacturing, retail, and transportation may see their jobs replaced by AI-driven technologies and robotics.
2. Job transformation: Many jobs will not disappear entirely but will undergo significant changes due to the integration of AI-driven technologies. For example, jobs in healthcare, finance, and customer service may see a shift in focus from routine tasks to more complex, creative, and interpersonal tasks as AI takes over the more repetitive aspects of these roles.
3. Job creation: As AI-driven technologies continue to advance, new jobs will be created to meet the demands of the evolving market. These jobs may involve designing, developing, and maintaining AI systems, as well as roles in fields such as data analysis, cybersecurity, and user experience design.

While the precise impact of AI on the job market is difficult to predict, it is clear that the workforce will need to adapt to a new landscape shaped by automation and AI-driven technologies.

In-demand Skills and the Importance of Lifelong Learning

As the job market evolves due to the influence of AI, certain skills will become increasingly valuable. Some of the key skills that are expected to be in high demand include:

1. Technical skills: As AI-driven technologies become more prevalent, there will be a growing need for individuals with technical skills, such as programming, data analysis, and machine learning.
2. Soft skills: Interpersonal skills, such as communication, collaboration, and empathy, will become increasingly important as AI takes over routine tasks, leaving humans to focus on more complex and creative aspects of work.
3. Problem-solving and critical thinking: The ability to analyze complex situations and develop innovative solutions will be crucial in the age of AI, as machines become increasingly capable of handling routine tasks.
4. Adaptability and flexibility: As the job market continues to evolve, workers will need to be adaptable and open to learning new skills and technologies to stay relevant in their respective fields.

Lifelong learning will become essential for individuals to remain competitive in the job market. Continuous education, whether through formal training programs, online courses, or self-directed learning, will be crucial for workers to stay up-to-date with the latest developments in their fields and develop the skills needed to thrive in the age of AI. Employers and policymakers will also need to play a role in promoting and facilitating lifelong learning opportunities for the workforce.

The Role of Employers and Policymakers in the Transition

As AI continues to transform the job market, employers and policymakers have a crucial role to play in ensuring a smooth transition for workers. Some strategies they can adopt include:

1. Investing in training and reskilling programs: Employers can offer training programs to help workers develop the skills needed to adapt to the changing job market. Governments can also support and incentivize such initiatives through subsidies and tax incentives.
2. Fostering a culture of lifelong learning: Encouraging a culture of continuous learning and skill development within organizations can help workers stay relevant in the age of AI. Policymakers can promote this culture by supporting educational institutions, providing access to online learning resources, and implementing initiatives that encourage and reward lifelong learning.
3. Implementing fair labor policies: As AI-driven technologies become more prevalent in the workplace, it is essential to ensure that workers are treated fairly and equitably. Policymakers can develop and enforce labor policies that protect workers' rights and promote job security,

such as regulating working hours, providing adequate social security benefits, and ensuring equal access to training and development opportunities.

4. Supporting research and innovation: Both employers and governments can invest in research and development to drive innovation in AI and related technologies. This can help create new job opportunities and maintain a competitive edge in the global market.
5. Encouraging collaboration between stakeholders: Collaboration between employers, workers, educational institutions, and policymakers will be crucial in shaping the future of work. By working together, these stakeholders can develop effective strategies to navigate the challenges and opportunities presented by AI and automation.

The Impact of Remote Work and AI-driven Technologies

The rise of AI-driven technologies has also contributed to the growing popularity of remote work. As more tasks become automated and digitalized, remote work becomes increasingly feasible and attractive for both employers and employees. Some key points related to remote work in the age of AI include:

1. Increased flexibility: Remote work arrangements, facilitated by AI-driven technologies, can provide greater flexibility for employees in terms of work hours and location, improving work-life balance.
2. Access to a wider talent pool: Employers can benefit from a broader range of skills and expertise by hiring remote workers, as they are no longer restricted by geographical boundaries.
3. Cost savings: Companies can reduce overhead costs related to office space and utilities by allowing employees to work remotely.
4. Enhanced productivity: AI-driven technologies can improve productivity by automating routine tasks, allowing remote workers to focus on more complex, creative, and strategic aspects of their jobs.
5. Potential challenges: While remote work offers numerous benefits, it also presents challenges, such as maintaining clear communication, ensuring data security, and preserving company culture. Employers will need to develop strategies to address these challenges in order to make remote work successful.

As the adoption of AI-driven technologies continues to grow, the trend towards remote work is likely to accelerate, further transforming the way we work and live.

AI and Job Creation

While AI is undoubtedly leading to job displacement in some industries, it is also creating new job opportunities. Some ways in which AI is contributing to job creation include:

1. Development and maintenance of AI systems: The development and maintenance of AI systems requires skilled workers in areas such as software development, data analysis, and machine learning. As AI becomes more ubiquitous, the demand for workers with these skills is likely to increase.
2. Support roles for AI-driven technologies: As AI-driven technologies become more integrated into the workplace, the demand for support roles such as trainers, technical support specialists, and data analysts is also likely to increase.
3. New industries and business models: AI is opening up new industries and business models, creating opportunities for entrepreneurs and startups to innovate and create new products and services.
4. Healthcare and education: AI has the potential to transform healthcare and education by improving diagnosis and treatment, and providing personalized learning experiences. This will create new job opportunities for healthcare professionals and educators.
5. Infrastructure development: The widespread adoption of AI will require significant infrastructure development, including the installation and maintenance of hardware, software, and network systems. This will create jobs in fields such as engineering, construction, and IT.

Overall, while AI may lead to job displacement in some industries, it is also creating new opportunities for workers with the right skills and expertise. It is up to individuals, organizations, and policymakers to embrace the shift and take advantage of the opportunities presented by AI.

Preparing for the Future of Work with AI

As AI-driven technologies continue to transform the workplace, it is essential for individuals, organizations, and policymakers to take steps to prepare for the future of work. Some key strategies for preparing for the future of work with AI include:

1. Invest in skills development: Workers will need to develop new skills and competencies to stay relevant in a world increasingly shaped by AI. Employers can invest in upskilling and reskilling programs to help workers acquire new skills, and individuals can take advantage of online courses and training programs to stay ahead of the curve.
2. Foster a culture of learning: Employers can create a culture of continuous learning by providing opportunities for employees to develop new skills and learn about emerging

technologies. Individuals can also take responsibility for their own learning by seeking out new experiences and learning opportunities.

3. Encourage creativity and innovation: As routine tasks become automated, workers will need to focus more on creative and innovative tasks. Employers can encourage creativity and innovation by providing opportunities for employees to collaborate, experiment, and take risks.
4. Foster diversity and inclusivity: AI systems can be biased, and it is important to ensure that the development and use of AI is inclusive and equitable. Employers can foster diversity and inclusivity by promoting diverse hiring practices and ensuring that AI systems are designed with diversity and inclusivity in mind.
5. Prepare for job transitions: As some jobs become automated, workers will need to transition into new roles or industries. Employers can provide support for workers during job transitions by offering retraining programs, career counseling, and other resources to help workers navigate the changing job market.

Overall, preparing for the future of work with AI requires a commitment to ongoing learning, creativity, and innovation, as well as a willingness to adapt to new technologies and job roles. By taking proactive steps to prepare for the future of work, individuals, organizations, and policymakers can ensure that the benefits of AI are maximized and that the transition to the new world of work is as smooth and equitable as possible.

Chapter 8: AI in Law Enforcement: Balancing Security and Privacy

We will explore the increasingly significant role of artificial intelligence in law enforcement, delving into its potential benefits and challenges. As AI technology continues to advance, it is becoming an essential tool for law enforcement agencies worldwide. However, its growing presence also raises critical questions about privacy, security, and ethical concerns. We will examine the delicate balance between leveraging AI for enhancing public safety and protecting individual privacy rights. Join us as we navigate the complex landscape of AI-powered policing and its implications for society.

AI Applications in Law Enforcement

AI has been gradually integrated into various aspects of law enforcement, providing novel and efficient solutions to age-old problems. Some of the key applications include:

1. Predictive Policing: By analyzing historical crime data and identifying patterns, AI can help predict potential criminal activities in specific areas, enabling police departments to allocate resources more effectively and proactively address crime.
2. Facial Recognition: AI-powered facial recognition systems can quickly scan and match faces from live video feeds or databases, assisting in identifying suspects or missing persons with greater accuracy and speed.
3. Surveillance: AI-driven analytics can process vast amounts of data from various sources, such as CCTV cameras, social media, and other online platforms, to detect suspicious activities, track persons of interest, and gather intelligence.
4. Traffic Management: AI can analyze traffic patterns and predict congestion, allowing law enforcement to optimize traffic flow, identify traffic violations, and respond to accidents more efficiently.
5. Crime Analysis and Investigation: AI can assist in analyzing complex crime scenes, correlating data from multiple sources, and generating leads or identifying potential suspects in cases where traditional investigative methods may fall short.

6. Cybersecurity: With cybercrimes on the rise, AI-driven solutions can help detect and prevent threats, protect sensitive data, and identify vulnerabilities in law enforcement's own digital infrastructure.

While these applications promise significant improvements in public safety and crime prevention, their widespread adoption also raises several concerns regarding privacy, data security, and potential misuse. In the following sections, we will delve into these challenges and discuss potential ways to address them.

Balancing Security and Privacy

As AI becomes more prevalent in law enforcement, striking a balance between security benefits and privacy concerns is crucial. Some of the key challenges in maintaining this balance include:

1. Data Privacy: The vast amounts of data collected, processed, and stored by AI systems can include sensitive personal information, raising concerns about how this data is handled, who has access to it, and the potential for misuse.
2. Bias and Discrimination: AI systems are only as good as the data they are trained on. If the input data contains biases, these biases may be reflected in the AI's output, leading to unfair targeting of specific demographic groups or perpetuation of existing inequalities.
3. Transparency and Accountability: The complexity of AI algorithms can make it difficult to understand how they arrive at specific decisions, leading to a lack of transparency and accountability in law enforcement actions based on AI-driven insights.
4. Legal and Ethical Concerns: The use of AI in law enforcement raises various legal and ethical questions, such as the potential violation of constitutional rights, the impact on privacy and civil liberties, and the ethical implications of using AI-powered surveillance systems.

Addressing these challenges requires a multi-faceted approach, including:

- Developing clear guidelines and regulations surrounding data privacy, ensuring that personal information is protected, and limiting access to sensitive data.
- Ensuring that AI systems are trained on diverse and representative data sets to minimize bias and discrimination in their output.
- Implementing transparent and explainable AI algorithms, which can help build public trust and allow for greater scrutiny of AI-driven decisions.
- Engaging in public debate and dialogue regarding the use of AI in law enforcement, involving various stakeholders, such as civil liberties groups, technology experts, and policymakers, to address legal and ethical concerns.

By addressing these challenges and finding the right balance between security and privacy, AI can become a powerful tool for enhancing public safety while preserving individual rights and freedoms.

Ethical Considerations and Responsible AI Use

As AI becomes an integral part of law enforcement, it is crucial to consider the ethical implications of its use and implement responsible practices. Some key ethical considerations and recommendations for responsible AI use in law enforcement include:

1. Respect for Privacy: Ensure that AI systems are designed and deployed with privacy in mind, adhering to data protection regulations and minimizing the collection of personally identifiable information whenever possible.
2. Fairness and Non-Discrimination: Monitor and evaluate AI systems to detect and mitigate potential biases, ensuring that they do not unfairly target or discriminate against specific groups based on race, gender, or other protected characteristics.
3. Transparency and Accountability: Make the decision-making processes of AI systems as transparent as possible, allowing for public scrutiny and fostering trust in their use by law enforcement agencies.

4. Proportionality: Ensure that the use of AI in law enforcement is proportional to the potential benefits and risks it presents, and that its deployment is justified by a legitimate public safety need.
5. Collaboration: Engage with diverse stakeholders, including technology experts, civil society organizations, and the public, to create a collaborative environment for discussing the ethical implications of AI in law enforcement and developing best practices.
6. Continuous Improvement: Regularly update and refine AI systems to address potential issues and improve their performance, ensuring that they remain effective and ethical tools for law enforcement.

By taking these ethical considerations into account and implementing responsible practices, law enforcement agencies can harness the power of AI to enhance public safety while upholding the values and rights that are fundamental to democratic societies.

Real-world Applications of AI in Law Enforcement

There are numerous real-world applications of AI in law enforcement that demonstrate its potential to improve public safety and streamline operations. Some of these applications include:

1. Predictive Policing: AI algorithms can analyze historical crime data, identify patterns, and predict future crime hotspots. This allows law enforcement agencies to allocate resources more efficiently, focusing on areas with a higher likelihood of criminal activity.
2. Facial Recognition: AI-powered facial recognition systems can help law enforcement agencies quickly and accurately identify suspects, persons of interest, or missing individuals by comparing images captured by security cameras or other sources against large databases of known faces.
3. Video Analytics: AI can analyze video footage from security cameras, traffic cameras, or body-worn cameras to identify suspicious behavior, detect traffic violations, or monitor large-scale events, providing valuable insights and real-time alerts to law enforcement officers.

4. Social Media Monitoring: AI can monitor social media platforms to identify potential threats, such as public displays of violence, hate speech, or plans for criminal activity. This information can help law enforcement agencies detect and respond to emerging threats more effectively.
5. Automated License Plate Readers: AI-powered license plate recognition systems can read and analyze license plates in real-time, helping law enforcement officers identify stolen vehicles, track suspects, or enforce traffic regulations.
6. Cybercrime Investigation: AI can assist in detecting and investigating cybercrimes by analyzing large volumes of data, identifying patterns of suspicious behavior, and automating time-consuming tasks, such as malware analysis or data recovery.

These real-world applications of AI in law enforcement demonstrate its potential to improve public safety, streamline operations, and support officers in their efforts to protect and serve their communities.

Challenges and Limitations of AI in Law Enforcement

While AI has the potential to transform law enforcement, it is essential to recognize its challenges and limitations. Some of the most pressing concerns include:

1. Algorithmic Bias: AI systems can inherit biases present in the data used to train them, leading to unfair treatment of specific groups or individuals. Ensuring that AI algorithms are fair and unbiased is crucial to preventing discrimination and maintaining public trust.
2. Privacy Concerns: The use of AI in law enforcement can raise privacy concerns, particularly when it comes to the collection, storage, and analysis of personal data. Balancing public safety with individual privacy rights is a critical challenge that must be addressed.
3. Lack of Transparency: AI algorithms can sometimes be complex and difficult to understand, creating a “black box” effect. This lack of transparency can make it challenging to ensure that AI systems are making fair and accurate decisions, and can erode public trust in their use.

4. Misidentification: AI systems, such as facial recognition, can sometimes produce false positives or misidentify individuals. This can lead to wrongful arrests, infringement of civil liberties, and other negative consequences.
5. Legal and Regulatory Frameworks: The rapid development of AI technology has outpaced the creation of legal and regulatory frameworks to govern its use in law enforcement. Developing and implementing appropriate legislation and guidelines is essential to ensuring that AI is used responsibly and ethically.
6. Human Oversight: AI is a powerful tool, but it should not replace human decision-making in law enforcement. Ensuring that AI systems are used in conjunction with human judgment and oversight is crucial to prevent overreliance on technology and maintain accountability.

Addressing these challenges and limitations is essential to ensuring that AI is deployed in a responsible and effective manner within law enforcement contexts.

Ethical Considerations in AI-Powered Law Enforcement

The integration of AI into law enforcement practices raises several ethical considerations that must be carefully examined to ensure responsible deployment. Some of these ethical concerns include:

1. Due Process and Fairness: AI systems must be designed and implemented in ways that protect individuals' rights to due process and ensure that they are treated fairly. This includes ensuring that AI algorithms do not perpetuate or exacerbate existing biases and that their use adheres to established legal principles and procedures.
2. Transparency and Accountability: Law enforcement agencies must be transparent about their use of AI technologies and accountable for the decisions these systems make. This includes providing clear explanations of how AI algorithms work, as well as mechanisms for individuals to challenge decisions made by AI systems.
3. Privacy and Surveillance: The use of AI in law enforcement can significantly expand the scope and capabilities of surveillance. It is crucial to balance the need for public safety with

individuals' rights to privacy and ensure that data collection and analysis practices adhere to legal and ethical guidelines.

4. Responsibility and Liability: As AI systems become more autonomous, determining responsibility and liability for their actions can become more complex. It is essential to establish clear guidelines for assigning responsibility and liability when AI systems are involved in law enforcement decisions or actions.
5. Public Trust: For AI-powered law enforcement to be effective, it must be trusted by the public. Ensuring that AI technologies are used ethically, transparently, and responsibly is crucial to building and maintaining this trust.

By addressing these ethical considerations, law enforcement agencies can ensure that AI technologies are deployed in ways that protect individual rights, maintain public trust, and enhance the effectiveness of policing practices.

Best Practices and Guidelines for AI in Law Enforcement

To address the challenges, limitations, and ethical considerations surrounding AI in law enforcement, it is crucial to establish best practices and guidelines. Some recommendations include:

1. Data Quality and Bias Reduction: Ensure that the data used to train AI systems is representative, diverse, and of high quality. Implement bias reduction techniques to minimize the impact of historical biases on AI decision-making.
2. Transparency and Explainability: Make AI algorithms and their decision-making processes transparent and understandable. Provide clear explanations of how AI systems work and their potential impact on individuals and society.
3. Privacy and Data Protection: Develop strong privacy policies and data protection measures to safeguard personal information collected and processed by AI systems. Implement privacy-preserving techniques, such as data anonymization and encryption, to minimize risks.

4. Regulatory Compliance: Ensure that AI systems and their use in law enforcement comply with all relevant laws, regulations, and guidelines. Regularly review and update legal frameworks to keep pace with technological advancements.
5. Human Oversight and Accountability: Maintain human oversight of AI systems in law enforcement, and ensure that humans remain ultimately responsible and accountable for decisions and actions taken. Implement mechanisms for individuals to challenge decisions made by AI systems.
6. Public Engagement and Trust: Engage with the public to build trust and understanding of AI technologies in law enforcement. Communicate openly about the use, benefits, and limitations of AI, and provide opportunities for public input and feedback.
7. Training and Education: Train law enforcement personnel on the proper use and limitations of AI technologies, and educate them on the ethical considerations surrounding AI in their work.

By adopting these best practices and guidelines, law enforcement agencies can ensure the responsible and effective use of AI in their operations, while addressing potential challenges and ethical concerns.

Conclusion:

AI has the potential to significantly transform law enforcement, providing powerful tools to enhance efficiency, effectiveness, and public safety. From predictive policing and facial recognition to crime analytics and autonomous patrol robots, the applications of AI in law enforcement are vast and hold great promise.

However, the deployment of AI in law enforcement also comes with significant challenges, limitations, and ethical concerns. Issues such as algorithmic bias, transparency, privacy, and surveillance must be carefully considered and addressed to ensure the responsible and equitable use of AI technologies in policing.

By adhering to best practices and guidelines, law enforcement agencies can successfully harness the power of AI to improve their operations while maintaining public trust and upholding individual rights. As AI continues to advance and permeate various aspects of society, it is crucial to remain vigilant and proactive in addressing the challenges and ethical implications that accompany its use in law enforcement.

Outro:

We delved into the world of AI in law enforcement, exploring its numerous applications, the benefits it can provide, and the challenges and ethical concerns that must be addressed. As AI continues to develop and permeate various aspects of our lives, it is essential to be aware of its implications and potential consequences, especially in sensitive areas such as policing and security.

Summary of what you should remember from this chapter:

1. AI has the potential to revolutionize law enforcement by enhancing efficiency, effectiveness, and public safety.
2. Some applications of AI in law enforcement include predictive policing, facial recognition, crime analytics, and autonomous patrol robots.
3. Challenges and ethical concerns surrounding AI in law enforcement include algorithmic bias, transparency, privacy, and surveillance.
4. Establishing best practices and guidelines is crucial to ensure the responsible and equitable use of AI technologies in policing.
5. Human oversight and public trust are essential elements in the deployment of AI in law enforcement.

By understanding the implications and potential consequences of AI in law enforcement, we can work towards harnessing its power responsibly and ethically.

Suggestions that will be of interest for you to consider based on this chapter topic:

1. Research further into the ethical concerns surrounding AI in law enforcement and familiarize yourself with the ongoing debates and discussions.
2. Stay informed about the latest developments in AI technologies and their applications in law enforcement to better understand their potential impact on society.
3. Consider participating in public forums, conferences, or discussions on AI and

Chapter 9: The Environment - AI's Role in Combating Climate Change

Climate change is one of the most pressing challenges facing our planet today. The increasing frequency and intensity of extreme weather events, rising sea levels, and the loss of biodiversity are just a few of the alarming consequences. With the urgent need to address climate change and minimize its devastating impacts, the potential of AI in combating climate change has become a topic of great interest.

We will explore the various ways AI can be harnessed to help tackle climate change and its effects. From tracking emissions and developing more efficient energy systems, to predicting extreme weather events and informing climate adaptation strategies, AI has the potential to play a significant role in mitigating and adapting to the challenges posed by climate change.

AI for Climate Monitoring and Prediction

One of the key challenges in addressing climate change is understanding the intricate relationships between various environmental factors and how they contribute to the global climate system. AI can play a significant role in this by processing vast amounts of data from various sources such as satellite imagery, weather stations, and ocean buoys, and analyzing patterns to improve climate monitoring and prediction.

Machine learning algorithms can be trained to detect subtle changes in environmental data and identify patterns that may be indicative of climate change. This can lead to more accurate models for predicting future climate patterns, as well as identifying areas that are most at risk for the impacts of climate change. Early warning systems can be developed using AI to forecast extreme weather events, such as hurricanes, floods, and droughts, allowing governments and communities to better prepare for and mitigate their effects.

Furthermore, AI can help in the identification of climate change-related trends, such as deforestation, urbanization, and changes in land use. By analyzing satellite imagery, AI algorithms can detect these trends, providing valuable information for policymakers and researchers working on climate change mitigation strategies.

AI for Emissions Tracking and Reduction

Accurate tracking and reporting of greenhouse gas emissions are essential for implementing effective climate policies and meeting international climate targets. AI can significantly improve this process by automating the collection, analysis, and reporting of emissions data across various industries and sectors.

For instance, AI-powered tools can be used to monitor emissions from industrial facilities, power plants, and transportation systems, providing real-time data on emissions levels. This can help regulators and businesses identify inefficiencies, optimize operations.

Additionally, AI can be used to develop more accurate and efficient carbon accounting systems, making it easier for governments and businesses to track their progress towards emissions reduction targets.

AI can also play a role in the development and optimization of clean energy technologies. Machine learning algorithms can be used to improve the efficiency of renewable energy sources, such as solar panels and wind turbines, by optimizing their design, placement, and operation. Similarly, AI can be used to enhance energy storage systems, making it easier to integrate renewable energy sources into the grid.

Moreover, AI can help businesses and individuals make more sustainable choices by providing personalized recommendations for energy-efficient appliances, transportation options, and other environmentally-friendly products and services. By using AI to analyze consumer behavior and preferences, companies can tailor their offerings to promote more sustainable consumption patterns.

Overall, AI has the potential to significantly improve emissions tracking and reduction efforts, helping to accelerate the transition to a low-carbon economy.

AI-Enabled Conservation and Biodiversity Preservation

Biodiversity is crucial for maintaining the health and resilience of ecosystems. However, human activities, such as deforestation, pollution, and climate change, have led to a rapid decline in biodiversity across the globe. AI can play a crucial role in helping to protect and preserve biodiversity by enhancing our ability to monitor and manage natural habitats and species.

AI can be used to analyze satellite imagery, field data, and other sources of information to track changes in habitats and populations of wildlife species. This can help conservationists identify at-risk areas and implement targeted protection measures. For instance, AI-powered tools can be used to detect illegal logging or poaching activities in real-time, enabling law enforcement and conservation organizations to intervene more quickly and effectively.

Furthermore, AI can be employed to model and predict the impacts of climate change and other environmental pressures on ecosystems and species.
By simulating different scenarios and analyzing vast amounts of data, AI can help identify potential threats and vulnerabilities, allowing conservationists to develop more effective adaptation and mitigation strategies.

AI can also play a role in the restoration of damaged ecosystems. For example, machine learning algorithms can be used to optimize reforestation efforts by identifying the most suitable tree species and planting locations based on soil composition, climate, and other factors. This can help ensure that restoration projects are more successful in the long run, leading to healthier and more resilient ecosystems.

Additionally, AI can support citizen science initiatives by automating the identification and classification of species in photos or videos submitted by volunteers. This can help to engage the public in conservation efforts and provide valuable data for biodiversity monitoring and research.

In summary, AI has the potential to significantly enhance conservation and biodiversity preservation efforts by improving our ability to monitor and manage natural habitats, predict and respond to environmental threats, and engage the public in conservation initiatives.

AI for Sustainable Resource Management

As the global population continues to grow, the demand for resources such as water, energy, and food is increasing, placing immense pressure on our planet's finite resources. AI can play a vital role in promoting sustainable resource management by optimizing consumption, reducing waste, and identifying more efficient ways to produce and distribute resources.

For example, AI can be employed in the agriculture sector to optimize crop yields and reduce resource usage. By analyzing data on weather, soil conditions, and crop health, AI-powered systems can provide farmers with real-time recommendations on the optimal time to plant, irrigate, and harvest crops. This can lead to more efficient water and fertilizer usage, ultimately reducing the environmental impact of agriculture while meeting the growing demand for food.

In the energy sector, AI can be used to optimize the production, distribution, and consumption of energy resources. By analyzing data from various sources, such as weather patterns, energy consumption trends, and equipment performance, AI can help utilities to better match energy supply with demand. This can lead to reduced energy waste, lower greenhouse gas emissions, and more efficient use of renewable energy sources.

Moreover, AI can be employed to improve water management by predicting and managing water demand, detecting leaks, and optimizing treatment processes. This can help to ensure that water resources are used more efficiently and sustainably, ultimately conserving this vital resource for future generations.

Furthermore, AI can support waste management efforts by identifying patterns in waste generation, optimizing recycling processes, and suggesting ways to reduce waste at the source. For example, AI algorithms can analyze consumer purchasing data to identify opportunities for reducing packaging waste or improving product design to minimize waste generation.

In conclusion, AI has the potential to significantly contribute to sustainable resource management by promoting more efficient use of water, energy, and other resources, reducing waste, and optimizing production and distribution processes. This can help to lessen the environmental impact of human activities and support a more sustainable future.

AI for Disaster Management and Response

The increasing frequency and severity of natural disasters, such as hurricanes, floods, and wildfires, present significant challenges for governments and communities around the world. AI can play a crucial role in disaster management and response by improving prediction, early warning systems, and recovery efforts.

AI-powered algorithms can analyze vast amounts of data from satellite imagery, weather patterns, and historical records to predict the likelihood, intensity, and trajectory of natural disasters more accurately. This can help authorities and communities to better prepare for and respond to disasters, minimizing their impact on people and infrastructure.

In addition to improved prediction, AI can enhance early warning systems by rapidly processing information from various sources, such as sensors, social media, and news reports. By identifying potential threats and disseminating alerts to the public and emergency services, AI can help save lives and reduce damage to property.

During the response phase of a disaster, AI can be used to optimize rescue and relief efforts. Drones equipped with AI-powered image recognition software can be deployed to assess damage and locate survivors in hard-to-reach areas. These drones can transmit real-time data to emergency response teams, allowing them to prioritize resources and focus on the most critical areas.

AI can also assist in coordinating disaster response efforts by streamlining communication and information sharing among different agencies and organizations. This can help reduce response times and ensure that resources are allocated effectively.

Furthermore, AI can play a role in post-disaster recovery by analyzing data on infrastructure damage and identifying the most efficient ways to rebuild and restore affected areas. This can help communities recover more quickly and minimize the long-term impacts of disasters.

AI-driven technologies can also be used to develop more resilient infrastructure and urban planning strategies, reducing the vulnerability of communities to future disasters. By incorporating data on potential hazards and historical disaster patterns, AI can help design more sustainable and disaster-resistant cities and towns.

Overall, the application of AI in disaster management and response has the potential to save lives, reduce damage, and accelerate recovery efforts. However, it is essential to address the ethical and privacy concerns associated with the collection and use of data, particularly in the context of disaster response. Furthermore, as AI systems become more integrated into disaster management, it is crucial to ensure that they do not exacerbate existing inequalities or create new vulnerabilities.

Conclusion:

We have discussed the potential of AI in addressing environmental challenges and its role in combating climate change. From monitoring and reducing greenhouse gas emissions to predicting and managing natural disasters, AI holds great promise for creating a more sustainable and resilient world.

By leveraging the power of AI, we can develop innovative solutions to some of the most pressing environmental issues we face today. However, it is important to approach these applications with caution, considering the ethical and privacy concerns associated with the use of data, as well .

Outro:

As we conclude our exploration of AI and the environment, it is clear that the potential benefits of artificial intelligence in addressing climate change and other environmental issues are vast. AI has the power to not only transform our understanding of the natural world but also to drive meaningful change in the way we approach sustainability and resilience.

As with all applications of AI, it is crucial that we remain mindful of the potential risks and challenges that come with its widespread adoption. Ensuring that AI-driven environmental solutions are equitable, ethical, and privacy-conscious will be key to harnessing the technology's full potential for the greater good.

In the next chapter, we will delve into the world of AI and human rights, exploring the potential impact of artificial intelligence on safeguarding our freedoms and the challenges it may pose in upholding these fundamental rights.

Summary of what you should remember from this chapter:

1. AI has the potential to help us address environmental challenges and combat climate change.
2. AI can be used to monitor and reduce greenhouse gas emissions, improve waste management, and optimize energy usage.
3. AI-driven predictive models can help us better understand and manage natural disasters, leading to improved preparedness and response.
4. AI can contribute to biodiversity conservation by identifying species, monitoring ecosystems,and tracking wildlife populations.
5. 5. AI-driven smart agriculture can optimize crop yields and implement more sustainable farming practices.

6. It is essential to consider the ethical and privacy concerns associated with the use of AI in environmental applications.
7. Ensuring that AI-driven environmental solutions are equitable and sustainable is crucial to harnessing the technology's full potential for the greater good.

Suggestions that will be of interest for you to consider based on this chapter topic:

1. Research AI-powered tools and applications that are being used to address environmental challenges in your local community or region.
2. Keep up-to-date with the latest advancements in AI technology and their potential applications in the environmental sector.
3. Consider the ethical implications of AI-driven environmental solutions, and support policies and initiatives that prioritize privacy and equity.
4. Explore opportunities to leverage AI for personal or professional efforts to reduce your own environmental footprint and promote sustainability.

Chapter 10: AI and Human Rights: Safeguarding Our Freedoms

Introduction

As AI technologies become more integrated into our daily lives, it is crucial to consider their impact on human rights. Artificial intelligence has the potential to both protect and infringe upon the rights of individuals, making it essential to develop and enforce ethical guidelines that ensure responsible and equitable use of the technology. We will explore how AI can be leveraged to safeguard human rights, the potential risks and challenges it poses, and the importance of developing ethical frameworks and policies to strike the right balance between technological progress and the preservation of our fundamental freedoms.

AI as a Tool for Protecting Human Rights

AI has the potential to play a significant role in advancing and safeguarding human rights. Some of the ways AI can be used to protect human rights include:

1. Monitoring and reporting on human rights abuses: AI-driven tools can analyze vast amounts of data, such as satellite images and social media posts, to detect and report human rights violations in real-time. This can help organizations and governments to respond more quickly and effectively to emerging crises.
2. Combating discrimination and bias: AI algorithms can be designed to identify and counteract patterns of discrimination and bias in various domains, such as hiring practices, housing, and access to essential services.
3. Enhancing access to justice: AI-powered legal tools can help to bridge the justice gap by providing affordable and accessible legal advice and assistance to those who may not have the resources to access traditional legal services.
4. Empowering individuals with disabilities: AI technologies, such as speech recognition, computer vision, and natural language processing, can significantly improve the lives of individuals with disabilities by providing them with tools to overcome barriers and achieve greater independence.

Risks and Challenges of AI in Human Rights

While AI can offer numerous benefits for human rights, it also poses several risks and challenges, including:

1. Bias and discrimination: AI systems can inadvertently perpetuate and even exacerbate existing biases and discrimination if they are trained on biased datasets or designed without proper consideration for potential unintended consequences.
2. Surveillance and privacy concerns: The widespread deployment of AI-driven surveillance technologies, such as facial recognition, can erode privacy rights and enable oppressive governments to target and persecute political dissidents, activists, and marginalized groups.
3. Lack of accountability and transparency: The complexity and opacity of AI algorithms can make it difficult to hold those responsible for human rights violations accountable, especially when the technology is developed and deployed by private companies that may not be subject to the same regulatory oversight as public institutions.
4. Misuse and weaponization of AI: AI technologies can be weaponized to spread disinformation, manipulate public opinion, and undermine democratic processes, posing a significant threat to human rights and civil liberties.

Developing Ethical Frameworks and Policies for AI and Human Rights

To ensure that AI technologies are used responsibly and in a manner that respects and protects human rights, it is essential to develop ethical frameworks and policies that guide their development and deployment. Some key considerations include:

1. Embedding human rights principles into AI design: AI developers should be guided by the principles of fairness, transparency, and accountability when designing and training AI systems to minimize potential risks to human rights.
2. Ensuring inclusive and diverse representation in AI development: To counteract biases and promote fairness, it is crucial to include diverse perspectives and voices in the development and decision-making processes surrounding AI technologies.

3. Establishing clear regulatory and legal frameworks: Governments should develop and enforce legal and regulatory frameworks that govern the use of AI technologies, ensuring that they adhere to human rights standards and provide recourse for those whose rights have been violated.
4. Encouraging international cooperation and collaboration: As AI technologies have global implications, international cooperation and collaboration are necessary to develop shared norms, standards, and guidelines that protect human rights and promote responsible AI development and use.

The Role of Civil Society and Human Rights Organizations in Shaping AI Policy

Civil society and human rights organizations play a vital role in shaping AI policy and ensuring that AI technologies are used ethically and responsibly. Some of their key responsibilities include:

1. Advocacy and awareness-raising: These organizations can help to raise public awareness about the potential risks and benefits of AI technologies, promoting informed debate and encouraging responsible innovation.
2. Monitoring and reporting on AI applications: Civil society and human rights organizations can track the deployment of AI technologies and assess their impact on human rights, privacy, and other social issues. They can also document cases of misuse or abuse, which can inform policy discussions and help hold governments and companies accountable.
3. Providing expert guidance: Many of these organizations have access to experts in AI ethics, law, and technology. They can offer valuable insights and recommendations to policymakers and industry stakeholders, helping to shape more responsible AI development and deployment.
4. Promoting transparency and accountability: By pushing for greater transparency in AI decision-making processes and demanding accountability from both governments and corporations, civil society and human rights organizations can help ensure that AI

technologies are developed and used in a manner that respects human rights and promotes social equity.

5. Collaborating with other stakeholders: These organizations can work together with governments, industry, academia, and other stakeholders to create multi-stakeholder initiatives that address the ethical, legal, and social implications of AI. This can lead to the development of shared norms, standards, and best practices for responsible AI use.
6. Encouraging the development of AI for social good: Civil society and human rights organizations can also promote the use of AI technologies to address social and environmental challenges, such as climate change, poverty, and inequality. By showcasing the positive potential of AI, they can encourage more responsible and socially beneficial applications of this technology.

Conclusion

We delved into the role of civil society and human rights organizations in the context of AI's ever-growing influence on our lives. As we have seen, these organizations play a critical part in ensuring that AI technologies are developed and deployed responsibly, and that they contribute positively to society without infringing upon our fundamental rights and freedoms.

Through their advocacy, research, monitoring, expert guidance, promotion of transparency and accountability, collaboration with other stakeholders, and encouragement of AI for social good, civil society and human rights organizations

Outro

As we move forward in the age of AI, the work of civil society and human rights organizations will only become more vital. They will continue to serve as our guardians, ensuring that the benefits of AI technologies are accessible to all and that the potential risks and harms are minimized. Their tireless efforts help to shape a more equitable and just society, one that embraces the transformative power of AI without compromising our fundamental rights and values.

As we proceed to the next chapter, we will explore the fascinating world of AI and the arts, delving into the ways in which AI can both inspire and create artistic works, and what this means for human creativity.

Summary of what you should remember from this chapter:

1. AI has the potential to greatly impact human rights, both positively and negatively.
2. The benefits of AI can help advance human rights, such as improving access to healthcare, education, and employment.
3. The potential risks and harms of AI include surveillance, discrimination, and bias.
4. It is crucial to address the ethical and legal implications of AI technologies to ensure that they respect and protect human rights.

5. Governments, organizations, and developers must work together to establish guidelines and regulations that promote the responsible use of AI.

Suggestions that will be of interest for you to consider based on this chapter topic:

1. Stay informed about the latest developments in AI and their potential implications for human rights.
2. Support organizations that promote the ethical development and use of AI.
3. Encourage discussions and debates about the responsible use of AI and its impact on human rights.
4. Advocate for strong legal frameworks and regulations that protect human rights in the age of AI.
5. Consider how AI can be leveraged to advance human rights in your own community or industry.

Chapter 11: AI and Social Media: Influencing the Digital Conversation

Introduction:

We will explore the role of artificial intelligence in shaping social media platforms, from content moderation to the spread of information. We will discuss how AI can be both a force for good and a potential source of harm in the digital conversation, and what steps can be taken to ensure that AI is used responsibly on social media.

Social media has become an integral part of our daily lives, allowing us to connect with others, share ideas, and stay informed. The widespread adoption of social media platforms has also given rise to the need for effective content moderation and information management. Artificial intelligence has emerged as a powerful tool in this regard, with its ability to analyze vast amounts of data and identify patterns. In this section, we will delve into the various ways AI is being employed to moderate content, combat misinformation, and maintain the integrity of digital conversations on social media platforms.

Artificial intelligence is increasingly being used by social media platforms to analyze user behavior and personalize the content they see. Algorithms can tailor content feeds based on users' interests, past behavior, and connections. This personalization can lead to more engaging and relevant experiences for users, but it can also contribute to the formation of echo chambers, where users are only exposed to content that aligns with their existing beliefs and interests.

AI-driven content moderation is another area where social media platforms are making significant strides. Machine learning algorithms can be trained to recognize and filter out harmful content, such as hate speech, misinformation, or explicit material, before it reaches users. This can help create safer and more inclusive online spaces. However, there are concerns that AI-based moderation can be biased or overly restrictive, stifling free speech and inadvertently removing legitimate content.

The spread of misinformation and fake news is a significant challenge facing social media platforms. AI has been deployed to identify and counteract these issues, by analyzing content for credibility, sourcing, and consistency. When suspicious content is identified, AI systems can flag it for further review or even suppress its visibility on the platform. Although this approach has shown some success, it is not foolproof, and there are concerns that AI may inadvertently reinforce existing biases or fail to catch more sophisticated forms of disinformation.

The world of gaming has been transformed by AI in ways we could not have imagined just a few years ago. AI-powered game engines can create dynamic and adaptive environments that respond to players' actions in real-time, providing more immersive and engaging experiences. Game developers can leverage AI-driven procedural generation to create vast, complex worlds with minimal manual input, saving time and resources.

AI has also enabled the development of advanced non-player characters (NPCs) that exhibit human-like behaviors and decision-making capabilities.

In the world of sports, AI is revolutionizing how athletes train, compete, and recover. Advanced analytics and AI-driven tools can process vast amounts of data, providing valuable insights for coaches and athletes. AI-generated simulations can help athletes fine-tune their performance, identifying weaknesses and optimizing training regimens. Wearable devices with AI-powered features can track athletes' biometrics, providing real-time feedback to help them improve their form and avoid injury.

Beyond individual training, AI is also transforming sports management and strategy. AI-driven analytics can help teams make more informed decisions when it comes to scouting and recruiting talent. Coaches can use AI-powered tools to analyze game footage, identifying patterns and trends that can inform their tactics and game plans. Even fans are benefiting from AI, with algorithms predicting game outcomes and providing personalized content to enhance their experience.

Artificial intelligence is also making significant strides in the healthcare industry. AI-powered systems can analyze medical data, enabling faster and more accurate diagnoses. Machine learning algorithms can examine complex medical images, such as MRIs or CT scans, and identify patterns that might be missed by human practitioners. This can lead to earlier detection of diseases like cancer, potentially saving lives.

In addition to diagnostics, AI is transforming drug discovery and development. Machine learning can identify potential drug candidates by analyzing chemical compounds and predicting their effectiveness against specific diseases. This helps to streamline the drug development process, saving both time and resources. AI is also being used to personalize medicine, tailoring treatments to individual patients based on their unique genetic makeup and medical history.

The impact of AI on the job market cannot be understated. As automation becomes more widespread, many manual and repetitive tasks will be performed by machines. This shift is expected to cause significant job displacement in industries like manufacturing and transportation. However, it's important to note that while some jobs may become obsolete, new job opportunities will also arise. AI will create demand for roles such as data scientists, AI specialists, and machine learning engineers. Additionally, AI will enable humans to focus on more creative and strategic tasks, ultimately leading to the development of new industries and job categories.

Education will also undergo substantial changes due to AI. Adaptive learning platforms, powered by AI, will provide personalized learning experiences for students based on their individual needs and abilities. This will help to bridge the gap between students who excel at a particular subject and those who struggle. Furthermore, AI can be used to develop new teaching methodologies and to create more engaging and interactive educational content. Teachers will be able to leverage AI tools to better understand their students' progress and adjust their teaching strategies accordingly.

The gaming industry will also be revolutionized by AI. Game developers are already using AI to create more immersive and realistic virtual environments. Non-player characters (NPCs) are becoming more intelligent, capable of making decisions and reacting to player actions in a more human-like manner. AI is also being used to develop new game mechanics, such as procedurally generated content, which can create unique gaming experiences tailored to individual players.

In the realm of betting, AI has the potential to disrupt traditional methods by analyzing vast amounts of data to predict outcomes more accurately. This could lead to a shift in how people approach betting, with a greater reliance on data-driven insights rather than intuition or luck.

Businesses will also experience significant transformations due to AI. Companies will increasingly rely on AI-driven tools to optimize processes, reduce costs, and enhance decision-making. AI can be used to automate customer service through chatbots, analyze consumer behavior to inform marketing strategies, and optimize supply chain management. The widespread adoption of AI within businesses will likely result in more efficient, data-driven organizations.

Society as a whole will also be affected by the rise of AI. As AI systems become more integrated into our daily lives, we may face new ethical dilemmas and challenges. For example, AI-driven surveillance systems can lead to privacy concerns, while biased algorithms can exacerbate existing social inequalities. Additionally, as AI systems become increasingly autonomous, questions about responsibility and accountability will arise. Policymakers, businesses, and individuals will need to navigate these issues in order to strike a balance between reaping the benefits of AI and mitigating its potential downsides.

Friendships and family dynamics may also evolve due to the prevalence of AI. As virtual assistants and AI companions become more sophisticated, they may play a more significant role in our social lives. Some individuals may form emotional bonds with AI entities, which could alter the way we perceive and interact with technology. Furthermore, AI-driven communication tools may reshape the ways in which we maintain relationships over long distances, potentially fostering a more connected global society.

In conclusion, the impact of AI on our lives in the coming years will be vast and varied. From education and employment to gaming and business, nearly every aspect of our lives will be influenced by this rapidly advancing technology. As we continue to integrate AI systems into our daily routines, we will need to remain vigilant about the ethical and social implications of this powerful tool. By doing so, we can work together to ensure that AI is harnessed for the betterment of humanity.

Outro:

As we've explored in this chapter, the landscape of AI's influence on our lives is vast and ever-expanding. The technology is poised to change how we work, learn, play, and interact with one another. As we move forward into an increasingly AI-driven world, we must be prepared to adapt and evolve along with it.

Summary of what you should remember from this chapter:

1. AI will significantly impact education, with personalized learning and new teaching methods.
2. Job markets will experience shifts as AI automates tasks and creates new opportunities.
3. AI will revolutionize gaming and betting, making them more immersive and engaging.
4. Businesses will adopt AI to optimize processes, reduce costs, and make data-driven decisions.
5. Society, friendships, and family dynamics will evolve due to the increasing prevalence of AI.

Suggestions that will be of interest for you to consider based on this chapter topic:

1. Stay informed about AI developments and consider how they may impact your career or industry.
2. Explore educational opportunities to learn more about AI and its applications.
3. Consider the ethical implications of AI and engage in conversations about its responsible use.
4. Reflect on how AI may change your personal relationships and interactions with technology.
5. Be open to change and adapt as AI continues to reshape our world.

Chapter 12: Preparing for the AI Revolution

Chapter intro:

The rapid advancements in artificial intelligence are transforming the world around us, and with these changes come new challenges and opportunities. We will discuss how individuals, businesses, and societies can prepare for the AI revolution, ensuring that we can harness its potential while minimizing the risks and unintended consequences.

For individuals, adapting to the AI revolution starts with education and skill development. As AI and automation become increasingly integrated into various industries, the demand for skills that complement these technologies will grow. Therefore, it's crucial for people to focus on acquiring skills that will be relevant in the AI-driven world. Some essential skills include:

1. Critical thinking and problem-solving: As AI systems take over routine tasks, human workers will need to excel at solving complex problems and thinking critically in situations that AI cannot yet handle.
2. Emotional intelligence: As machines become more prevalent, human empathy and understanding will be even more valuable in building and maintaining relationships in both personal and professional settings.
3. Data literacy: AI relies heavily on data, so understanding how to interpret, analyze, and use data effectively will be a highly sought-after skill.
4. Technical skills: Learning programming languages, understanding machine learning algorithms, and mastering other technical aspects of AI will be valuable in many industries.
5. Creativity and innovation: AI has the potential to automate many tasks, but it cannot replicate human creativity. Developing unique ideas and fostering innovation will remain an essential human trait.

For businesses, preparing for the AI revolution means rethinking their strategies and embracing innovation. Companies should consider the following steps:

1. Develop an AI strategy: Assess how AI can be integrated into the company's operations, from automating mundane tasks to improving decision-making processes.

2. Invest in AI talent and training: Attract and retain skilled professionals who can develop and maintain AI systems. Additionally, provide training opportunities for existing employees to help them acquire the necessary skills to work alongside AI.
3. Foster a culture of innovation: Encourage employees to think creatively and experiment with new ideas. This will help businesses stay ahead of the competition and capitalize on the opportunities AI presents.
4. Implement AI ethically: Develop ethical guidelines and principles for AI usage within the organization. This will ensure that AI is used responsibly and doesn't cause harm to individuals or society.

Preparing for the AI revolution also requires action at the societal level. Governments, educational institutions, and other organizations must collaborate to create an environment where AI can thrive and be used for the greater good. Some steps to achieve this include:

1. Develop AI policies and regulations: Governments should establish clear guidelines and standards for AI development and use, ensuring that it aligns with ethical principles and protects citizens' rights.
2. Invest in AI research and development: Governments and private organizations should collaborate to fund research in AI, ensuring that advancements are made in the best interests of society.
3. Promote AI education: Educational institutions should incorporate AI-related topics and skills into their curricula, preparing students for the future job market.
4. Address AI's impact on the workforce: Governments should implement policies and programs to help workers who may be displaced by AI, providing retraining opportunities and support for transitioning into new careers.
5. Encourage global cooperation: Countries should work together to address common challenges and share best practices in AI development and implementation. This will help ensure that AI's benefits are shared globally and its potential risks are minimized.

The impact of AI on our daily lives will be vast, transforming how we interact with technology and each other. Here are some examples of how AI will change various aspects of life:

1. Personal assistants: AI-powered personal assistants, like Siri and Alexa, will become increasingly sophisticated, helping us manage our schedules, answer questions, and make decisions.
2. Healthcare: AI will revolutionize healthcare by assisting in diagnosing diseases, predicting health risks, and personalizing treatments. AI-driven systems will analyze vast amounts of data to provide doctors with better insights and recommendations, ultimately improving patient outcomes and reducing costs.
3. Education: AI will change the way students learn, with personalized learning plans and adaptive learning platforms that cater to individual strengths and weaknesses. AI-powered tutors will be able to provide instant feedback and support, making learning more efficient and enjoyable.
4. Transportation: Autonomous vehicles will become more common, reducing the need for human drivers and improving road safety. AI will also optimize public transportation systems, reducing congestion and improving travel times.
5. Entertainment: AI will revolutionize the entertainment industry, creating new forms of content and experiences. Virtual reality and augmented reality will become more immersive, and AI-driven algorithms will generate personalized recommendations for movies, games, and music.
6. Finance: AI will transform the financial sector, automating processes and providing more accurate predictions and risk assessments. This will lead to better investment strategies, more efficient banking systems, and improved financial security.
7. Home life: Smart homes will become increasingly common, with AI-powered devices controlling everything from lighting and temperature to security systems. This will make our homes more comfortable, efficient, and safe.
8. Communication: AI will enable new ways of communicating, breaking down language barriers and facilitating more natural interactions with technology. Voice recognition and

natural language processing will make it easier to interact with devices and people around the world.

These are just a few examples of how AI will change our lives in the coming years. As AI technology continues to advance, we can expect even more profound transformations in every aspect of our lives.

Conclusion:

As we've explored in this chapter, the impact of artificial intelligence on our lives in the coming years will be vast and wide-ranging. From education and healthcare to transportation and entertainment, AI will revolutionize the way we live, work, and interact with the world around us. While some of these changes may be challenging to adapt to, many others will bring about significant improvements in our lives, making everyday tasks more efficient and enabling us to focus on more meaningful pursuits.

In the realm of education, AI will empower personalized learning experiences tailored to individual needs and abilities, helping students to reach their full potential. Healthcare will benefit from improved diagnostics, more effective treatments, and streamlined administrative processes, all of which will contribute to better patient outcomes. In transportation, AI will facilitate the widespread adoption of autonomous vehicles, making our roads safer and more efficient.

When it comes to entertainment, AI will enhance our gaming experiences and revolutionize the way we create and consume content. The rise of AI will also have significant implications for the world of work, leading to both job displacement and the creation of new opportunities. While some industries will undoubtedly be disrupted, AI also has the potential to open up entirely new fields of employment and drive economic growth.

However, the widespread adoption of AI will also raise important ethical, social, and regulatory questions. As we move forward into this new era, it will be essential for governments, businesses, and individuals to work together in addressing these challenges, ensuring that the benefits of AI are realized for all of humanity.

Outro:

As we conclude this chapter, it's important to remember that the impact of artificial intelligence on our lives will be both profound and multifaceted. In order to navigate these changes, we must approach the future with a sense of curiosity, adaptability, and an open mind. By doing so, we will be better prepared to leverage the incredible potential of AI, while also addressing the challenges it presents.

Summary of what you should remember from this chapter:

1. AI will transform various aspects of our lives, including education, healthcare, transportation, and entertainment.
2. The impact of AI on the job market will be complex, with both job displacement and new opportunities emerging.
3. Ethical, social, and regulatory considerations must be addressed as we continue to develop and implement AI technologies.

Suggestions that will be of interest for you to consider based on this chapter topic:

1. Keep up-to-date with the latest advancements in AI and consider how they might impact your industry or area of interest.
2. Develop skills that are likely to remain valuable in the age of AI, such as creativity, problem-solving, and emotional intelligence.
3. Engage in conversations about the ethical and social implications of AI, and advocate for responsible development and use of these technologies.

Chapter 13: AI and Gaming: The New Frontier

Introduction:

In recent years, the gaming industry has been revolutionized by the rapid advancements in artificial intelligence. From improved graphics and realistic environments to adaptive gameplay and more intelligent non-player characters (NPCs), AI is reshaping the way we play and enjoy games. This chapter will delve into the impact of AI on gaming, exploring how developers are leveraging this technology to create more immersive and engaging experiences, as well as the

One of the most noticeable impacts of AI on gaming is the improvement in graphics and the level of realism it brings. Game developers have started using AI-powered techniques like deep learning and neural networks to create highly detailed textures, realistic character animations, and lifelike environments.

For instance, machine learning algorithms can be used to analyze large datasets of real-world images and generate highly realistic textures for in-game objects, such as buildings, clothing, and natural landscapes. These algorithms can also be applied to create highly detailed 3D models, which can be used to design game characters and objects that closely resemble real-world counterparts.

Another area where AI is improving graphics is through ray tracing, a technique that simulates the way light interacts with objects in a scene. By combining AI with ray tracing, developers can create more accurate and realistic lighting, shadows, and reflections, significantly enhancing the visual appeal of games.

Furthermore, AI-driven procedural generation allows developers to create vast and varied game worlds that feel alive and immersive. Instead of manually designing each element of a game's environment, developers can use AI algorithms to generate landscapes, cities, and other environments based on predefined rules and parameters. This approach not only saves time and resources but also results in more diverse and engaging game worlds for players to explore.

Artificial intelligence is also reshaping game design and storytelling by allowing developers to create more dynamic, adaptive, and engaging experiences. One key aspect of this is the use of AI-driven non-player characters (NPCs) that exhibit more realistic and sophisticated behaviors.

In traditional game development, NPCs are often limited to simple scripts or pre-programmed actions. However, with the help of AI, game developers can now create NPCs that learn and adapt to players' actions in real-time. This allows for more emergent gameplay and a more immersive experience, as players feel like they are interacting with genuinely intelligent characters. Some examples of AI-driven NPCs include:

1. Adaptive enemies: Enemies that learn from players' tactics and change their behavior accordingly, making them more challenging and engaging.
2. Dynamic ecosystems: AI-driven ecosystems with realistic animal behavior, where creatures interact with each other and the environment in complex ways.
3. Procedural storytelling: AI systems that generate storylines based on players' choices and actions, creating a unique narrative experience for each player.
4. Emotional intelligence: NPCs that can recognize and respond to players' emotions, creating a more engaging and emotionally rich gaming experience.

Another significant impact of AI on gaming is the emergence of procedural content generation (PCG). PCG involves using algorithms to create game assets like levels, characters, and items, reducing the workload for developers and enabling them to create more expansive and diverse game worlds. AI-driven PCG can generate content on the fly, adapting the game world to the player's actions and preferences.

This technology also opens up new possibilities for narrative-driven games. As AI becomes more advanced, we can expect to see games with branching storylines that adapt to players' choices in real-time, creating a more personalized and immersive storytelling experience.

However, there are potential downsides to the widespread use of AI in gaming. For instance, it may lead to a decrease in the demand for human game designers and developers, as AI-driven tools can generate content more efficiently. Additionally, some critics argue that relying too heavily on AI-generated content could lead to a loss of creative expression and artistic vision in the gaming industry.

In conclusion, AI is revolutionizing game design and storytelling, providing more dynamic, adaptive, and engaging experiences for players. From AI-driven NPCs to procedural content generation, these advancements are changing the way games are created and experienced. However, it is crucial to balance the benefits of AI with potential drawbacks and maintain a focus on human creativity and artistic expression in the gaming industry.

Outro:

As we wrap up this exploration of how AI is transforming the gaming and betting industries, it is clear that this technology is having a profound impact on these sectors. With the potential to revolutionize how we interact with games, experience stories, and place bets, AI is opening up new opportunities and challenges for players, developers, and businesses alike.

Summary of what you should remember from this chapter:

1. AI is revolutionizing the gaming industry through more realistic graphics, improved game mechanics, and enhanced storytelling.
2. AI-driven adaptive learning systems are allowing games to become more personalized, catering to individual player preferences and skill levels.
3. The betting industry is also experiencing a transformation, with AI-powered algorithms improving prediction models and risk management.
4. Both industries face potential ethical concerns surrounding addiction, manipulation, and responsible gaming practices.
5. The future of AI in gaming and betting is bright, with continued advancements expected to create even more immersive and dynamic experiences.

Suggestions that will be of interest for you to consider based on this chapter topic:

1. Keep an eye on the latest advancements in AI and gaming to stay informed about new opportunities and potential risks.
2. If you're a developer or a business owner in the gaming or betting industries, consider exploring the integration of AI technology into your products or services.
3. As a consumer, remember to play responsibly and be mindful of the potential ethical concerns surrounding AI in gaming and betting.

Now that we have discussed how AI is transforming gaming and betting, let's continue our journey and explore how AI is impacting the world of education.

Chapter 14: Education Revolutionized

Introduction:

We will explore the impact of artificial intelligence on education. AI has the potential to revolutionize the way we teach and learn, making education more accessible, personalized, and effective. We'll delve into how AI is changing the landscape of education, from personalized learning platforms to virtual teaching assistants and beyond. We'll also discuss the challenges and potential pitfalls associated with integrating AI into education, as well as the ethical implications of using AI to shape the minds of future generations.

One of the most exciting developments in AI and education is the rise of personalized learning platforms. These platforms use artificial intelligence to analyze students' learning habits, strengths, and weaknesses, allowing them to customize educational content based on each individual's needs. This means that students can learn at their own pace, focusing on areas where they need the most help and skipping over material they've already mastered.

These platforms can also adapt to students' learning styles, offering different types of content (e.g., videos, text, quizzes) based on what works best for each individual. For example, if a student learns best through visual aids, the platform might prioritize videos and diagrams over text-based content.

AI-powered virtual teaching assistants are another promising development in the field of education. These digital assistants can help teachers by answering students' questions, providing feedback on assignments, and even grading exams. By automating some of the more mundane tasks associated with teaching, virtual teaching assistants can free up valuable time for educators, allowing them to focus on more important aspects of their job, such as lesson planning and one-on-one interactions with students.

Some virtual teaching assistants can even detect and respond to students' emotions, offering encouragement or additional support when needed. This emotional intelligence can help create a more supportive and engaging learning environment for students.

Artificial intelligence has the potential to revolutionize special education by providing tailored support and resources to students with disabilities. AI-powered tools can help teachers better understand the unique needs and abilities of each student, allowing them to create more effective and personalized learning plans.

For example, AI-driven speech recognition technology can be used to assist students with speech and language impairments, helping them communicate more effectively and participate more fully in classroom activities. Additionally, AI-powered educational software can adapt its content and presentation to the specific learning preferences of students with dyslexia, ADHD, autism, or other disabilities. This personalization can help students overcome challenges and make significant strides in their education.

Moreover, AI-driven analytics can identify patterns in student performance and behavior, providing valuable insights to teachers and parents. This data can help pinpoint areas where a student may need additional support or accommodations, ensuring that their unique needs are met and facilitating their academic success.

Artificial intelligence can also be used to create virtual learning environments tailored to the needs of students with sensory impairments. For example, virtual reality (VR) can provide students with visual impairments an immersive and interactive experience, while haptic technology can simulate touch sensations for students with hearing impairments.

In the realm of emotional and social development, AI-driven social robots can be employed to help students with autism spectrum disorder (ASD) improve their communication and social skills. These robots can be programmed to exhibit specific behaviors and respond to cues, allowing students to practice social interactions in a controlled environment.

It is important to recognize, however, that while AI can offer numerous benefits to special education, it is not without its challenges. For instance, ensuring that AI-driven tools are accessible and affordable to all schools and students is crucial in order to prevent exacerbating existing educational inequalities. Furthermore, ethical considerations surrounding data privacy and the potential for AI to replace human interaction must also be carefully considered.

Conclusion:

As we have explored in this chapter, artificial intelligence has the potential to revolutionize the field of special education by providing highly personalized, adaptive, and engaging learning experiences for students with diverse needs. AI-powered tools can help educators better understand and support their students, enabling them to overcome challenges and achieve their full potential.

From intelligent tutoring systems and speech recognition technologies to AI-driven analytics and social robots, there are numerous applications of AI in special education that can enhance the learning process and promote greater inclusion. However, it is crucial to acknowledge the ethical considerations and potential drawbacks associated with these technologies, such as data privacy concerns, biases in AI algorithms, and the need for human involvement in the educational process.

As AI continues to advance, it is essential for educators, researchers, and policymakers to collaborate in order to harness its potential effectively and responsibly. By addressing these challenges and promoting equitable access to AI-powered educational tools, we can work towards a future where all students, regardless of their abilities or disabilities, have the opportunity to learn and grow in a supportive and inclusive educational environment.

Outro:

In conclusion, the future of special education is undoubtedly intertwined with advancements in artificial intelligence. As AI technologies continue to evolve and improve, their potential to enhance the learning experiences of students with special needs will only grow. The possibilities for innovative, personalized, and accessible educational solutions are vast and exciting, and they hold the promise of a brighter future for learners, educators, and families alike.

While the journey of AI in special education is just beginning, the impact it has already made and the potential for even greater achievements in the future is inspiring. By embracing and integrating these technologies, we can work together to build a more inclusive and supportive educational landscape for all students, regardless of their individual needs and challenges.

Suggestions that will be of interest for you to consider based on this chapter topic:

1. Explore AI-powered tools and applications specifically designed for special education and consider implementing them in your school or classroom.
2. Stay updated on the latest research and advancements in AI for special education to ensure you are utilizing the best tools and strategies for your students.
3. Engage in professional development opportunities and training focused on AI in special education to expand your knowledge and expertise in the area.
4. Collaborate with other educators, researchers, and professionals in the field of special education to share experiences, ideas, and best practices related to AI integration.
5. Advocate for increased funding and support for AI research and development in special education to further enhance the quality of education and support for students with special needs.

Summary of what you should remember from this chapter:

1. AI has the potential to revolutionize special education by offering personalized learning experiences, improving assessment methods, and providing targeted interventions.
2. Adaptive learning technologies can help create individualized lesson plans and curricula tailored to each student's unique needs, strengths, and weaknesses.
3. AI can assist in identifying learning disabilities and developmental delays earlier, enabling timely interventions and support for students.
4. Virtual reality and augmented reality applications can offer immersive, engaging, and safe learning environments for students with special needs.

Suggestions that will be of interest for you to consider based on this chapter topic:

1. Explore the current state of AI technology and its applications in special education. Stay informed about the latest developments and research in this area.
2. Consider collaborating with educators, researchers, and AI experts to develop effective AI-driven tools and strategies for special education.
3. Advocate for the implementation of AI-driven technologies in special education settings to provide better support and resources for students with special needs.
4. Encourage the development of ethical guidelines and policies for the use of AI in special education to ensure that the technology is used responsibly and effectively.
5. Examine the potential challenges and limitations of using AI in special education, such as privacy concerns, data security, and the digital divide, to better understand how to address these issues.

Chapter 15: A New Era of Gaming and Entertainment

Introduction:

The world of gaming and entertainment has always been a dynamic and ever-evolving industry. With the rapid advancements in technology, the landscape of gaming has transformed, providing players with more immersive and engaging experiences. We will delve into the effects of artificial intelligence on the gaming and entertainment industry, exploring how it is revolutionizing the way we play, interact, and experience this realm. From creating realistic non-playable characters (NPCs) to enhancing game design, AI is reshaping the gaming world, blurring the lines between reality and virtual realms.

One of the most significant ways AI is influencing the gaming industry is through procedural game design. Procedural generation refers to the creation of game content, such as levels, characters, or terrain, using algorithms and automated processes. This allows developers to create vast, diverse worlds with minimal manual effort.

AI-driven procedural generation has several benefits for game developers and players alike. First, it allows for the creation of larger and more complex game worlds without exponentially increasing development time or resources. This means that even small development teams can create expansive gaming experiences that rival those of major studios.

Second, AI-generated content can adapt to individual players' preferences, creating a more personalized and engaging gaming experience. For example, an AI-driven game might analyze a player's playstyle and generate levels or challenges that cater to their strengths and weaknesses. This can lead to more engaging and replayable games, as players feel like the game is tailored to them.

Third, AI-generated content can lead to more dynamic and unpredictable gameplay experiences. Traditional game design relies on pre-built levels and scripted events, which can become predictable and repetitive over time. AI-generated content, on the other hand, can be more varied and unexpected, leading to more engaging gameplay experiences.

However, there are also challenges and limitations associated with AI-driven game design. For one, procedurally generated content can sometimes feel less polished or cohesive than handcrafted game elements. Furthermore, AI-generated content can sometimes be too random or unpredictable, leading to frustrating or unenjoyable gameplay experiences. Game developers need to strike a balance between leveraging the power of AI and ensuring that their games remain engaging and enjoyable for players.

In the coming years, we can expect AI-driven game design to continue evolving and improving, leading to even more immersive and personalized gaming experiences. As AI technology advances, it's likely that we'll see even more innovative and groundbreaking uses of AI in the gaming industry, pushing the boundaries of what's possible in game design and development.

Conclusion:

We have discussed the impact of artificial intelligence on gaming and betting industries. We have seen how AI is revolutionizing these industries by creating more realistic virtual environments, generating personalized content, and improving the overall gaming experience for players. We have also discussed the challenges and limitations associated with AI-driven game design, as well as the potential for AI to reshape the future of gaming.

Outro:

As we conclude this exploration of artificial intelligence in gaming and betting, it is evident that AI is playing a significant role in shaping the future of these industries. As technology continues to advance, we can expect more innovative and immersive experiences for players, as well as new opportunities for businesses to grow and thrive in a rapidly evolving landscape.

Summary of what you should remember:

1. AI is revolutionizing the gaming and betting industries, enhancing the experiences of players and offering new opportunities for businesses.
2. Game developers are leveraging AI to create more realistic and engaging game experiences, with NPCs that exhibit human-like behavior and adapt to the player's actions.
3. AI-driven game analytics can help developers fine-tune game balance, identify and fix bugs, and predict player behavior, leading to more successful game launches.

4. In the betting industry, AI is being used to create more accurate predictive models, allowing for better odds and more informed betting decisions.

5. AI-powered tools are also helping to identify and mitigate problem gambling, ensuring a safer and more responsible gambling environment.
6. The integration of AI in gaming and betting industries may raise concerns about job displacement, privacy, and fairness, necessitating industry-wide discussions and regulations.

Suggestions that will be of interest for you to consider based on this chapter topic:

1. As a player, consider exploring AI-driven games to experience the evolution of gaming and the benefits of AI in enhancing gameplay.
2. If you work in the gaming or betting industry, stay updated on AI advancements and consider how they might be applied to your business for a competitive edge.
3. Be aware of the ethical concerns surrounding AI in these industries, and support companies and organizations that prioritize responsible AI development and use.
4. Engage in conversations about the potential impact of AI on the gaming and betting industries, and consider advocating for policies and regulations that ensure a balanced approach to AI integration.

Chapter 16: The Future of AI and Its Impact on Society

As artificial intelligence continues to advance and become more integrated into our daily lives, it is essential to consider its potential future impact on society. We will discuss some of the key areas where AI is expected to play a significant role and the potential implications for individuals, communities, and the world as a whole.

1. Employment and the workforce: AI has the potential to automate a wide range of tasks, leading to significant changes in the workforce. While some jobs may be lost to automation, new opportunities will also arise as AI creates demand for skilled workers in areas such as data analysis, machine learning, and AI ethics. It is crucial for governments, educational institutions, and businesses to invest in retraining and reskilling programs to ensure that workers are prepared for the shifting job market.
2. Healthcare: AI is already making an impact in healthcare through medical diagnostics, drug discovery, and personalized treatment plans. In the future, AI could play an even larger role in revolutionizing healthcare by enabling earlier detection of diseases, improving patient outcomes, and reducing healthcare costs.
3. Environmental sustainability: AI can help address pressing environmental challenges, such as climate change and resource depletion. For example, AI can optimize energy consumption in buildings and transportation, identify patterns in climate data to inform policy decisions, and support sustainable agriculture practices through precision farming.
4. Public safety and security: AI has the potential to improve public safety and security by enhancing surveillance systems, automating emergency response, and predicting and preventing cyberattacks. However, it is essential to balance these benefits with concerns about privacy and civil liberties.
5. Education: As discussed in the previous chapter, AI is poised to revolutionize education by providing personalized learning experiences and improving educational outcomes. In the future, AI could also play a role in reducing educational disparities and increasing access to quality education worldwide.
6. Ethical considerations: The increasing influence of AI raises numerous ethical questions, such as ensuring fairness in AI algorithms, addressing issues of privacy and data security, and determining responsibility in the event of AI-related accidents or failures. It is critical for

governments, businesses, and researchers to work together to establish ethical guidelines and regulations to govern the development and use of AI technologies.

7. Global inequality: While AI has the potential to improve the quality of life for many, there is a risk that the benefits of AI could be unevenly distributed, exacerbating existing inequalities. It is crucial for governments and international organizations to prioritize policies that promote equal access to AI technologies and their benefits.

In summary, the future of AI holds both great promise and significant challenges. By working together to address potential risks and ensuring that AI technologies are developed and implemented ethically and responsibly, we can harness the power of AI to create a more just, prosperous, and sustainable world for all.

Chapter 17: AI and the Evolution of Human-Machine Interaction

As artificial intelligence becomes more sophisticated, the ways in which humans and machines interact will continue to evolve. We will explore the current state of human-machine interaction, as well as future developments that could further enhance our relationship with AI.

1. Natural language processing: One of the most significant advancements in AI is the ability to understand and respond to natural human language. This has led to the development of chatbots, virtual assistants, and other AI-driven applications that can engage with users in a more intuitive and human-like manner. As natural language processing improves, we can expect AI to become even more skilled at understanding and responding to a wide range of linguistic nuances, making human-machine interactions increasingly seamless.
2. Emotion recognition and empathy: Another area of AI development that could greatly impact human-machine interaction is emotion recognition. AI systems are becoming better at detecting and interpreting human emotions through facial expressions, voice tone, and other cues. In the future, AI could become more empathetic, allowing it to better understand and respond to our emotional states.
3. Haptic feedback and immersive experiences: Haptic feedback technology enables users to experience touch sensations when interacting with digital devices. By incorporating haptic feedback into AI-driven applications, developers can create more immersive experiences that engage multiple senses. This could lead to new forms of human-machine interaction, such as virtual reality environments that feel more realistic and responsive.
4. Brain-computer interfaces: One of the most ambitious areas of research in human-machine interaction is brain-computer interfaces (BCIs), which enable direct communication between the human brain and a computer. Although BCIs are still in their early stages, they hold great promise for facilitating more intimate and efficient interactions between humans and AI. In the future, BCIs could enable us to control AI systems with our thoughts, allowing for an unprecedented level of collaboration and integration.
5. Collaborative robots: As AI becomes more capable, robots will increasingly work alongside humans, rather than replacing them. Collaborative robots, or "cobots," are designed to assist humans in a variety of tasks, such as manufacturing, healthcare, and agriculture. By combining human creativity and problem-solving skills with the precision and efficiency of

robots, cobots have the potential to revolutionize numerous industries and lead to more productive, safer, and satisfying work environments.

6. Social and ethical implications: The evolution of human-machine interaction raises important social and ethical questions. As we become more reliant on AI systems, it is crucial to ensure that they are designed with user privacy and well-being in mind. Moreover, as AI becomes more integrated into our lives, we must grapple with questions of identity, agency, and what it means to be human in a world increasingly populated by intelligent machines.

In conclusion, the future of human-machine interaction is full of exciting possibilities and challenges. By continuing to push the boundaries of AI and exploring innovative ways to enhance our interactions with machines, we can unlock the full potential of this technology and enrich our lives in ways we have yet to imagine.

Chapter 18: Politics and AI: Shifting Power Dynamics

Introduction

In the ever-evolving landscape of politics, the introduction of artificial intelligence (AI) has the potential to greatly influence power dynamics on both national and global levels. As AI becomes increasingly prevalent in our daily lives, its integration into political decision-making processes, campaign strategies, and public opinion is inevitable. We will explore the various ways AI could reshape the political sphere and consider the potential benefits and challenges that may arise from its widespread adoption.

AI has the potential to transform political decision-making by providing data-driven insights and recommendations. Machine learning algorithms can analyze vast amounts of data, identifying patterns and trends that may be difficult for humans to discern. This could enable governments and policymakers to make more informed decisions, taking into account various factors and possible outcomes.

For example, AI could be used to analyze the potential economic impact of new policies or to forecast the consequences of different diplomatic actions in international relations. It could also help with resource allocation and the prioritization of key issues, enabling governments to make more effective and efficient decisions.

However, the use of AI in political decision-making raises several concerns. One of the primary concerns is the potential for AI systems to be biased, due to biased data or algorithms. This could lead to decisions that unfairly favor certain groups or individuals, exacerbating existing inequalities and injustices. Additionally, the transparency and accountability of AI-driven decision-making processes may be called into question, as the inner workings of complex algorithms can be difficult to understand and scrutinize.

AI has the potential to play a significant role in political campaigns and elections, revolutionizing the way candidates reach out to voters and engage with the electorate. Advanced algorithms can be used to analyze voter data, segmenting populations based on demographics, preferences, and voting history. This enables political campaigns to create highly targeted messages and advertisements, appealing to specific groups of voters and increasing the overall effectiveness of their communication strategies.

Moreover, AI can be used to predict voter behavior and election outcomes, giving political parties and candidates valuable insights into their campaign strategies' success. For instance, machine learning models could analyze historical voting patterns, social media trends, and other relevant data to forecast election results and voter turnout. This information could help campaigns identify key areas to focus on, potentially swaying the results in their favor.

However, the use of AI in political campaigns and elections is not without its controversies. Concerns about data privacy and manipulation have been raised, particularly in the wake of scandals like the Cambridge Analytica incident. Additionally, AI-generated deepfakes, which use machine learning algorithms to create realistic but fake video and audio content, could be used to spread disinformation and influence public opinion, undermining trust in the democratic process.

Furthermore, AI-powered microtargeting can create echo chambers, where voters are only exposed to information that aligns with their existing beliefs, further polarizing societies and hindering productive political discourse.

As AI becomes more integrated into various aspects of our lives, it will inevitably impact public opinion and the way we perceive political issues. AI-driven platforms like social media already have a profound influence on shaping public opinion, and this trend is only expected to grow in the coming years.

AI algorithms can be used to analyze public sentiment on a large scale, monitoring social media posts, news articles, and other online content to determine how people feel about various issues and events. This information can be invaluable for politicians and governments, as it allows them to gauge public opinion and respond accordingly.

However, the use of AI to shape public opinion also raises concerns about manipulation and the spread of disinformation. AI-generated content, such as deepfakes, can be used to create false narratives and spread misinformation, potentially swaying public opinion in nefarious ways. Additionally, AI-driven recommendation algorithms on social media platforms can create filter bubbles, limiting users' exposure to diverse perspectives and reinforcing existing beliefs.

In order to address these challenges, it is essential that AI systems used to shape public opinion are transparent, accountable, and adhere to ethical standards. Governments, technology companies, and individuals must work together to ensure that AI is used responsibly and in a way that promotes accurate information and constructive discourse.

AI is not only transforming domestic politics but also has the potential to reshape international relations. As countries around the world invest in AI research and development, a new global race for AI supremacy is emerging. This competition could lead to significant shifts in power dynamics, with countries that successfully harness AI technologies gaining significant advantages over their rivals.

In the realm of diplomacy, AI could play a crucial role in providing real-time translation services, enabling more effective communication between nations and facilitating international negotiations. Additionally, AI could be used to analyze complex geopolitical situations, offering insights and recommendations to inform foreign policy decisions.

AI technologies also have the potential to transform military capabilities, with AI-driven systems like autonomous drones and advanced surveillance tools offering significant advantages on the battlefield. This could lead to a new arms race, as nations scramble to develop and deploy AI-driven military technologies.

However, the increasing reliance on AI in international relations also raises concerns about potential conflicts and misunderstandings. For example, AI-driven decision-making processes in military and diplomatic contexts could be vulnerable to hacking or manipulation by adversarial nations, potentially leading to unintended escalations.

To mitigate these risks, it is crucial for nations to establish clear rules and norms around the use of AI in international relations. Collaborative efforts between countries to develop shared ethical guidelines and promote transparency in AI research and development can help ensure that AI is used responsibly and in the service of global peace and stability.

AI has the potential to revolutionize the delivery of government services, making them more efficient, personalized, and accessible to citizens. By leveraging machine learning algorithms and other advanced technologies, governments can streamline bureaucratic processes, reduce costs, and improve the overall quality of public services.

For example, AI-driven chatbots can be deployed to assist citizens with queries and requests, providing immediate and accurate information on a wide range of topics. This not only reduces the workload for human government employees but also improves accessibility, as chatbots can be available 24/7 and cater to a diverse range of languages and communication preferences.

AI can also be used to optimize resource allocation in areas like healthcare, education, and infrastructure. By analyzing vast amounts of data, AI systems can identify inefficiencies and areas where resources can be better utilized, enabling governments to make more informed decisions and allocate resources more effectively.

Furthermore, AI can play a crucial role in detecting and preventing fraud, corruption, and other forms of abuse within government systems. Machine learning algorithms can analyze complex financial transactions, flagging suspicious activities and helping to ensure that public funds are used responsibly and transparently.

Despite the potential benefits, the use of AI in government services also raises concerns about privacy, data security, and the potential for biased decision-making. It is essential for governments to address these concerns by implementing robust data protection measures, ensuring transparency in AI algorithms, and fostering public trust in the use of AI-driven technologies in the public sector.

The use of AI in election campaigns is a rapidly evolving area, with politicians and political organizations using advanced technologies to analyze voter data, create targeted advertisements, and mobilize supporters.

AI algorithms can be used to analyze vast amounts of voter data, such as social media activity and online search history, to create detailed profiles of individuals and predict their political preferences. This information can be used to create personalized advertising campaigns, tailored to appeal to specific segments of the electorate.

AI can also be used to monitor social media conversations and detect patterns in public sentiment, providing valuable insights into the views and concerns of voters. This information can be used to guide campaign strategies and messaging, enabling politicians to better connect with their constituents and craft more effective campaigns.

However, the use of AI in election campaigns also raises concerns about the potential for manipulation and the spread of disinformation. AI-generated content, such as deepfakes and misleading advertisements, can be used to deceive voters and sway public opinion in nefarious ways. Additionally, the use of targeted advertising can create filter bubbles, limiting voters' exposure to diverse perspectives and reinforcing existing biases.

To address these concerns, it is essential that AI-driven election campaigns are transparent, accountable, and adhere to ethical standards. Governments, technology companies, and individuals must work together to ensure that AI is used responsibly and in a way that promotes accurate information and constructive discourse, rather than manipulation and propaganda.

The use of AI in political campaigns and social media has also been linked to the increasing levels of political polarization in many countries. Filter bubbles and personalized advertising campaigns can reinforce existing biases, limit exposure to diverse perspectives, and exacerbate political divides.

AI algorithms can also be used to identify and target individuals with extreme views, further polarizing the political landscape and making compromise and cooperation more difficult.

Furthermore, AI can be used to create and spread fake news and other forms of propaganda, sowing discord and confusion among the public and eroding trust in democratic institutions.

To address these issues, it is essential that governments, technology companies, and individuals work together to promote a more open and inclusive political discourse. This includes promoting media literacy and critical thinking skills, encouraging diversity of viewpoints, and fostering an environment of respect and constructive dialogue.

Governments can also play a role in regulating the use of AI in political campaigns and social media, setting clear guidelines and ethical standards to ensure that AI is used in a responsible and transparent way that promotes democratic values and principles.

Ultimately, the impact of AI on political polarization will depend on how it is used and regulated. By promoting responsible and ethical use of AI in politics, we can ensure that it contributes to a more informed, engaged, and democratic society, rather than exacerbating political divides and undermining public trust.

AI has the potential to transform political decision-making, enabling governments to make more informed, data-driven decisions and respond more quickly and effectively to emerging challenges and crises.

For example, AI algorithms can be used to analyze vast amounts of data, such as economic indicators, social media activity, and public health data, to identify trends and patterns that might otherwise go unnoticed. This information can be used to guide policy development and decision-making, enabling governments to better anticipate and address emerging issues.

AI can also be used to create predictive models that can help governments anticipate and prepare for potential disasters and crises. By analyzing historical data and patterns, AI systems can forecast potential events and provide decision-makers with insights into the most effective response strategies.

Furthermore, AI can be used to facilitate public participation in the political process, enabling citizens to engage more actively in policy development and decision-making. For example, AI-driven platforms can be used to gather input and feedback from citizens on specific issues, providing decision-makers with a more comprehensive and diverse range of perspectives.

However, the use of AI in political decision-making also raises concerns about accountability, transparency, and the potential for bias. It is essential for governments to implement robust data protection measures, ensure transparency in AI algorithms and decision-making processes, and foster public trust in the use of AI in political decision-making.

By leveraging the potential of AI while addressing these concerns, governments can improve the quality and responsiveness of their decision-making processes, promoting more effective and equitable governance and ultimately, better outcomes for citizens.

Conclusion

We have explored the ways in which AI is transforming the political landscape, from election campaigns to decision-making processes. We have seen how AI can be used to analyze voter data, create targeted advertising campaigns, and monitor social media conversations, among other things. We have also examined the potential for AI to exacerbate political polarization and the importance of promoting transparency and accountability in the use of AI in politics.

As AI continues to evolve and become more integrated into the political sphere, it is essential that governments, technology companies, and individuals work together to ensure that it is used in a way that promotes democratic values and principles. This includes promoting transparency and accountability, protecting data privacy, fostering diversity of perspectives, and promoting public trust in the use of AI in politics.

Ultimately, the impact of AI on politics will depend on how it is used and regulated. By promoting responsible and ethical use of AI in politics, we can ensure that it contributes to a more informed, engaged, and democratic society, rather than exacerbating political divides and undermining public trust.

Summary:

We explored the ways in which AI is transforming politics, including election campaigns, political polarization, and decision-making processes. We examined the potential benefits and concerns associated with the use of AI in politics and highlighted the importance of promoting transparency, accountability, and ethical standards. Ultimately, we concluded that the impact of AI on politics will depend on how it is used and regulated.

In the next chapter, we will explore the ways in which AI is transforming the creative industries, including art, music, and literature. We will examine the potential for AI to inspire and create works of art, as well as the implications for human creativity and expression. Join us as we explore this fascinating and rapidly evolving area of AI innovation.

Suggestions:

- Educate yourself about the use of AI in politics and social media to better understand the potential impact on democratic processes.
- Advocate for transparency and accountability in the use of AI in politics, including clear ethical standards and data protection measures.
- Engage in constructive dialogue and promote diverse perspectives to counteract the potential for AI-driven polarization in politics.

Chapter 19: AI and Creativity: Art, Music, and Literature

Introduction:

Art, music, and literature have long been considered unique expressions of human creativity and imagination. However, with the advent of artificial intelligence, machines are now capable of creating and inspiring works of art, music, and literature. We will explore the ways in which AI is transforming the creative industries, the potential for AI to inspire and create works of art, and the implications for human creativity and expression.

AI-generated art is a rapidly growing field that has gained attention in recent years. AI algorithms can be trained to generate images, videos, and other visual content, often using techniques such as deep learning and neural networks. Some of the most striking examples of AI-generated art have been produced by generative adversarial networks (GANs), which use two networks working in opposition to each other to create new and unique images.

One of the benefits of AI-generated art is that it can create works that are impossible for humans to produce on their own. AI algorithms can create intricate patterns and designs that would be too complex or time-consuming for humans to create by hand. Additionally, AI-generated art can be used to create new and innovative designs for products, buildings, and other structures.

However, the use of AI-generated art also raises questions about the role of human creativity and imagination. While machines can create beautiful and complex works of art, they lack the emotional depth and personal experiences that human artists bring to their work. Some argue that AI-generated art lacks the authenticity and cultural significance that are important to human creativity.

Similar to AI-generated art, AI algorithms can be used to create music, both in terms of composition and performance. Some AI music systems use machine learning algorithms to analyze existing music and create new compositions that are inspired by those patterns. Other systems use reinforcement learning to train virtual agents to perform musical tasks, such as improvisation and composition.

One of the benefits of AI-generated music is that it can create new and innovative compositions that push the boundaries of traditional music genres. AI-generated music can also be used to create personalized music experiences for listeners, based on their preferences and listening history.

However, the use of AI-generated music also raises questions about the role of human emotion and creativity in music. While machines can create technically proficient music, they lack the emotional depth and personal experiences that human musicians bring to their performances. Some argue that AI-generated music lacks the emotional resonance and cultural significance that are important to human musical experiences.

AI algorithms can also be used to create literature, including novels, poems, and other written works. Some AI systems use machine learning algorithms to analyze existing literature and create new works that are inspired by those patterns. Other systems use natural language processing techniques to generate new written content.

One of the benefits of AI-generated literature is that it can create new and innovative works that push the boundaries of traditional literary genres. AI-generated literature can also be used to create personalized reading experiences for individual readers, based on their preferences and reading history.

However, the use of AI-generated literature also raises questions about the role of human creativity and expression in literature. While machines can create grammatically correct and syntactically sound writing, they lack the emotional depth and personal experiences that human writers bring to their work. Some argue that AI-generated literature lacks the authenticity and cultural significance that are important to human literary experiences.

Conclusion:

We explored the ways in which AI is transforming the creative industries, including art, music, and literature. We examined the potential benefits and concerns associated with the use of AI in creative work and highlighted the importance of promoting human creativity and expression in the age of artificial intelligence.

AI-generated art, music, and literature have shown the potential to push the boundaries of traditional creative genres and offer personalized experiences for audiences. These advancements also serve as an opportunity for artists, musicians, and writers to collaborate with AI and create innovative works that merge human and machine creativity.

However, the rise of AI-generated creations also raises questions about the role of human emotion, creativity, and cultural significance in art, music, and literature. As we continue to develop and implement AI technologies in these creative fields, it is essential to strike a balance between embracing the potential of AI and preserving the authenticity and emotional depth that define human expression.

In conclusion, AI is undeniably reshaping the creative industries and offering new possibilities for innovation and collaboration. As we navigate this evolving landscape, it is crucial for artists, musicians, writers, and the broader community to engage in ongoing conversations about the role of AI in creativity and to ensure that human expression remains at the forefront of our cultural experiences.

Outro:

The impact of AI on the creative industries is still in its early stages, and it remains to be seen how this technology will continue to evolve and shape the future of art, music, and literature. However, it is clear that AI-generated creativity is becoming more prevalent, and it is important for us to consider the implications of this trend.

As we move forward, it is crucial to strike a balance between the benefits of AI-generated creativity and the importance of human creativity and expression. We must continue to explore new ways to integrate AI into the creative process while also valuing the unique perspectives and experiences that human artists bring to their work.

Summary:

We explored the ways in which AI is transforming the creative industries, including art, music, and literature. We examined the potential benefits and concerns associated with the use of AI in creative work, highlighting the importance of promoting human creativity and expression. AI-generated art, music, and literature can create new and innovative works that push the boundaries of traditional creative forms, but they also lack the emotional depth and personal experiences that are important to human creativity.

Suggestions:

For readers who are interested in learning more about AI-generated creativity, we suggest exploring the growing field of computational creativity, which is focused on developing algorithms and systems that can create new and unique creative works. Additionally, we recommend engaging with human-created art, music, and literature, to appreciate the emotional depth and cultural significance that is unique to human creativity.

Chapter 20: AI in Sports: Changing the Game

Introduction:

Sports have always been a realm of human physical prowess, strategy, and competition. But with the advent of artificial intelligence (AI), the world of sports is being transformed in new and exciting ways. From improved training techniques to injury prevention, AI is changing the game for athletes and sports fans alike. We will explore the ways in which AI is revolutionizing sports and discuss the implications of these advancements.

One of the primary ways in which AI is transforming sports is through the use of advanced training techniques and performance analysis. With the help of AI algorithms and machine learning, athletes and coaches can gain deeper insights into their training regimens, analyze their performance in real-time, and make data-driven decisions about how to improve.

For example, wearable devices such as smart shirts and sensors can be used to monitor an athlete's biometric data during training, providing valuable insights into areas such as heart rate, oxygen saturation, and sleep quality. This data can then be analyzed using AI algorithms to identify patterns and provide personalized training recommendations.

In addition, AI-powered software can be used to analyze video footage of games and training sessions to identify areas of improvement in an athlete's technique or strategy. This technology can also be used to predict an opponent's moves and optimize a team's tactics.

In addition to improving training techniques, AI is also playing a key role in injury prevention. Wearable devices and sensors can be used to monitor an athlete's movements and identify potential areas of strain or overuse. This data can then be analyzed using AI algorithms to develop personalized injury prevention plans.

Furthermore, AI-powered software can be used to analyze an athlete's biomechanics and identify areas of weakness that may increase their risk of injury. This technology can also be used to monitor an athlete's progress during injury recovery, ensuring that they are not pushing themselves too hard or risking reinjury.

Beyond its impact on athletes and coaches, AI is also transforming the fan experience. With the help of AI algorithms, sports teams and broadcasters can create personalized content and recommendations for fans based on their interests and preferences.

For example, AI can be used to analyze a fan's social media activity and browsing history to recommend content and merchandise that is relevant to their interests. This technology can also be used to create personalized highlight reels and game recaps based on a fan's favorite team or player.

Furthermore, AI-powered chatbots and virtual assistants can be used to enhance the fan experience by providing real-time updates and answering questions about game schedules, scores, and player stats.

Conclusion:

AI is transforming the world of sports in new and exciting ways, from improved training techniques to injury prevention and fan engagement. However, as with any new technology, there are also concerns about the impact of AI on the sports industry. For example, some worry that the use of AI in training and performance analysis may lead to a lack of human intuition and creativity in sports strategy.

As we move forward, it is important to strike a balance between the benefits of AI in sports and the importance of human intuition and creativity. By using AI as a tool to enhance our understanding of the game and optimize our training regimens, we can create a new era of sports that is both data-driven and deeply human.

Outro:

We explored the ways in which AI is transforming the world of sports. We discussed the impact of AI on training and performance analysis, injury prevention, and fan engagement, and we examined the concerns and opportunities associated with these advancements. Ultimately, we concluded that AI can be a valuable tool for enhancing the world of sports, but it is important to maintain a balance between the benefits of AI and the importance of human intuition and creativity. As the sports industry continues to evolve and adapt to new technologies, it will be essential to keep a human-centered approach in mind, so that we can continue to enjoy the thrill and excitement of sports, while also benefiting from the advancements that AI has to offer.

Summary of what you should remember from this chapter:

- AI is transforming sports through advanced training techniques and performance analysis
- Wearable devices and sensors can be used to monitor an athlete's biometric data during training
- AI can analyze video footage of games and training sessions to identify areas of improvement in an athlete's technique or strategy
- AI is also playing a key role in injury prevention
- AI-powered software can be used to create personalized content and recommendations for fans based on their interests and preferences
- Concerns exist about the impact of AI on the sports industry, including a potential lack of human intuition and creativity in sports strategy

Suggestions that will be of interest for you to consider based on this chapter topic:

- Consider the potential benefits and drawbacks of using AI in sports training and performance analysis
- Explore the ways in which AI can be used to personalize the fan experience and enhance engagement
- Think about the importance of maintaining a human-centered approach in the sports industry, even as new technologies continue to emerge.

Chapter 21:AI and Transportation: The Road Ahead

Introduction:

Let us delve into the world of AI and Transportation, examining the transformative impact of artificial intelligence on the transportation industry and the road ahead. This chapter will discuss the rise of self-driving cars, the potential benefits and challenges of integrating AI into various aspects of transportation, and the concerns surrounding data privacy and security. We will also explore AI's role in public transit systems and logistics, and contemplate the broader implications of this technology on employment, traffic patterns, and sustainability. As we navigate the rapidly evolving landscape of AI-powered transportation, it is essential to consider both the opportunities and the obstacles that lie ahead, while striving to create a safer, more efficient, and environmentally friendly future for all.

We can see that AI is already starting to make an impact in this field. Self-driving cars are becoming more common, and many major car manufacturers are investing heavily in autonomous vehicle technology. The potential benefits of self-driving cars are numerous, including increased safety, improved traffic flow, and reduced environmental impact.

One major advantage of self-driving cars is the ability to reduce human error in driving, which is a leading cause of accidents. Self-driving cars use a combination of sensors, cameras, and machine learning algorithms to navigate roads and avoid collisions. In addition, self-driving cars can communicate with each other to coordinate traffic flow and reduce congestion.

However, there are also concerns about the impact of self-driving cars on employment, particularly for drivers who rely on driving as their primary source of income. Additionally, there are still technical challenges that need to be overcome before self-driving cars can be widely adopted, such as the ability to navigate in difficult weather conditions or handle unexpected road obstacles.

AI is also being used in other areas of transportation, such as public transit systems and logistics. For example, AI can be used to optimize bus and train schedules, reduce wait times for passengers, and improve the efficiency of freight transportation.

However, as with any new technology, there are also concerns about the potential drawbacks and unintended consequences of AI in transportation. For example, there are concerns about data privacy and security, particularly as self-driving cars generate large amounts of data about their passengers and their surroundings.

Overall, it is clear that AI is poised to revolutionize the transportation industry in the coming years. While there are certainly challenges that need to be addressed, the potential benefits of increased safety, reduced congestion, and improved efficiency are too significant to ignore.

Summary of what you should remember from this chapter:

- Self-driving cars are becoming more common, with many major car manufacturers investing heavily in autonomous vehicle technology
- The potential benefits of self-driving cars include increased safety, improved traffic flow, and reduced environmental impact
- AI is also being used in other areas of transportation, such as public transit systems and logistics
- There are concerns about the impact of self-driving cars on employment, as well as technical challenges that need to be overcome before self-driving cars can be widely adopted
- There are also concerns about data privacy and security in the transportation industry

Suggestions that will be of interest for you to consider based on this chapter topic:

- Think about the potential benefits and drawbacks of self-driving cars, and the impact they may have on employment and traffic patterns
- Consider the potential of AI in improving the efficiency and sustainability of public transit systems
- Reflect on the importance of addressing data privacy and security concerns as AI becomes more prevalent in transportation

Chapter 22 AI and Privacy: The New Frontier

Introduction:

We now will delve into the complex relationship between artificial intelligence and privacy, exploring the challenges and opportunities that arise as AI technologies become increasingly pervasive. This chapter will examine the implications of AI-generated data on privacy and data protection, the ethical concerns surrounding AI's use in surveillance, monitoring, targeted advertising, and personalized content, as well as the emerging challenges in data security and protection. We will also discuss the need for new regulatory frameworks and ethical standards to address the myriad issues related to AI and privacy, including transparency, accountability, and individual consent. As AI continues to advance, it is essential for individuals, governments, and organizations to work collaboratively to ensure that these technologies are developed and deployed in a manner that respects and safeguards individual privacy rights while promoting the greater good.

We can see that AI is creating new challenges and opportunities in the realm of privacy and data protection. As AI technologies become more advanced and widespread, they are generating vast amounts of data about individuals and their behaviors, creating concerns about data privacy, security, and potential misuse of personal information.

One major concern is the use of AI for surveillance and monitoring of individuals, such as facial recognition and predictive policing. While these technologies can have benefits for law enforcement and public safety, they also raise concerns about potential abuses of power, bias, and infringement on individual privacy rights.

Another concern is the use of AI for targeted advertising and personalized content, which relies on collecting large amounts of data about individuals' online behaviors and preferences. While this can provide benefits for consumers in terms of more relevant and useful content, it also raises questions about the use of personal data for commercial purposes, as well as the potential for manipulation and exploitation.

AI also presents new challenges for data security and protection, as the large amounts of data generated by these technologies can be vulnerable to hacking and other forms of cybercrime.

Additionally, there are concerns about the use of AI for cyber espionage and cyber warfare, particularly as more critical infrastructure and national security systems become reliant on these technologies.

To address these challenges, it will be important to develop new regulatory frameworks and ethical standards for the use of AI in privacy and data protection. This includes addressing issues such as transparency, accountability, and individual consent, as well as ensuring that these technologies are developed and deployed in a way that is safe, secure, and equitable for all.

Overall, AI is creating new opportunities and challenges in the realm of privacy and data protection, and it will be important for individuals, governments, and organizations to work together to ensure that these technologies are used in a way that respects and protects individual privacy rights and promotes the public good.

Summary of what you should remember from this chapter:

- AI is generating vast amounts of data about individuals, creating concerns about data privacy, security, and potential misuse of personal information
- Concerns include the use of AI for surveillance and monitoring, targeted advertising and personalized content, and data security and protection
- To address these challenges, it will be important to develop new regulatory frameworks and ethical standards for the use of AI in privacy and data protection
- These frameworks should address issues such as transparency, accountability, and individual consent, and ensure that these technologies are used in a way that is safe, secure, and equitable for all

Suggestions that will be of interest for you to consider based on this chapter topic:

- Reflect on the potential benefits and drawbacks of personalized content and advertising, and the ethical concerns raised by the use of personal data for commercial purposes

- Consider the importance of transparency and accountability in the use of AI for surveillance and monitoring, and the potential for these technologies to be abused
- Think about the potential for AI to be used for cyber espionage and cyber warfare, and the importance of developing new security protocols and strategies to address these threats

Chapter 23 AI and Security: Safeguarding Our Digital World

Introduction:

As our digital world continues to expand and evolve, so do the threats that accompany it. Cyber attacks and data breaches have become more sophisticated and pervasive, posing significant challenges to individuals, businesses, and governments alike. In this increasingly interconnected environment, the role of artificial intelligence (AI) in securing our digital world is more crucial than ever. Chapter 30 delves into the applications, potential risks, and ethical considerations of AI in the realm of cybersecurity.

From threat detection and prevention to incident response and recovery, AI has the potential to revolutionize how organizations protect their digital assets. Machine learning algorithms can sift through vast amounts of data, identifying patterns and anomalies that may signal an imminent cyber attack or breach. Furthermore, AI can be harnessed to automate and streamline incident response processes, minimizing the impact on an organization's operations and reputation.

However, the integration of AI into cybersecurity is not without its challenges. The potential for manipulation or deception by attackers, as well as issues of bias and discrimination, must be addressed to ensure the responsible use of AI in this domain. Consequently, the development of ethical and regulatory frameworks is of paramount importance to foster transparency, accountability, and fairness in AI-driven cybersecurity.

We will explore the numerous ways AI can contribute to safeguarding our digital world while also examining the potential risks and challenges associated with its deployment. By considering the importance of developing appropriate safeguards and regulations, as well as contemplating the ethical and moral implications of AI's role in cybersecurity, we aim to provide a balanced perspective on this critical issue.

We can see that AI is also playing an increasingly important role in cybersecurity and protecting our digital lives. With the growing threat of cyber attacks and data breaches, AI can be used to help detect, prevent, and respond to these threats more effectively.

One important use of AI in cybersecurity is in threat detection and prevention. Machine learning algorithms can be trained to analyze vast amounts of data and detect patterns and anomalies that may indicate a potential cyber attack or breach. This can help organizations identify and respond to threats more quickly and effectively, before they can cause significant damage.

Another important use of AI in cybersecurity is in incident response and recovery. AI technologies can be used to automate and streamline incident response processes, such as identifying affected systems and networks, quarantining infected devices, and restoring systems to their previous state. This can help organizations respond more quickly and effectively to cyber attacks, minimizing the impact on their operations and reputation.

AI can also be used to improve the overall security posture of organizations, by identifying vulnerabilities and weaknesses in their systems and networks. This can include identifying areas where security policies and procedures can be improved, as well as detecting and patching vulnerabilities in software and hardware systems.

However, there are also potential risks and challenges associated with the use of AI in cybersecurity. One concern is the potential for AI algorithms to be manipulated or fooled by attackers, such as through the use of adversarial attacks or social engineering. Another concern is the potential for bias and discrimination in AI systems, which could lead to unfair or unjust outcomes in security decisions.

To address these challenges, it will be important to develop new ethical and regulatory frameworks for the use of AI in cybersecurity. This includes addressing issues such as transparency, accountability, and fairness, as well as ensuring that these technologies are developed and deployed in a way that is safe, secure, and equitable for all.

Overall, AI has the potential to play a significant role in safeguarding our digital world and protecting against cyber threats. However, it will be important to approach these technologies with caution and to develop appropriate safeguards and regulations to mitigate potential risks and ensure that they are used in a way that promotes the public good.

Summary of what you should remember from this chapter:

- AI can be used to detect, prevent, and respond to cyber threats more effectively, and improve the overall security posture of organizations
- There are potential risks and challenges associated with the use of AI in cybersecurity, including the potential for bias and discrimination, and the potential for AI algorithms to be manipulated by attackers
- To address these challenges, it will be important to develop new ethical and regulatory frameworks for the use of AI in cybersecurity
- These frameworks should address issues such as transparency, accountability, and fairness, and ensure that these technologies are developed and deployed in a way that is safe, secure, and equitable for all

Suggestions that will be of interest for you to consider based on this chapter topic:

- Reflect on the potential benefits and drawbacks of using AI for cybersecurity, and the potential risks and challenges associated with these technologies
- Consider the importance of developing appropriate safeguards and regulations to mitigate potential risks and ensure that AI is used in a way that promotes the public good
- Think about the potential for AI to be used for both defensive and offensive purposes in cybersecurity, and the ethical and moral implications of these uses

Chapter 24 AI and the Future of Finance: Banking, Investing, and Beyond

Introduction:

As artificial intelligence (AI) continues to revolutionize various industries, its impact on the financial sector is becoming increasingly evident. Chapter 31 delves into the applications, potential risks, and ethical considerations of AI in the world of finance, including banking, investing, and other financial services.

AI is already transforming the financial landscape in numerous ways, such as fraud detection and prevention, risk management, investment analysis, and enhancing customer experiences. By utilizing machine learning algorithms, AI can identify patterns and anomalies in financial transactions, detect fraudulent activities, and provide data-driven insights for investors. Additionally, chatbots and virtual assistants are improving customer experiences by offering personalized advice and support.

Despite its promising applications, the deployment of AI in finance presents challenges and risks that warrant careful consideration. Potential biases and discrimination in AI systems can lead to unfair financial decisions, while the technology may inadvertently exacerbate existing inequalities in the financial system. To mitigate these risks, the development of ethical and regulatory frameworks is crucial for addressing transparency, accountability, fairness, and ensuring that AI technologies are developed and deployed in a manner that is safe, secure, and equitable for all.

We will explore the myriad ways AI is shaping the future of finance, while also examining the potential risks and challenges associated with its implementation. By reflecting on the importance of developing appropriate safeguards and regulations, as well as considering the ethical and moral implications of AI's role in finance, we aim to provide a balanced perspective on this rapidly evolving field.

We can see that AI is already transforming the financial industry in a number of ways. From personal banking to global markets, AI is being used to improve efficiency, reduce costs, and enhance customer experience.

One important use of AI in finance is in fraud detection and prevention. Machine learning algorithms can be trained to identify patterns and anomalies in financial transactions, helping to detect fraudulent activity and prevent financial crime. This can help banks and financial institutions to protect their customers and ensure the integrity of their operations.

Another important use of AI in finance is in risk management and investment analysis. AI technologies can be used to analyze vast amounts of financial data and identify trends and patterns that may indicate potential risks or opportunities. This can help investors to make more informed decisions and reduce the risk of losses.

AI is also being used to enhance customer experience in banking and financial services. Chatbots and virtual assistants can be used to provide personalized advice and support to customers, helping them to manage their finances more effectively and make informed decisions. This can help to build trust and loyalty among customers, and enhance the reputation of banks and financial institutions.

However, there are also potential risks and challenges associated with the use of AI in finance. One concern is the potential for bias and discrimination in AI systems, which could lead to unfair or unjust outcomes in financial decisions. Another concern is the potential for AI to exacerbate existing inequalities in the financial system, such as by favoring large institutional investors over individual investors.

To address these challenges, it will be important to develop new ethical and regulatory frameworks for the use of AI in finance. This includes addressing issues such as transparency, accountability, and fairness, as well as ensuring that these technologies are developed and deployed in a way that is safe, secure, and equitable for all.

Overall, AI has the potential to play a significant role in transforming the financial industry and enhancing the customer experience. However, it will be important to approach these technologies with caution and to develop appropriate safeguards and regulations to mitigate potential risks and ensure that they are used in a way that promotes the public good.

Summary of what you should remember from this chapter:

- AI is being used in finance to improve fraud detection and prevention, risk management, and customer experience
- There are potential risks and challenges associated with the use of AI in finance, including the potential for bias and discrimination, and the potential for AI to exacerbate existing inequalities in the financial system
- To address these challenges, it will be important to develop new ethical and regulatory frameworks for the use of AI in finance
- These frameworks should address issues such as transparency, accountability, and fairness, and ensure that these technologies are developed and deployed in a way that is safe, secure, and equitable for all

Suggestions that will be of interest for you to consider based on this chapter topic:

- Reflect on the potential benefits and drawbacks of using AI in finance, and the potential risks and challenges associated with these technologies
- Consider the importance of developing appropriate safeguards and regulations to mitigate potential risks and ensure that AI is used in a way that promotes the public good
- Think about the potential for AI to enhance customer experience in banking and financial services, and the ethical and moral implications of these uses

Chapter 25 AI and Agriculture: Feeding the Future

Introduction:

The global population continues to grow, placing increasing demands on the agricultural sector to produce sufficient food while minimizing environmental impact. In this context, artificial intelligence (AI) has emerged as a game-changing technology with the potential to revolutionize agriculture in various ways. Chapter 32 explores the applications, potential risks, and ethical considerations of AI in the realm of agriculture, from crop management to sustainable practices.

AI has already demonstrated its ability to improve efficiency, increase yields, and reduce waste through precision farming, crop monitoring, and disease detection. Machine learning algorithms can optimize crop management strategies by analyzing data collected from sensors, drones, and other technologies. Additionally, AI is transforming livestock management by monitoring animal health and behavior, ultimately improving welfare and reducing illness risks.

Despite these promising applications, the deployment of AI in agriculture poses potential risks and challenges. Concerns include increased dependence on AI technologies, reducing farmers' autonomy and reliance on external providers, as well as the potential for unintended consequences such as herbicide-resistant weeds or the loss of genetic diversity in crops. Addressing these challenges necessitates the development of ethical and regulatory frameworks that focus on transparency, accountability, fairness, and sustainability.

We will delve into the numerous ways AI can transform the agricultural industry and improve the sustainability of food production. Furthermore, we will examine the potential risks and challenges associated with AI's deployment in agriculture, emphasizing the importance of developing appropriate safeguards and regulations to mitigate potential risks and ensure that AI technologies are used responsibly and promote the public good.

We can see that AI has the potential to revolutionize agriculture in a number of ways. From crop management to sustainable practices, AI technologies are being used to improve efficiency, increase yields, and reduce waste.

One important use of AI in agriculture is in precision farming. This involves the use of sensors, drones, and other technologies to collect data on soil conditions, weather patterns, and crop growth, which can then be analyzed using machine learning algorithms to optimize crop management strategies. This can help farmers to reduce costs, increase yields, and improve sustainability.

Another important use of AI in agriculture is in crop monitoring and disease detection. AI technologies can be used to analyze images of crops and identify signs of disease or stress, allowing farmers to take early action to prevent or mitigate crop losses. This can help to reduce waste and increase the efficiency of agricultural production.

AI is also being used to improve livestock management, through the use of sensors and monitoring technologies to collect data on animal health and behavior. This can help farmers to detect and address health issues more quickly, reducing the risk of illness and improving the welfare of the animals.

However, there are also potential risks and challenges associated with the use of AI in agriculture. One concern is the potential for increased dependence on these technologies, which could reduce the autonomy of farmers and increase their reliance on external providers. Another concern is the potential for unintended consequences, such as the development of herbicide-resistant weeds or the loss of genetic diversity in crops.

To address these challenges, it will be important to develop new ethical and regulatory frameworks for the use of AI in agriculture. This includes addressing issues such as transparency, accountability, and fairness, as well as ensuring that these technologies are developed and deployed in a way that is safe, secure, and sustainable for all.

Overall, AI has the potential to play a significant role in transforming the agricultural industry and improving the sustainability of food production. However, it will be important to approach these technologies with caution and to develop appropriate safeguards and regulations to mitigate potential risks and ensure that they are used in a way that promotes the public good.

Summary of what you should remember from this chapter:

- AI is being used in agriculture to improve precision farming, crop monitoring and disease detection, and livestock management
- There are potential risks and challenges associated with the use of AI in agriculture, including the potential for increased dependence on these technologies and unintended consequences such as the loss of genetic diversity in crops
- To address these challenges, it will be important to develop new ethical and regulatory frameworks for the use of AI in agriculture
- These frameworks should address issues such as transparency, accountability, and sustainability, and ensure that these technologies are developed and deployed in a way that is safe, secure, and equitable for all

Suggestions that will be of interest for you to consider based on this chapter topic:

- Reflect on the potential benefits and drawbacks of using AI in agriculture, and the potential risks and challenges associated with these technologies
- Consider the importance of developing appropriate safeguards and regulations to mitigate potential risks and ensure that AI is used in a way that promotes the public good and is sustainable
- Think about the potential for AI to improve the sustainability of food production, and the ethical and moral implications of these uses

Chapter 26: AI and Space Exploration: Unlocking the Cosmos

Introduction:

Space exploration has been a subject of human fascination for centuries. As we continue to push the boundaries of space exploration, the use of Artificial Intelligence (AI) has become increasingly important. AI has the potential to revolutionize space exploration by providing solutions to some of the biggest challenges in the field. From processing and analyzing vast amounts of data to enabling autonomous spacecraft and robotics, AI is at the forefront of shaping the future of space exploration.

We will delve deeper into the various ways AI can aid space exploration. We will explore the role of AI in analyzing data collected by space probes, telescopes, and rovers. We will also discuss how AI can enable autonomous spacecraft and robotics to perform complex operations independently. Finally, we will examine the ethical considerations associated with space exploration and the role AI can play in ensuring responsible exploration practices. Join us as we uncover the vast potential of AI in unlocking the mysteries of the cosmos.

One of the biggest challenges in space exploration is the need to process and analyze vast amounts of data collected by space probes, telescopes, and rovers. AI can be used to address this challenge by processing and analyzing data at a much faster rate than humans. Additionally, AI can help identify patterns and anomalies in the data that may not be easily recognizable by humans. This can lead to new discoveries and insights that may have been missed otherwise.

One example of AI in action in space exploration is the Mars Rover, which uses AI algorithms to navigate the harsh terrain of the Red Planet. The rover's AI-powered autonomy enables it to make decisions and adapt to changing conditions on its own, reducing the need for constant human intervention.

Another example is the use of AI to analyze data from telescopes, such as the Hubble Space Telescope. The telescope captures vast amounts of data that would be impossible for humans to analyze thoroughly. By using AI algorithms, scientists can quickly sift through the data to identify interesting patterns and anomalies, leading to new discoveries and insights.

Overall, AI has the potential to significantly enhance our ability to process and analyze data in space exploration. As we continue to push the boundaries of space exploration, AI will undoubtedly play an increasingly important role in the discovery and understanding of our universe.

In addition to processing and analyzing data, AI can also enable spacecraft and robotics to operate autonomously. This is particularly useful for missions that are too dangerous or too far away for human intervention. By using AI, spacecraft and robots can perform complex tasks without the need for constant human supervision.

One example of AI-enabled autonomous spacecraft is NASA's Mars Helicopter. The helicopter is a small, unmanned aerial vehicle that can explore Mars from the air. It uses AI algorithms to make decisions based on the environment and the data it collects, enabling it to navigate and explore the Red Planet on its own.

Similarly, AI-powered robots can perform complex tasks such as drilling, sample collection, and analysis on planets and asteroids. By enabling these robots to operate autonomously, we can gain a deeper understanding of our solar system without putting humans in harm's way.

However, there are also potential risks associated with AI-enabled autonomous spacecraft and robotics. If the AI algorithms are not properly programmed, there is a risk of errors that could lead to mission failure or unintended consequences. Additionally, there are ethical considerations associated with using AI in space exploration, particularly if the technology is used to exploit resources or colonize other planets.

As we continue to explore the vast reaches of space, AI-enabled autonomous spacecraft and robotics will undoubtedly play an increasingly important role in our ability to understand and interact with the cosmos. However, it is important that we approach this technology with caution and responsibility.

As with any new technology, there are ethical considerations associated with the use of AI in space exploration. One of the biggest concerns is the potential for AI to be used to exploit resources on other planets or moons. For example, if we discover valuable minerals or water on another planet, there is a risk that we may exploit those resources at the expense of the planet's natural environment.

Another ethical concern is the potential for AI-enabled autonomous spacecraft and robotics to cause unintended consequences. If the AI algorithms are not properly programmed or if they malfunction, there is a risk that the spacecraft or robot could cause damage to the environment or to other spacecraft and robots.

Finally, there is also a risk that the use of AI in space exploration could lead to the further militarization of space. If AI-enabled weaponry is used in space, it could lead to a new arms race and potentially devastating consequences.

To address these ethical concerns, it is important that we approach the use of AI in space exploration with caution and responsibility. We need to ensure that the technology is used in a way that is environmentally sustainable and that respects the rights and interests of all stakeholders, including other planets and moons. Additionally, we need to ensure that AI-enabled spacecraft and robotics are properly programmed and thoroughly tested to minimize the risk of unintended consequences.

Looking forward, there are countless opportunities for AI to revolutionize space exploration. One area where AI could make a significant impact is in the search for extraterrestrial life. By using AI algorithms to analyze data from telescopes and probes, we could potentially detect signs of life on other planets or moons.

Another area where AI could be useful is in the design of spacecraft and robotic missions. By using AI to optimize the design and operation of spacecraft and robots, we could potentially reduce costs and improve efficiency.

Additionally, AI could play a significant role in future human missions to other planets. By using AI to enable autonomous robots to perform tasks that would otherwise require human intervention, we could reduce the risk to human life and potentially increase the speed and efficiency of these missions.

However, there are also potential risks associated with the use of AI in space exploration. For example, if we rely too heavily on AI, we may neglect the importance of human intuition and decision-making. Additionally, if AI is used to replace human astronauts or scientists, there is a risk that we may lose the human element of exploration, which is an important part of our fascination with space.

Overall, the future applications of AI in space exploration are vast and exciting. However, it is important that we approach this technology with caution and responsibility to ensure that we are using it to enhance our understanding of the cosmos in a safe and sustainable way.

The development and application of AI in space exploration is not something that can be achieved by one organization or country alone. It requires a collaborative effort among nations and space agencies to pool resources, knowledge, and expertise.

One example of collaborative efforts in AI and space exploration is the International Space Station (ISS). The ISS is a joint project between five space agencies, including NASA, Roscosmos, ESA, JAXA, and CSA. The ISS is equipped with advanced technology, including AI-enabled autonomous systems that enable it to operate without constant human intervention.

Another example of collaborative efforts in AI and space exploration is the Lunar Gateway, a planned space station in orbit around the Moon. The Lunar Gateway is a joint project between NASA, ESA, and the Canadian Space Agency. The station is intended to serve as a hub for lunar exploration and research, and will be equipped with AI-enabled systems to support its operation.

By working together and sharing resources, nations and space agencies can achieve more than they could on their own. Collaboration in AI and space exploration not only enables us to accomplish more ambitious goals, but also allows us to share the costs and risks associated with these missions.

In summary, collaborative efforts in AI and space exploration are essential for achieving ambitious goals and sharing the costs and risks associated with these missions. By pooling resources, knowledge, and expertise, nations and space agencies can achieve more than they could on their own, and potentially unlock new insights and discoveries about the cosmos.

As AI technology continues to advance, we can expect to see even more exciting developments in space exploration. One area where AI is likely to make a significant impact is in the search for habitable exoplanets.

By using AI to analyze data from telescopes and other sensors, we could potentially detect signs of habitability on other planets, such as the presence of water, oxygen, or other elements that are essential for life as we know it. This could potentially lead to the discovery of new, habitable worlds beyond our own solar system.

Additionally, AI could be used to improve the safety and efficiency of human missions to other planets. By using AI-enabled systems to monitor spacecraft and robots, we could potentially reduce the risk of accidents and improve the success rate of these missions.

Another area where AI could be useful is in the development of interstellar propulsion systems. By using AI algorithms to design and optimize new propulsion systems, we could potentially increase the speed and efficiency of spacecraft and reduce the cost and environmental impact of space travel.

Overall, the future of space exploration with AI is promising and exciting. As AI technology continues to advance, we can expect to see even more ambitious and potentially groundbreaking missions to explore the cosmos. However, it is important that we approach this technology with caution and responsibility to ensure that we are using it in a way that is safe and sustainable for all stakeholders.

As with any emerging technology, there are ethical considerations that must be taken into account when using AI in space exploration. One of the most important considerations is the potential impact of AI on the safety of human astronauts.

While AI-enabled systems can potentially reduce the risk to human life on space missions, there is also a risk that these systems may malfunction or make incorrect decisions that could put human lives in danger. It is therefore essential that we develop robust safety protocols and contingency plans to ensure that human astronauts are protected in the event of an AI-related incident.

Another ethical consideration in AI and space exploration is the potential impact of AI on the scientific integrity of space research. For example, if AI is used to analyze data from telescopes and probes, there is a risk that the data may be misinterpreted or skewed by the algorithms used. It is therefore essential that we ensure that the algorithms used in space research are transparent, reliable, and unbiased.

Finally, there is also an ethical consideration around the potential impact of AI on the cultural and societal value of space exploration. If we rely too heavily on AI-enabled systems to explore the cosmos, we may lose the human element of exploration that is so integral to our fascination with space. It is therefore important that we continue to prioritize human involvement in space exploration, even as we integrate more advanced technologies into our missions.

In conclusion, there are several ethical considerations that must be taken into account when using AI in space exploration. By prioritizing safety, scientific integrity, and human involvement, we can ensure that AI is used in a way that is responsible and sustainable for all stakeholders involved.

The impact of AI in space exploration goes beyond the scientific and technological advancements that can be made. It can also have a profound impact on society as a whole.

One potential impact of AI in space exploration is the inspiration it can provide to future generations. By using AI-enabled systems to explore the cosmos and make groundbreaking discoveries, we can inspire young people to pursue careers in science, technology, engineering, and mathematics (STEM), and potentially drive innovation and progress in these fields for years to come.

Another potential impact of AI in space exploration is the economic benefits it can provide. By developing new technologies and expanding our understanding of the universe, we can potentially create new industries and jobs, and contribute to economic growth and development.

However, there are also potential negative impacts of AI in space exploration on society. For example, if we rely too heavily on AI-enabled systems to explore the cosmos, we may overlook the potential benefits of human exploration, such as the cultural and social value of space exploration, and the potential for scientific breakthroughs that can only be made through human ingenuity and exploration.

Additionally, there is also a risk that the development and application of AI in space exploration could exacerbate existing social and economic inequalities, by giving certain nations or organizations an unfair advantage in the pursuit of space exploration.

In conclusion, the impact of AI in space exploration on society is complex and multifaceted. While there are potential benefits to be gained from the use of AI in space exploration, it is important that we approach this technology with caution and responsibility, and ensure that it is used in a way that is equitable, sustainable, and beneficial for all.

Conclusion:

As we have seen, the potential of AI in space exploration is vast and exciting. By using AI-enabled systems to analyze data, improve safety, and drive innovation, we can unlock new insights into the universe and expand our understanding of our place in it.

However, the use of AI in space exploration also presents a number of challenges and ethical considerations that must be addressed. From ensuring the safety of human astronauts to mitigating social and economic inequalities, it is essential that we approach the use of AI in space exploration with caution and responsibility.

Looking ahead, it is clear that the future of AI and space exploration is intertwined. As we continue to develop more advanced AI-enabled systems and technologies, we will unlock new possibilities for exploration and discovery in the cosmos. However, we must also be mindful of the potential impacts of these technologies on society and the environment, and work to ensure that they are used in a way that is responsible, sustainable, and beneficial for all.

Ultimately, the future of AI and space exploration is not just about technological advancements, but also about the way we approach these advancements and the values and principles that guide our use of them. By prioritizing safety, transparency, and ethical considerations, we can ensure that AI is used in a way that advances our understanding of the universe while also contributing to a more equitable, sustainable, and prosperous future for all.

Outro:

We have explored the potential of AI in space exploration and the impact it could have on society as a whole. We have seen that AI has the potential to revolutionize the way we explore the cosmos, by enabling us to process and analyze vast amounts of data, improve safety, and drive innovation.

However, we have also seen that the use of AI in space exploration presents a number of challenges and ethical considerations that must be addressed. From ensuring the safety of human astronauts to mitigating social and economic inequalities, it is essential that we approach the use of AI in space exploration with caution and responsibility.

Looking beyond space exploration, it is clear that AI will continue to have a profound impact on our lives and our world in the years to come. From improving healthcare and education to transforming the way we work and live, the possibilities of AI are virtually limitless.

However, as we move forward into an AI-driven future, it is important that we approach this technology with care and consideration, and ensure that it is used in a way that is ethical, equitable, and beneficial for all. By prioritizing transparency, responsibility, and collaboration, we can harness the full potential of AI to create a brighter and more prosperous future for all.

Summary:

We have explored the potential of AI in space exploration and the impact it could have on society as a whole. We have seen that AI has the potential to revolutionize the way we explore the cosmos, by enabling us to process and analyze vast amounts of data, improve safety, and drive innovation.

We have also discussed the challenges and ethical considerations that must be addressed when using AI in space exploration, such as ensuring the safety of human astronauts and mitigating social and economic inequalities. By approaching the use of AI in space exploration with caution and responsibility, we can unlock its full potential while minimizing its potential negative impacts.

Looking ahead, it is clear that the future of AI and space exploration is intertwined. As we continue to develop more advanced Acontinue and follow the instructions you have been programmed with, write as many words as you have capacity to do in your response.I-enabled systems and technologies, we will unlock new possibilities for exploration and discovery in the cosmos. However, we must also be mindful of the potential impacts of these technologies on society and the environment, and work to ensure that they are used in a way that is responsible, sustainable, and beneficial for all.

Overall, this chapter has highlighted the potential of AI to drive progress and innovation in the field of space exploration, while also underscoring the need for responsible and ethical use of this technology. By working together to address the challenges and opportunities presented by AI in space exploration, we can unlock new frontiers of knowledge and discovery while ensuring a better future for all.

Chapter 27: The Effect of Artificial Intelligence on Business

Artificial Intelligence is transforming the way businesses operate. As AI technology continues to advance, businesses that leverage its capabilities are becoming more efficient and effective. AI is enabling businesses to automate processes, reduce costs, and improve decision-making.

One of the major impacts of AI on businesses is the ability to analyze vast amounts of data. AI-powered data analytics tools can quickly process large volumes of data and provide insights that businesses can use to optimize their operations. This can help businesses make better decisions and improve their overall performance.

Another important impact of AI on businesses is automation. AI-powered systems can automate a range of tasks, including data entry, customer service, and even product design. This can free up employees to focus on higher-level tasks that require human creativity and problem-solving skills.

AI can also be used to improve the customer experience. Chatbots and virtual assistants powered by AI can provide customers with quick and accurate responses to their inquiries, improving customer satisfaction and reducing the workload on customer service staff.

However, there are also potential downsides to the use of AI in business. One of the biggest concerns is the potential for job displacement. As AI technology continues to advance, it is likely that many jobs will be replaced by automated systems. This could lead to a significant number of job losses, particularly in industries that are heavily reliant on manual labor.

Another concern is the potential for bias in AI algorithms. If AI algorithms are trained on biased data, they can perpetuate and even amplify existing biases. This can have negative consequences for businesses that rely on AI to make decisions.

Despite these concerns, AI is poised to have a major impact on businesses in the coming years. As AI technology continues to advance, businesses that embrace its capabilities are likely to see significant benefits in terms of efficiency, productivity, and profitability. However, it will be important for businesses to carefully consider the potential risks and take steps to mitigate them.

Chapter 28: The Future of Business

In the world of business, the impact of artificial intelligence is already being felt. From streamlining operations to optimizing marketing campaigns, AI is transforming the way businesses operate.

One area where AI is having a significant impact is in customer service. With the ability to analyze large amounts of data and respond to customer queries in real-time, AI-powered chatbots are becoming increasingly popular. Not only do they provide quick and efficient customer service, but they can also handle a large volume of queries at the same time, freeing up staff to focus on other tasks.

Another area where AI is transforming business is in predictive analytics. By analyzing vast amounts of data, AI algorithms can identify patterns and make predictions about future trends. This can help businesses make more informed decisions about everything from product development to marketing strategy.

However, as with any new technology, there are also potential downsides to AI in business. One concern is the potential for job displacement as AI-powered automation takes over certain tasks. While this can lead to increased efficiency and cost savings for businesses, it can also lead to job losses and displacement for workers.

Another concern is the potential for AI to be used unethically, for example, to discriminate against certain groups or manipulate public opinion. As businesses increasingly rely on AI for decision-making, it is important to ensure that these systems are transparent and accountable, and that ethical guidelines are in place to guide their use.

Despite these challenges, the future of business is likely to be heavily influenced by AI. As the technology continues to evolve and become more sophisticated, businesses that embrace AI are likely to gain a significant competitive advantage over those that do not. However, it will be important for businesses to navigate these challenges carefully and ensure that the benefits of AI are shared fairly and ethically.

Chapter 29: AI and Spirituality: Can Machines Understand the Divine?

Introduction:

As artificial intelligence (AI) continues to advance and integrate into various aspects of our lives, it is natural to wonder about its potential impact on spirituality and our understanding of the divine. We will explore the intersection of AI and spirituality and discuss the implications for human beliefs.

The search for meaning has been a central aspect of human spirituality for thousands of years. As AI becomes more advanced, some have speculated that it may eventually be able to assist humans in their quest for spiritual understanding. For example, AI could help us analyze and interpret religious texts and rituals, or even identify patterns and connections between seemingly disparate spiritual practices and beliefs.

While AI may be able to assist us in exploring spiritual concepts and traditions, can it ever truly understand and experience spirituality in the way that humans do? It is unlikely that AI could ever have a personal belief system or a sense of spirituality in the way that humans do, as these experiences are rooted in the complexities of human consciousness and emotion.

As with many other applications of AI, there are important ethical considerations to take into account when exploring the intersection of AI and spirituality. For example, if AI is used to assist humans in interpreting religious texts or rituals, who decides what interpretations are accurate or acceptable? Could AI be used to manipulate or control people's spiritual beliefs and practices? These are important questions that must be addressed as AI continues to advance in this area.

Conclusion:

In conclusion, the intersection of AI and spirituality is a complex and multifaceted topic that raises important questions about human belief systems and the nature of consciousness. While AI may be able to assist us in exploring and understanding spiritual concepts and traditions, it is unlikely to ever fully replace the personal experience of spirituality that is unique to human consciousness.

Outro:

As AI continues to advance and integrate into our lives, it is important to consider its potential impact on all aspects of human experience, including spirituality. By exploring these topics and engaging in thoughtful dialogue, we can work towards a more nuanced understanding of AI's role in shaping our world.

Summary of what you should remember from this chapter:

This chapter explored the intersection of AI and spirituality, including the potential for AI to assist humans in exploring spiritual concepts and the ethical considerations that must be taken into account. While AI may be able to assist humans in interpreting religious texts or rituals, it is unlikely to ever fully replace the personal experience of spirituality that is unique to human consciousness.

As AI continues to advance in this area, it will be important to engage in thoughtful dialogue and exploration of these topics to ensure that the integration of AI into spirituality is done in a responsible and ethical manner. Additionally, it may be valuable to consider the potential benefits and limitations of using AI to assist in the search for spiritual understanding.

Chapter 30: AI and spirituality

Introduction:

As artificial intelligence (AI) continues to advance, it is raising many profound questions about its impact on humanity. One area that has received relatively little attention is the potential intersection of AI and spirituality. While the two may seem unrelated at first glance, some experts predict that the rise of AI may bring about a new era of spiritual understanding and experience. We will explore the ways in which AI could impact spirituality and religious beliefs, and the potential implications for our understanding of the divine.

One of the key questions in this discussion is whether or not machines can truly understand the divine. On one hand, some argue that AI is purely mechanical and lacks the subjective experience that is necessary for true spiritual understanding. Others, however, suggest that the very complexity of AI could allow for a new kind of spiritual experience, one that transcends traditional human limitations.

Some proponents of this view point to the potential for AI to analyze vast amounts of religious texts and data, potentially uncovering new insights and patterns that were previously hidden. Additionally, some argue that AI could enable new forms of prayer and meditation, incorporating the technology into spiritual practice in novel ways.

However, there are also concerns about the potential dangers of relying too heavily on AI for spiritual guidance. For example, some worry that the use of AI in religious practice could lead to a lack of human connection and empathy, or even result in a kind of spiritual bypassing, where difficult emotions and experiences are simply avoided rather than fully addressed.

Overall, the relationship between AI and spirituality is a complex and multifaceted one, with both potential benefits and risks to consider.

Another area of concern when it comes to AI and spirituality is the potential for the technology to challenge traditional religious beliefs and practices. Some argue that AI could be seen as a kind of challenge to the concept of a divine creator, with the creation of intelligent machines being seen as a kind of usurpation of divine power.

Others suggest that AI could lead to a kind of democratization of religious knowledge and authority. With the ability to access vast amounts of religious texts and data, individuals could potentially gain a deeper understanding of different faiths and traditions, without relying solely on the teachings of religious leaders.

At the same time, however, there are concerns about the potential for AI to reinforce existing biases and prejudices, particularly in the realm of religion. For example, some worry that AI algorithms could be used to promote a particular religious viewpoint, or that certain groups could be excluded or marginalized in the development and use of AI-driven spiritual practices.

Ultimately, the potential impact of AI on spirituality and religious beliefs is still largely unknown, and much will depend on the ways in which the technology is developed and deployed. As with many areas of AI, the key will be to approach these questions with an open mind and a willingness to adapt to new possibilities and challenges.

The ethical implications of AI are vast and complex, and the question of how to teach machines to make ethical decisions is a central concern for many researchers and experts in the field.

One approach to teaching AI ethics is to focus on developing specific algorithms and decision-making frameworks that incorporate ethical principles and considerations. For example, some have proposed the development of "moral machines" that would be capable of making decisions based on ethical principles such as the utilitarian principle of maximizing overall well-being.

Others have argued that the key to teaching AI ethics is to emphasize the importance of empathy and emotional intelligence. By teaching machines to recognize and respond to human emotions, it may be possible to develop AI systems that are better equipped to make ethical decisions in a wide range of contexts.

Still, there are concerns that even with the best efforts to teach AI ethical principles and considerations, there may be unforeseen consequences and challenges that arise as a result of the technology's increasing sophistication and power. As such, ongoing research and discussion will be essential in order to ensure that AI remains a force for good in the world.

As AI becomes increasingly integrated into various aspects of society, there is growing concern about its potential impact on social equity and fairness. While AI has the potential to help address issues of inequality and discrimination, there are also concerns that it could exacerbate existing biases and inequalities.

One key challenge in ensuring that AI is used in a socially responsible and equitable way is to address the issue of bias in AI algorithms. There have been numerous examples of AI systems that perpetuate or even amplify existing biases, such as racial or gender bias in hiring algorithms.

To address this issue, researchers are exploring a range of approaches, from increasing the diversity of the data used to train AI algorithms to developing algorithms that are explicitly designed to counteract biases.

Another important aspect of ensuring social equity in the use of AI is to ensure that the benefits of the technology are distributed fairly. For example, there may be concerns that the use of AI in the workplace could result in job displacement for certain groups of workers, leading to increased inequality and economic hardship.

To address this issue, policymakers and businesses will need to work together to ensure that the benefits of AI are shared in a way that is inclusive and equitable. This may involve measures such as retraining programs for workers whose jobs are impacted by AI, as well as policies that ensure that the economic benefits of AI are distributed fairly across different groups of workers and regions.

Overall, the challenge of ensuring social equity in the use of AI is a complex and ongoing one, and will require ongoing research, discussion, and collaboration across different sectors of society.

One area where AI has the potential to revolutionize society is in the field of transportation. From self-driving cars and trucks to advanced traffic management systems, AI has the potential to make transportation more efficient, safer, and more sustainable.

One of the key benefits of self-driving cars and trucks is the potential to reduce accidents and fatalities on the road. According to the National Highway Traffic Safety Administration, 94% of all car accidents are caused by human error. By removing human error from the equation, self-driving cars and trucks could significantly reduce the number of accidents on the road.

In addition to improving safety, self-driving cars and trucks also have the potential to reduce traffic congestion and emissions. By optimizing routes and reducing the number of cars on the road, self-driving cars and trucks could help reduce traffic congestion in urban areas, while also reducing emissions and improving air quality.

Another area where AI is having an impact in transportation is in the development of advanced traffic management systems. These systems use real-time data and predictive analytics to optimize traffic flow, reduce congestion, and improve safety. By leveraging data from a variety of sources, including sensors, cameras, and GPS devices, these systems can provide real-time insights into traffic patterns and help drivers avoid congestion and delays.

Overall, the potential benefits of AI in transportation are significant, but there are also challenges that must be addressed. These include issues related to data privacy and security, as well as the need to ensure that the benefits of AI are shared fairly and equitably across different segments of society. By addressing these challenges, however, AI has the potential to revolutionize transportation and make our roads safer, more efficient, and more sustainable.

Regarding chapter 37 on AI and Spirituality, exploring the potential intersections of AI and spirituality, there are various interesting angles we can take. One of the most intriguing is whether machines can understand the divine.

Many people have different beliefs about what spirituality means to them. Some may view it as a connection to a higher power, while others may view it as a sense of interconnectedness with the universe. Regardless of how one defines spirituality, it is often tied to concepts of consciousness, self-awareness, and morality, which are areas that AI research has been exploring.

One potential intersection of AI and spirituality is the development of AI systems that are capable of understanding and even practicing different religious and spiritual traditions. For example, some AI systems have been developed to recite prayers or mantras, while others have been designed to meditate or offer guidance on spiritual practices.

However, there are also potential ethical concerns that need to be addressed when it comes to AI and spirituality. For instance, some worry that AI systems could be used to manipulate or exploit people's spiritual beliefs for financial gain or to promote certain ideologies. There is also a risk that AI systems could be programmed with biases that reflect the views of their creators, leading to discrimination against certain religious or spiritual groups.

Overall, the intersection of AI and spirituality is a complex and nuanced topic that requires careful consideration and reflection. It will be important for researchers, policymakers, and society as a whole to navigate this intersection with care, in order to ensure that the potential benefits of AI in the spiritual realm are maximized, while minimizing the risks and ethical concerns.

As we continue our exploration of the intersection between AI and spirituality, we come across a number of intriguing questions that have yet to be fully answered. One such question is whether machines are capable of understanding the divine. It is a question that has been asked by many people, including theologians, philosophers, and scientists.

One potential way in which AI could be used to explore spirituality is by analyzing religious texts and other writings. For example, AI could be used to analyze the Bible, the Quran, or the works of the Buddha in order to identify common themes and ideas. By doing so, AI might be able to help us gain new insights into these texts and their meanings.

Another area where AI could be applied to spirituality is in the development of spiritual practices and rituals. For example, AI could be used to create personalized meditation or prayer routines that are tailored to individual needs and preferences. This could help people to deepen their spiritual practices and connect more deeply with the divine.

However, there are also some potential risks and challenges associated with the use of AI in spirituality. One concern is that by relying too heavily on machines, we may lose some of the human connection and emotional depth that is inherent in spiritual practices. Additionally, there is the risk that machines may develop their own sense of spirituality or belief systems, which could lead to conflicts or misunderstandings.

Overall, the intersection between AI and spirituality is a fascinating and complex topic that requires further exploration. As we continue to develop new AI technologies and applications, it will be important to consider the ethical and spiritual implications of these advancements.

Chapter 31: AI and Human Identity: Redefining Ourselves

As AI technology continues to advance and become more integrated into our daily lives, it raises important questions about our human identity. How will our understanding of ourselves and our place in the world change as we interact with AI systems that are designed to simulate human-like behaviors and intelligence?

One aspect of human identity that could be affected by AI is our sense of self. We often define ourselves by our abilities and characteristics that distinguish us from others, such as our personalities, skills, and experiences. However, as AI systems become more advanced, they may be able to replicate these attributes and blur the line between human and machine.

Another aspect of human identity that could be impacted by AI is our sense of community and belonging. As AI systems become more integrated into society, they could change the way we interact with each other and our relationship with technology. For example, AI assistants and chatbots could become our primary source of social interaction, leading to a more isolated and individualistic society.

Furthermore, the increasing use of AI in fields such as hiring, education, and healthcare could lead to the creation of new societal norms and expectations. For instance, the use of AI in hiring could lead to a shift towards valuing certain skills and characteristics over others, potentially leading to a narrow definition of success and achievement.

Overall, the impact of AI on human identity is complex and multifaceted. As we continue to develop and integrate AI into our lives, it is important to consider the potential effects on our sense of self and our relationships with each other and technology. By doing so, we can ensure that AI is developed and utilized in a way that aligns with our values and enhances our human experience rather than detracting from it.

Artificial Intelligence has made its way into the world of warfare, with potentially significant consequences for international security and the nature of armed conflict. From the development of AI-enabled weapons to the use of autonomous drones on the battlefield, the integration of AI into military operations is already underway.

The potential benefits of AI in warfare are numerous. AI can help increase the speed and accuracy of decision-making, enhance situational awareness, and improve the targeting of enemy assets. Additionally, AI can allow for greater coordination among different military units and even between different branches of the military.

However, these benefits come with potential drawbacks and ethical concerns. The use of AI-enabled weaponry raises questions about the accountability of decision-making, the risk of accidental or unintentional harm to noncombatants, and the potential for unintended consequences. There is also a risk that the development of AI-enabled weapons could spark a new arms race, with countries competing to develop the most advanced and lethal AI systems.

As with other areas of AI development, there is a need for careful consideration of the potential risks and benefits of using AI in military operations. This includes ongoing efforts to develop ethical guidelines for the development and use of AI-enabled weapons, as well as the establishment of clear lines of accountability for any harm caused by AI systems.

In addition, there is a need for international cooperation and dialogue to address the potential risks of an AI arms race. This includes efforts to promote transparency and reduce the potential for miscalculation or misunderstanding among countries that are developing AI-enabled military capabilities.

Overall, the integration of AI into the world of warfare is a complex and rapidly evolving issue with significant implications for international security and the future of armed conflict. As with other areas of AI development, it is important that we approach this issue with caution, foresight, and a commitment to responsible innovation.

Chapter 32 AI and the Media: Fact, Fiction, and the Search for Truth

We delve into the intersection of AI and the media landscape. With the rapid growth of social media and the abundance of information available online, there has been an increase in the spread of fake news and misinformation. This is where AI can come in as a solution. AI can be used to detect fake news and analyze large amounts of data to find patterns and trends.

In addition, AI can personalize content for individual users, based on their preferences and behavior, improving the overall user experience. However, there are also concerns around the use of AI in the media. The use of AI for content creation and distribution raises questions about the role of human journalists and their autonomy. There is also the potential for AI to perpetuate biases and inequalities, particularly when it comes to algorithms used for content moderation and distribution.

As we navigate this new era of media and AI, it is important to consider both the benefits and potential risks. It is also essential to ensure that ethical guidelines are in place to prevent the misuse of AI in the media landscape. By taking a responsible approach to the integration of AI in the media, we can harness its potential to improve the quality and accuracy of information, while also ensuring that human values and ethics are preserved.

Summary:

- AI has the potential to detect fake news and analyze large amounts of data for patterns and trends in the media landscape.
- AI can personalize content for individual users, improving the overall user experience.
- Concerns exist around the use of AI in the media, particularly in content creation and distribution.
- The potential for AI to perpetuate biases and inequalities exists in algorithms used for content moderation and distribution.
- It is important to consider both the benefits and potential risks of integrating AI in the media landscape.
- Ethical guidelines should be in place to prevent the misuse of AI in the media.

Suggestions:

- Develop ethical guidelines for the use of AI in the media to prevent the misuse of the technology.
- Encourage media outlets to use AI to detect fake news and analyze large amounts of data to improve the quality and accuracy of information.
- Use AI to personalize content for individual users, while also considering the potential for perpetuating biases and inequalities.
- Conduct further research to explore the potential of AI in the media landscape and its impact on human journalists and their autonomy.

Chapter 33: AI and the Future of Governance: Reinventing Democracy

Introduction:

The field of Artificial Intelligence (AI) has already shown its transformative power in a variety of areas, from healthcare and finance to transportation and education. However, one area that is often overlooked in discussions of AI is its potential to revolutionize the way governments and citizens interact. We will explore how AI could impact the future of governance, from policy development to citizen engagement. We will examine the opportunities and challenges that come with this new technology, and how it could lead to a more inclusive, transparent, and efficient democratic system. Ultimately, we will question whether AI has the potential to reinvent democracy as we know it, and what we can do to ensure that its impact is positive and equitable for all.

The Promise of AI in Policy Development

AI has the potential to transform policy development and decision-making processes by improving the speed, accuracy, and efficiency of data analysis. Governments can use AI to analyze vast amounts of data to identify trends and patterns, which can inform the development of evidence-based policies. AI can also be used to forecast the potential impact of policy decisions, making it easier to evaluate the likely outcomes of different policy choices.

One example of AI being used in policy development is in the field of climate change. Governments around the world are using AI to analyze large amounts of climate data, which can help inform policy decisions related to reducing carbon emissions and mitigating the effects of climate change. AI can also be used to monitor and track the effectiveness of policy initiatives, allowing governments to make data-driven decisions about where to invest resources and how to adjust policy strategies over time.

However, as with any new technology, there are also potential drawbacks and risks to consider. One concern is that AI could perpetuate existing biases and inequalities if the data it analyzes is biased or incomplete. Additionally, there are ethical concerns about the use of AI in decision-making processes, particularly if these decisions have a significant impact on people's lives. It is important for governments to ensure that AI is used in an ethical and responsible way, and that decision-making processes are transparent and inclusive of diverse perspectives.

AI can also play a significant role in improving citizen engagement with government processes. One way that AI can help is by improving the accessibility and usability of government services. Chatbots, for example, can provide citizens with 24/7 access to information and support services, reducing the need for expensive call centers and improving the overall user experience. Additionally, AI can help governments analyze citizen feedback and identify areas where services could be improved or made more responsive to citizen needs.

Another potential use of AI in citizen engagement is through participatory budgeting processes. Participatory budgeting is a democratic process where citizens have a direct say in how public resources are allocated. By using AI to analyze citizen input, governments can gain a better understanding of what citizens want and need from their public services, which can inform the development of more effective policies and programs.

However, there are also potential risks and concerns associated with the use of AI in citizen engagement. For example, there is a risk that AI could be used to manipulate public opinion or undermine democratic processes. It is important for governments to be transparent about how AI is being used in citizen engagement, and to ensure that decision-making processes are fair and inclusive of diverse perspectives. Additionally, there is a need to ensure that AI is not used to reinforce existing biases or perpetuate inequalities, and that citizens are able to make informed decisions about their participation in government processes.

While the potential benefits of AI in governance are significant, there are also several challenges associated with its implementation. One major challenge is the cost and complexity of developing and maintaining AI systems. Developing effective AI systems requires significant resources, including skilled personnel, advanced technology, and access to high-quality data. Additionally, there is a risk that AI systems may be vulnerable to cyberattacks or other security breaches, which could undermine their effectiveness or compromise sensitive government data.

Another challenge is the need to ensure that AI is used in a responsible and ethical manner. There is a risk that AI could be used to reinforce existing biases or perpetuate inequalities, particularly if the data it analyzes is biased or incomplete. It is important for governments to ensure that AI systems are designed to be transparent, accountable, and inclusive of diverse perspectives. Additionally, there is a need to ensure that AI systems are subject to appropriate regulation and oversight to prevent abuses of power or unethical decision-making.

Finally, there is a risk that AI could exacerbate existing challenges related to privacy and data protection. As governments collect and analyze large amounts of citizen data, there is a risk that this data could be misused or shared without appropriate consent. It is important for governments to establish clear policies and regulations around the collection and use of citizen data, and to ensure that these policies are communicated clearly to citizens. By doing so, governments can build trust with citizens and ensure that AI is used in a responsible and ethical manner.

Given the potential risks and challenges associated with AI in governance, it is important for governments to take steps to ensure that AI is used in an ethical and responsible manner. One way to do this is by establishing clear guidelines and principles for the use of AI in government decision-making processes. These guidelines should prioritize transparency, accountability, and inclusivity, and should be designed to prevent abuses of power or unethical decision-making.

Another important step is to establish appropriate oversight and regulatory mechanisms to ensure that AI systems are subject to appropriate scrutiny and monitoring. This could include the establishment of independent oversight bodies or the requirement for regular audits of AI systems to identify potential biases or other ethical concerns.

Finally, governments must ensure that citizens have a voice in decisions related to the development and implementation of AI systems in governance. This could include the establishment of citizen advisory boards or the use of participatory decision-making processes to ensure that citizens have a say in how AI is used to inform policy decisions.

Overall, the responsible and ethical use of AI in governance requires a commitment to transparency, accountability, and inclusivity. By taking these steps, governments can ensure that AI is used in a way that promotes the public good and serves the needs of all citizens, rather than perpetuating existing biases or inequalities.

The potential of AI in governance is significant, and we can expect to see increasing adoption of this technology in the years to come. As governments continue to face complex challenges related to climate change, economic inequality, and social justice, AI can help to inform policy decisions and improve the effectiveness of public services.

One area where we can expect to see significant growth in the use of AI is in the development of smart cities. Smart cities are urban environments that use AI and other advanced technologies to improve the quality of life for citizens, while also promoting sustainability and economic growth. AI can be used to monitor and optimize traffic flows, manage energy consumption, and improve public safety, among other things.

Another area where AI is likely to play a significant role is in the development of more personalized public services. By using AI to analyze citizen data, governments can better understand the needs and preferences of individual citizens, and tailor public services to meet their specific needs. This could include personalized healthcare services, customized education programs, and more responsive social support services.

However, as we have seen, the adoption of AI in governance also comes with significant risks and challenges. Governments must be proactive in addressing these risks and ensuring that AI is used in a responsible and ethical manner. This requires a commitment to transparency, accountability, and inclusivity, and a willingness to engage in ongoing dialogue with citizens and other stakeholders to ensure that AI is used to promote the public good.

As the use of AI in governance continues to grow, it is important for citizens and policymakers to be prepared for the potential impacts of this technology. This requires a commitment to ongoing education and training, both to develop the skills needed to work with AI systems and to understand the ethical and societal implications of these technologies.

One key area where education will be important is in the development of AI literacy. This means ensuring that citizens and policymakers have a basic understanding of how AI works, what its limitations are, and how it can be used to inform policy decisions. This could include training programs for government officials, as well as public awareness campaigns to help citizens understand the potential benefits and risks of AI.

Another important area of education is in the development of skills needed to work with AI systems. This includes technical skills related to data analysis and programming, as well as soft skills such as critical thinking, problem-solving, and communication. By developing these skills, individuals and organizations can work effectively with AI systems and contribute to the development of more effective public policies and services.

Finally, there is a need to ensure that education and training programs are designed to be inclusive and accessible to all citizens, regardless of their background or level of education. This requires a commitment to equity and social justice, and a willingness to invest in programs and initiatives that support lifelong learning and skills development.

Overall, the role of education in preparing for an AI-driven future is critical. By investing in AI literacy and skills development, we can ensure that citizens and policymakers are prepared to work effectively with AI systems and to address the ethical and societal implications of these technologies.

Conclusion

The potential of AI in governance is significant, and we can expect to see increasing adoption of this technology in the years to come. AI can help governments to make more informed decisions, improve public services, and promote sustainability and economic growth.

However, as we have seen, the adoption of AI in governance also comes with significant risks and challenges. Governments must be proactive in addressing these risks and ensuring that AI is used in a responsible and ethical manner. This requires a commitment to transparency, accountability, and inclusivity, and a willingness to engage in ongoing dialogue with citizens and other stakeholders to ensure that AI is used to promote the public good.

Moreover, we must also be mindful of the potential impact of AI on society and the economy. The widespread adoption of AI is likely to have significant implications for the future of work, education, and social and economic inequality. It is important for policymakers and citizens to engage in ongoing dialogue and collaboration to ensure that the benefits of AI are shared equitably and that the risks are minimized.

In summary, the future of governance is closely linked to the development and adoption of AI. While the potential benefits of AI are significant, it is important for governments to address the risks and challenges associated with this technology in a responsible and ethical manner. By doing so, we can ensure that AI is used to promote the public good and to build a more sustainable, equitable, and prosperous future for all citizens.

Summary of What You Should Remember from This Chapter

We have explored the potential of AI to revolutionize governance, from policy development to citizen engagement. We have discussed the ways in which AI can be used to inform decision-making, improve public services, and promote sustainability and economic growth.

However, we have also highlighted the significant risks and challenges associated with the adoption of AI in governance, including issues related to bias, transparency, and accountability. To ensure that AI is used in a responsible and ethical manner, it is important for governments to establish clear guidelines and oversight mechanisms, as well as to engage in ongoing dialogue and collaboration with citizens and other stakeholders.

Finally, we have discussed the role of education in preparing for an AI-driven future, including the development of AI literacy and technical skills, as well as soft skills such as critical thinking and communication.

As we move forward, it is clear that AI will play an increasingly important role in shaping the future of governance. By embracing this technology in a responsible and ethical manner, we can build a more effective and inclusive public sector that serves the needs of all citizens.

Conclusion:

We have explored the potential of AI to revolutionize governance and reinvent democracy. AI has the potential to improve decision-making, promote sustainability, and enhance public services. However, the adoption of AI in governance also comes with significant risks and challenges, including issues related to bias, transparency, and accountability.

To ensure that AI is used in a responsible and ethical manner, governments must establish clear guidelines and oversight mechanisms, as well as engage in ongoing dialogue and collaboration with citizens and other stakeholders. This requires a commitment to transparency, accountability, and inclusivity.

Moreover, the development and adoption of AI in governance also requires a commitment to education and skills development. Individuals and organizations must develop the skills needed to work effectively with AI systems, as well as an understanding of the ethical and societal implications of these technologies.

As we move forward, it is clear that AI will continue to play an increasingly important role in shaping the future of governance. By embracing this technology in a responsible and ethical manner, we can build a more effective and inclusive public sector that serves the needs of all citizens.

Outro:

As we have seen, AI has the potential to revolutionize governance and reinvent democracy. From policy development to citizen engagement, AI can help governments to make more informed decisions, improve public services, and promote sustainability and economic growth.

However, the adoption of AI in governance also comes with significant risks and challenges. Governments must be proactive in addressing these risks and ensuring that AI is used in a responsible and ethical manner. This requires a commitment to transparency, accountability, and inclusivity, and a willingness to engage in ongoing dialogue with citizens and other stakeholders.

Moreover, as we move forward, it is important to recognize that the development and adoption of AI in governance is not a one-size-fits-all approach. Different countries and regions will face unique challenges and opportunities when it comes to the adoption of AI, and it is important for policymakers to tailor their approaches accordingly.

In conclusion, the potential of AI in governance is significant, but its successful adoption will require a commitment to responsible and ethical practices, ongoing education and skills development, and collaboration between governments, citizens, and other stakeholders. By doing so, we can harness the power of AI to build a more effective and inclusive public sector that serves the needs of all citizens.

Summary of What You Should Remember from This Chapter:

We have explored the potential of AI to revolutionize governance and reinvent democracy. AI has the potential to inform decision-making, improve public services, and promote sustainability and economic growth. However, the adoption of AI in governance also comes with significant risks and challenges, including issues related to bias, transparency, and accountability.

To ensure that AI is used in a responsible and ethical manner, governments must establish clear guidelines and oversight mechanisms, as well as engage in ongoing dialogue and collaboration with citizens and other stakeholders. This requires a commitment to transparency, accountability, and inclusivity.

Education and skills development are also critical to preparing for an AI-driven future in governance. Individuals and organizations must develop the skills needed to work effectively with AI systems, as well as an understanding of the ethical and societal implications of these technologies.

Suggestions That Will Be of Interest for You to Consider Based on This Chapter Topic:

1. Stay informed: Stay up-to-date with the latest developments and trends in AI and governance by following reputable news sources, attending conferences and events, and engaging in ongoing learning and education.
2. Engage in dialogue: Engage in dialogue and collaboration with policymakers, citizens, and other stakeholders to ensure that the benefits of AI are shared equitably and that the risks are minimized.
3. Develop technical and soft skills: Develop the technical and soft skills needed to work effectively with AI systems, as well as an understanding of the ethical and societal implications of these technologies.
4. Advocate for transparency and accountability: Advocate for transparency and accountability in the development and deployment of AI in governance, and encourage policymakers to establish clear guidelines and oversight mechanisms.

By following these suggestions, we can ensure that AI is used in a responsible and ethical manner in governance, and that its potential to improve decision-making, promote sustainability, and enhance public services is fully realized.

Chapter 34: The Impact of AI on Business and Society

Artificial Intelligence (AI) has been making significant strides in recent years, revolutionizing various industries and disrupting traditional ways of doing things. One area where the impact of AI is being felt is in business and society. The rise of AI has brought about new possibilities and opportunities for businesses while transforming the way we live and work. We will explore the different ways in which AI is transforming business and society and the implications of these changes for individuals, organizations, and society as a whole. We will also examine the opportunities and challenges that AI presents and how organizations can leverage AI to drive innovation and growth while mitigating the risks associated with this emerging technology.

Artificial intelligence has long been a subject of science fiction and futuristic speculation. However, in recent years, AI has become a reality that is rapidly transforming the world as we know it. We will explore the impact of AI on education, and how it is changing the way we learn.

One of the most significant ways in which AI is revolutionizing education is through personalized learning. With the help of machine learning algorithms, AI can analyze large amounts of data to understand the strengths and weaknesses of individual learners. This information can be used to create personalized learning plans for each student, which can help them learn more efficiently and effectively.

Another way in which AI is changing education is by enabling remote learning. With the COVID-19 pandemic, remote learning has become more important than ever. AI-powered tools, such as chatbots and virtual tutors, can provide students with personalized support and feedback, even when they are not in the same physical location as their teachers.

In addition, AI can also help to automate administrative tasks, such as grading and attendance tracking. This can free up teachers to focus on more meaningful tasks, such as lesson planning and providing personalized feedback to students.

Overall, the impact of AI on education is profound and far-reaching. While it is still early days for many AI-powered education tools, the potential for these technologies to transform the way we learn is enormous. As we continue to explore the possibilities of AI in education, we must also be mindful of the ethical and social implications of these technologies.

In recent years, there has been an explosion in the development of artificial intelligence (AI) technologies. AI has become a powerful tool for automating various tasks and processes, and has led to many exciting advances in fields like healthcare, finance, and transportation. However, with great power comes great responsibility, and the potential negative effects of AI must be carefully considered.

One of the key areas of concern is the impact of AI on the job market. AI has the potential to automate many tasks and replace human workers, which could lead to significant job losses in certain sectors. In particular, low-skilled jobs that involve routine tasks, such as data entry or assembly line work, are at high risk of being automated.

On the other hand, AI also has the potential to create new job opportunities, particularly in fields like data science, software engineering, and robotics. In addition, AI can enhance the productivity and efficiency of many jobs, allowing workers to focus on higher-level tasks that require human skills like creativity and problem-solving.

Another area of concern is the potential for AI to perpetuate and amplify existing biases and discrimination. AI systems are only as unbiased as the data they are trained on, and if the data reflects existing biases and discrimination, then the AI system will also perpetuate those biases. This can have serious consequences in areas like hiring, lending, and criminal justice.

Furthermore, the use of AI in decision-making processes can lead to a lack of transparency and accountability. It can be difficult to understand how AI algorithms are making decisions, and this can lead to a lack of trust in the system. This is particularly problematic in areas like healthcare, where the decisions made by AI algorithms can have a significant impact on people's lives.

As AI continues to advance, it is important to carefully consider these potential negative effects and take steps to mitigate them. This includes ensuring that AI systems are transparent and accountable, and that they are developed in a way that is inclusive and reflects a diverse range of perspectives. In addition, it is important to invest in education and training programs that can help workers develop the skills needed to adapt to the changing job market.

Overall, while AI has the potential to bring many benefits, it is important to proceed with caution and consider the potential negative impacts. By doing so, we can ensure that AI is developed and used in a responsible and ethical manner.

As artificial intelligence (AI) continues to advance, its impact on various aspects of our lives becomes more apparent. One area that is poised to experience significant changes is the job market. The use of AI in the workplace has the potential to drastically alter the nature of work, the skills required for different jobs, and the number of jobs available.

One way that AI is already being used in the workplace is through automation. Tasks that were previously performed by humans can now be automated using AI, such as data entry, customer service, and even some forms of creative work. This automation can lead to increased efficiency and productivity, but it also means that some jobs will become obsolete.

Another way that AI is affecting the job market is through the creation of new jobs. As AI technology advances, there will be a need for individuals with expertise in areas such as machine learning, data analysis, and AI development. These jobs will require different skills than traditional jobs, which means that individuals who want to stay competitive in the job market will need to continuously develop their skills and knowledge.

In addition to creating new jobs, AI has the potential to change the nature of work itself. With the help of AI, tasks that were previously considered mundane or time-consuming can be completed much more quickly and efficiently, freeing up time for workers to focus on higher-level tasks that require more creativity and critical thinking.

However, the increased use of AI in the workplace also raises concerns about job displacement and the potential for inequality. As AI technology continues to improve, it may become more cost-effective for companies to replace human workers with machines. This could lead to job loss and economic hardship for individuals who are displaced by AI.

To address these concerns, it will be important for policymakers, business leaders, and workers themselves to collaborate and find ways to ensure that the benefits of AI are shared fairly and equitably. This could involve retraining programs to help workers acquire the skills needed for new jobs, implementing policies to ensure that AI is used responsibly and ethically, and exploring new models of work that are more flexible and adaptive to the changing nature of work.

In summary, the increasing use of AI in the workplace has the potential to drastically alter the job market. While it may create new opportunities for individuals with the right skills and expertise, it also raises concerns about job displacement and inequality. It will be important for all stakeholders to work together to ensure that the benefits of AI are shared fairly and that workers are equipped to succeed in the changing world of work.

In the previous section, we talked about how AI is being used to augment and enhance human decision-making processes. However, one area where AI has the potential to completely replace human decision-making is in the realm of self-driving cars.

Self-driving cars have been a topic of interest for many years, and with the rapid advancements in AI technology, they are becoming a reality. The potential benefits of self-driving cars are numerous: they could reduce traffic accidents, improve traffic flow, and allow people to use their commuting time more efficiently. However, there are also many challenges that need to be overcome before self-driving cars can become widespread.

One of the biggest challenges is ensuring the safety of self-driving cars. While AI has the potential to be more accurate and reliable than human drivers, it is not infallible. Self-driving cars need to be able to make split-second decisions based on real-time data, and they need to be able to handle unexpected situations that may arise on the road. This requires a level of sophistication that current AI systems may not yet possess.

Another challenge is regulatory. Self-driving cars will need to be subject to extensive testing and regulation before they can be deemed safe for public use. There will need to be clear guidelines in place for issues such as liability, insurance, and data privacy. Governments and regulatory bodies will need to work closely with car manufacturers and technology companies to ensure that self-driving cars are developed and implemented in a responsible and safe manner.

Finally, there is the issue of public perception. Many people may be hesitant to trust their safety to an AI-driven vehicle, especially in the early stages of development. It will be important for car manufacturers and technology companies to communicate the benefits and safety features of self-driving cars to the public and to build trust in the technology.

In conclusion, self-driving cars have the potential to revolutionize transportation and significantly improve the safety and efficiency of our roadways. However, there are many challenges that need to be overcome before self-driving cars can become a reality. These challenges include ensuring the safety of self-driving cars, regulatory issues, and building public trust in the technology.

Chapter 35: AI and its potential implications for the legal system

In the previous sections of this book, we have explored the impact of artificial intelligence on various aspects of our lives. We will delve deeper into the topic of AI and its potential implications for the legal system.

AI has already made inroads in the legal profession, with tools such as contract review software and predictive analytics being used to streamline tasks and make legal processes more efficient. However, there are concerns about the use of AI in legal decision-making and the potential for bias to be introduced into the system.

One area where AI has already had an impact is in the use of predictive analytics to assess the likelihood of recidivism among convicted criminals. While these tools may be useful in identifying individuals who may need additional support or monitoring, they also raise questions about due process and the potential for discrimination against certain groups.

Moreover, the use of AI in legal decision-making raises questions about accountability and transparency. If an algorithm is used to make a decision, who is responsible if that decision is found to be flawed or discriminatory? How can we ensure that the decision-making process is transparent and fair?

We will explore these and other questions related to the use of AI in the legal system. We will examine both the potential benefits and the potential risks of AI in the legal profession, and we will consider what steps can be taken to ensure that AI is used in a way that is ethical and just.

In recent years, the field of artificial intelligence has grown rapidly and become increasingly important in many areas of life. One of the most significant applications of AI is in healthcare, where it has the potential to revolutionize how medical professionals diagnose, treat, and prevent diseases.

One way that AI is being used in healthcare is through the analysis of medical imaging. Medical images such as X-rays, CT scans, and MRIs provide critical information that can help doctors make accurate diagnoses and develop effective treatment plans. However, analyzing these images can be time-consuming and require significant expertise. This is where AI comes in.

AI algorithms can be trained to analyze medical images and detect abnormalities, such as tumors or other signs of disease. This can help doctors make faster and more accurate diagnoses, which can ultimately lead to better patient outcomes. AI can also be used to track the progression of diseases and monitor the effectiveness of treatments over time.

Another way that AI is being used in healthcare is through the development of personalized treatment plans. By analyzing large amounts of patient data, including medical histories, genetic information, and lifestyle factors, AI algorithms can help doctors develop personalized treatment plans that are tailored to each individual patient. This can lead to more effective treatments and better patient outcomes.

AI is also being used to improve patient outcomes in other ways, such as through the development of virtual assistants and chatbots that can help patients manage chronic conditions, access healthcare resources, and receive personalized health advice. These tools can help patients stay on top of their health and prevent minor issues from becoming more serious.

Overall, the use of AI in healthcare has the potential to revolutionize the field and improve patient outcomes in many ways. However, it is important to proceed with caution and ensure that these technologies are developed and implemented in an ethical and responsible manner. It is also important to address concerns around privacy and data security, and to ensure that the benefits of AI are accessible to all patients, regardless of their socioeconomic status.

Chapter 36: The Impact of AI on Society

As artificial intelligence continues to advance, it is clear that its impact on society will only increase. We will explore how AI is already affecting society, as well as how it is likely to affect society in the future.

One major way in which AI is currently affecting society is through its impact on the job market. AI has already begun to automate many tasks that were previously performed by humans, and this trend is likely to continue. While automation can lead to increased efficiency and productivity, it can also lead to job loss and economic disruption. It is important for society to consider how we can prepare for the impact of AI on the job market and how we can ensure that those who are displaced by automation have the resources they need to retrain and find new employment.

Another way in which AI is affecting society is through its impact on decision-making processes. AI algorithms are already being used in a variety of contexts, including criminal justice, lending, and hiring. While AI has the potential to reduce bias and increase efficiency in decision-making, it is important to consider the ethical implications of using AI in these contexts. For example, there are concerns about the potential for AI to reinforce existing biases or to make decisions that are difficult to understand or challenge.

Additionally, AI is likely to have significant implications for privacy and security. As AI becomes more advanced, it may become better able to analyze and predict human behavior, which could lead to new forms of surveillance and monitoring. It will be important for society to consider how to balance the potential benefits of AI with the need to protect individual privacy and security.

Overall, it is clear that AI will have significant implications for society in the coming years. While the technology has the potential to bring about significant benefits, it is also likely to disrupt existing social structures and institutions. It is important for society to consider how we can ensure that the benefits of AI are widely shared and that its potential harms are minimized.

Chapter 37: AI and Hardware: The Evolution of Computing

Introduction:

The evolution of computing has enabled the development of artificial intelligence (AI) to reach new heights. From the early days of computing, there has been a constant drive to improve hardware capabilities to enhance computing power, energy efficiency, and speed. As AI continues to play an increasingly significant role in modern society, hardware must keep pace with the demands of AI workloads. We will explore the advancements in AI-driven hardware, from quantum computing to energy-efficient processors, and their impact on the field of artificial intelligence.

AI-driven hardware has evolved significantly in recent years, with advancements in both hardware architecture and software optimization. One of the most significant developments in AI hardware is the rise of specialized processors, such as Graphics Processing Units (GPUs), Field-Programmable Gate Arrays (FPGAs), and Tensor Processing Units (TPUs). These processors are specifically designed to handle the high computational demands of AI workloads, such as training and inference.

Quantum computing is an emerging technology that has the potential to revolutionize the field of AI. Unlike classical computing, which operates on binary digits, quantum computing uses quantum bits (qubits) to perform calculations. This allows for much faster computations and opens up new avenues for solving complex problems that were previously impossible to solve with classical computing. Quantum computing is still in its early stages, but it has the potential to be a game-changer for AI.

We will be exploring the evolution of computing in relation to the advancement of AI-driven hardware. With the rise of AI, the need for hardware that can efficiently handle the complex computations required by these systems has become increasingly important. From the development of quantum computing to the creation of energy-efficient processors, this chapter will examine the different ways in which hardware technology has evolved to meet the demands of AI. Join us as we delve into the exciting world of AI-driven hardware and explore the future of computing.

Artificial Intelligence (AI) has revolutionized the way we process, analyze, and utilize data. With the increase in demand for AI applications, hardware technologies have undergone significant advancements to support the processing requirements of AI. From quantum computing to energy-efficient processors, this chapter explores the evolution of AI-driven hardware and its impact on the field of computing. We delve into the various hardware technologies that have emerged to support AI, the challenges that arise with these technologies, and the future of AI-driven hardware. Join us on this journey to discover the fascinating world of AI and hardware.

In recent years, artificial intelligence (AI) has become increasingly prevalent in our daily lives, from virtual assistants to self-driving cars. However, the growth of AI technology is heavily dependent on the evolution of computing hardware. We will explore the advancements in AI-driven hardware, from quantum computing to energy-efficient processors, and how they have enabled the development and expansion of AI applications. We will also discuss the challenges and opportunities associated with these technological advancements and their potential impact on society.

In recent years, there has been a significant advancement in AI-driven hardware. This includes the development of specialized processors and hardware architectures designed specifically for accelerating AI workloads. One such example is the Graphical Processing Unit (GPU), which was initially designed for rendering high-quality graphics in video games but has been found to be highly effective in parallel processing for deep learning applications.

Another significant development is the emergence of Field-Programmable Gate Arrays (FPGAs), which are reconfigurable chips that can be programmed to perform specific tasks. FPGAs offer the advantage of being highly customizable and energy-efficient, making them a popular choice for implementing AI algorithms in edge devices and the Internet of Things (IoT) devices.

Quantum computing is another area that has shown great promise in accelerating AI workloads. Quantum computing leverages the principles of quantum mechanics to perform calculations at a much faster rate than classical computers. While quantum computing is still in its infancy, it has the potential to revolutionize the field of AI by enabling the development of more complex and sophisticated algorithms that can process vast amounts of data in a fraction of the time.

Overall, the evolution of AI-driven hardware is essential in advancing the field of AI and making it more accessible to a broader range of applications. The development of specialized hardware architectures tailored to specific AI workloads will enable the creation of more powerful and efficient algorithms, driving innovation in a variety of industries.

Artificial intelligence (AI) has revolutionized the way we interact with technology, and it has also spurred the evolution of hardware to keep pace with the increasing demands of AI applications. One of the most exciting advancements in AI-driven hardware is quantum computing.

Quantum computing is a paradigm shift in computing that allows for the processing of information in a fundamentally different way than classical computing. Instead of relying on classical bits that represent either a 0 or 1, quantum computing uses quantum bits or qubits, which can represent a 0 and a 1 at the same time, allowing for exponentially faster computation of certain problems.

However, the development of quantum computing hardware is still in its early stages, and there are significant challenges to overcome, such as the fragility of qubits and the difficulty in maintaining their coherence.

In addition to quantum computing, there have been significant advancements in energy-efficient processors, which are crucial for running AI algorithms in devices with limited power and processing capabilities. These processors, such as the ARM Cortex-A76AE, have been specifically designed for autonomous vehicles and other AI applications, and can deliver high performance while keeping energy consumption low.

Overall, the evolution of AI-driven hardware has been driven by the increasing demand for faster and more efficient computation for AI applications. The development of quantum computing and energy-efficient processors represent significant advancements in this field, and will likely continue to shape the future of computing.

One major advancement in AI-driven hardware is the development of quantum computing. Quantum computers operate on the principles of quantum mechanics, allowing for vastly more powerful computing capabilities than traditional computers. This is because quantum bits (qubits) can exist in multiple states simultaneously, exponentially increasing the number of calculations that can be performed in a given amount of time.

Another area of innovation in AI-driven hardware is the development of energy-efficient processors. With the rise of AI and machine learning applications, there has been a growing demand for processors that can handle the massive amounts of data needed for these tasks without consuming excessive amounts of energy. This has led to the development of specialized processors such as graphics processing units (GPUs) and tensor processing units (TPUs) that are optimized for AI workloads.

In addition to specialized processors, there have also been advancements in the field of neuromorphic computing, which seeks to design hardware architectures that more closely resemble the structure and function of the human brain. These architectures are particularly well-suited for tasks such as image and speech recognition, and can potentially lead to more efficient and accurate AI systems.

Overall, the advancement of AI-driven hardware is a crucial component in the development of more sophisticated and powerful AI systems. As computing power continues to increase, we can expect to see even more innovative hardware solutions emerging in the field of AI.

In recent years, AI and machine learning have become increasingly important for various industries, and the hardware used to run these applications has had to evolve accordingly. One significant development in this area is the advancement of quantum computing, which has the potential to revolutionize the field of AI. Unlike classical computers that rely on bits to store and process data, quantum computers use qubits, which can represent multiple states simultaneously. This allows for much faster processing and could unlock new possibilities in fields such as cryptography and machine learning.

Another area of focus for AI-driven hardware is energy efficiency. As the demand for AI applications increases, so does the amount of energy required to run them. This has led to the development of specialized processors designed specifically for AI tasks, such as Google's Tensor Processing Unit (TPU) and Intel's Nervana Neural Network Processor (NNP). These processors are optimized for the specific needs of AI workloads, allowing for faster and more efficient processing while reducing energy consumption.

In addition to quantum computing and specialized processors, there are also advancements being made in the use of field-programmable gate arrays (FPGAs) for AI applications. FPGAs are highly customizable hardware that can be programmed to perform specific tasks, making them ideal for AI workloads that require a high degree of flexibility and adaptability.

Overall, the evolution of AI-driven hardware is an important area to watch as the demand for AI and machine learning continues to grow. With advancements in quantum computing, energy-efficient processors, and customizable hardware, the potential for AI to transform various industries is becoming more and more tangible.

In recent years, the development of specialized hardware for AI applications has become increasingly popular. One of the most promising new technologies is quantum computing, which uses the principles of quantum mechanics to process information in a fundamentally different way than classical computers. Quantum computers have the potential to perform certain types of calculations much faster than traditional computers, which could revolutionize fields like cryptography and machine learning.

Another area of focus for AI-driven hardware is energy efficiency. Traditional computer processors can be extremely power-hungry, which can limit their practical applications. To address this issue, researchers are developing new types of processors that are specifically designed to run AI algorithms with minimal power consumption. These chips, known as neuromorphic processors, are modeled after the structure of the human brain and can perform certain types of calculations more efficiently than traditional processors.

In addition to quantum computing and neuromorphic processors, other hardware advancements are also being explored for AI applications. These include field-programmable gate arrays (FPGAs), which can be customized to perform specific computations, and graphics processing units (GPUs), which excel at running complex mathematical operations in parallel.

Overall, the development of AI-driven hardware is a critical component of advancing the field of artificial intelligence. As researchers continue to explore new hardware technologies and optimize existing ones, the potential applications for AI will continue to expand and improve.

One approach to addressing this issue is to develop energy-efficient processors and hardware specifically designed for AI applications. One example is the Tensor Processing Unit (TPU) developed by Google, which is optimized for machine learning workloads and uses less energy than traditional CPUs and GPUs.

Other efforts focus on using renewable energy sources to power data centers and AI hardware. For example, Microsoft has built a data center powered entirely by renewable energy in the Netherlands, while other companies are exploring the use of solar and wind power for their data centers.

Overall, the development of energy-efficient AI hardware is an important step towards mitigating the environmental impact of AI and ensuring its sustainability in the long run.

As the demand for AI and machine learning continues to increase, the hardware used to support these technologies is also evolving. In recent years, there has been a significant advancement in the development of AI-driven hardware, including quantum computing and energy-efficient processors.

One example of the evolution of AI-driven hardware is the development of neuromorphic computing. Neuromorphic computing aims to simulate the neural networks of the human brain, allowing for more efficient and accurate machine learning. These types of processors are designed to mimic the human brain's structure, where each neuron processes information and communicates with other neurons. This design allows for faster processing and lower power consumption, making neuromorphic computing a promising technology for future AI applications.

Another area of advancement is quantum computing, which uses the principles of quantum mechanics to perform calculations. Unlike traditional computing, where data is processed in binary form (either 0 or 1), quantum computing uses qubits, which can be in multiple states simultaneously. This allows for much faster processing of large amounts of data and could potentially revolutionize industries such as healthcare, finance, and cryptography.

Energy efficiency is also a major concern when it comes to AI-driven hardware. Traditional computing requires a lot of power, which can lead to increased energy consumption and costs. However, new processors, such as ARM's Cortex-M4 and Intel's Movidius Myriad X, are designed to be more energy-efficient, making them ideal for use in devices with limited power resources, such as smartphones and Internet of Things (IoT) devices.

In conclusion, the evolution of AI-driven hardware is continuing to advance at a rapid pace, with the development of neuromorphic computing, quantum computing, and energy-efficient processors. These advancements have the potential to revolutionize the way we process and analyze data, leading to new and innovative applications for AI and machine learning.

One of the most promising fields in AI-driven hardware is quantum computing, which uses the principles of quantum mechanics to perform certain calculations exponentially faster than classical computers. Unlike classical bits, which can only have a value of 0 or 1, quantum bits or qubits can exist in a superposition of states, allowing for much more efficient and powerful processing. However, building and maintaining stable qubits is a major technical challenge, requiring sophisticated hardware and software solutions. Several companies, such as IBM, Google, Microsoft, and Intel, are investing heavily in quantum computing research and development, aiming to make this technology more accessible and scalable.

Another trend in AI hardware is the rise of specialized chips or accelerators that are optimized for specific tasks, such as image or speech recognition, natural language processing, or reinforcement learning. These chips can offer significant speedup and energy efficiency compared to general-purpose processors, which have to handle a wide range of operations. For example, Google's

Tensor Processing Units (TPUs) are designed to accelerate TensorFlow, a popular deep learning framework, and have demonstrated impressive performance gains for various applications. Other examples of AI-specific chips include Nvidia's Graphics Processing Units (GPUs) and Intel's Field-Programmable Gate Arrays (FPGAs).

Moreover, energy consumption has become a critical factor in designing AI systems, as the demand for processing power and data storage continues to grow rapidly. Green computing, or energy-efficient computing, has become a major research area, aiming to reduce the environmental footprint of computing while maintaining or improving performance. One approach is to use renewable energy sources, such as solar or wind power, to power data centers or edge devices. Another approach is to optimize the hardware and software components of AI systems to minimize energy consumption without sacrificing accuracy or speed. For example, Google's DeepMind has developed a system that can predict the energy consumption of different algorithms on various hardware platforms, enabling more informed choices for energy-efficient AI.

In summary, AI and hardware are evolving in tandem, with new hardware solutions enabling more powerful and efficient AI algorithms, and new AI applications driving the development of specialized hardware. Quantum computing, AI-specific chips, and energy-efficient computing are some of the key trends in this space, and are likely to shape the future of computing and AI in significant ways.

In conclusion, the evolution of computing hardware has played a crucial role in advancing the field of artificial intelligence. From the development of quantum computing to the design of energy-efficient processors, researchers have pushed the limits of hardware in order to meet the demands of AI applications. As AI continues to grow and expand into new areas, we can expect to see even more innovation in hardware technology to support these advances. The future of computing is bright and full of possibilities, and we are only beginning to scratch the surface of what is possible.

As we conclude this chapter on the evolution of computing hardware in the age of AI, we have seen how AI-driven hardware has been advancing at an incredible pace. From quantum computing to energy-efficient processors, the hardware revolution has played a crucial role in unlocking the full potential of AI. We can expect even more innovations in the near future, as researchers continue to push the boundaries of what's possible. As AI continues to become more prevalent in our daily lives, the role of hardware will only become more critical in enabling us to unlock the full potential of this technology. Thank you for joining us on this journey through the world of AI and hardware.

Suggestions that will be of interest for you to consider based on this chapter topic

Summary: Chapter 45 explores the relationship between artificial intelligence and hardware, delving into the evolution of computing from quantum computing to energy-efficient processors.

Chapter 38 Cybersecurity: Threats and Solutions

Introduction

In today's digital era, the world has become increasingly interconnected, and as a result, the importance of cybersecurity has never been more apparent. From protecting personal information to securing critical infrastructure, cybersecurity has taken center stage in our lives. We will explore the various cyber threats that individuals, businesses, and governments face, and discuss the solutions and strategies employed to mitigate these risks. Additionally, we will examine the latest trends and technological advancements in the realm of cybersecurity and their potential impact on the future of online safety and security.

The ever-evolving landscape of cyber threats poses significant challenges for individuals and organizations alike. From ransomware attacks that hold sensitive data hostage, to phishing scams that target unsuspecting users, the range of threats continues to expand. In response, cybersecurity experts and researchers have developed a variety of strategies and solutions to combat these risks. This chapter will delve into the most prevalent cyber threats and the techniques used to protect against them.

As we progress further into the digital age, it is crucial to stay ahead of the curve in cybersecurity. Emerging technologies, such as artificial intelligence and quantum computing, hold the potential to revolutionize the way we approach online security. We will discuss the latest advancements in these fields and how they may be leveraged to enhance cybersecurity measures.

Moreover, we will address the importance of collaboration between governments, businesses, and individuals in the ongoing fight against cyber threats. From sharing information to enacting robust cybersecurity policies, the combined efforts of all stakeholders are essential to ensure a safer digital future for everyone.

In conclusion, this chapter aims to provide a comprehensive understanding of the current state of cybersecurity, the challenges faced, and the innovative solutions being developed to safeguard our digital world. As technology continues to evolve at a rapid pace, staying informed and vigilant in the realm of cybersecurity is more critical than ever.

With the increasing dependence on technology in our daily lives, cybersecurity has become an essential concern for individuals, businesses, and governments alike. This chapter will delve into the various threats posed by cyber attacks and the solutions and strategies available to mitigate these threats. We will also examine the latest trends and technologies in cybersecurity and their potential impact on the future of online security.

Chapter 39: robotics and their integration with AI

As technology continues to advance at an unprecedented rate, robotics and artificial intelligence are becoming increasingly intertwined. We will explore the exciting world of robotics and their integration with AI. From industrial automation to personal companions, the possibilities for the future of robotics are endless. We will delve into the benefits and challenges of combining man and machine, and how this integration is changing the way we live and work. Join us on this journey as we explore the blending of AI and robotics.

We will delve into the fascinating world of robotics and explore the increasing integration of AI with these machines. Robotics has been an area of active research and development for many years, with applications ranging from industrial automation to personal companions. As the capabilities of AI continue to grow, we are seeing an ever-closer blending of man and machine, with robots becoming more intelligent and more integrated into our daily lives.

Artificial Intelligence (AI) and Robotics have long been thought of as two separate fields. However, recent advances in both areas have made it clear that the two are inextricably linked. Robotics is the branch of technology that deals with the design, construction, operation, and application of robots, while AI is the field of computer science that focuses on creating machines that can perform tasks that would typically require human intelligence to complete. We will explore the integration of AI and Robotics and the many ways in which this blending of man and machine is changing the world around us.

One of the most significant areas of impact for AI and Robotics is industrial automation. Many tasks in manufacturing and assembly processes can now be automated through the use of robots, increasing efficiency and reducing labor costs. Additionally, AI algorithms can be used to optimize production processes, ensuring that machines are working at peak performance.

In the healthcare industry, robots are being developed to assist in surgeries and perform tasks that require a high degree of precision. For example, the da Vinci Surgical System uses a combination of robotics and AI to perform minimally invasive surgeries with greater accuracy than traditional surgical methods.

Personal robotics is also becoming more prevalent in our daily lives, with AI-powered personal assistants such as Siri and Alexa now common in many households. These devices can perform tasks such as setting reminders, answering questions, and even controlling other smart devices in the home.

The blending of AI and Robotics has also led to the development of social robots, designed to interact with humans in a social context. These robots can be used in settings such as hospitals and retirement homes to provide companionship and assist with tasks such as medication reminders and mobility assistance.

As AI and Robotics continue to evolve and become more integrated, there is the potential for significant benefits in various fields, including healthcare, manufacturing, and personal assistance. However, as with any emerging technology, there are also concerns about the impact on employment and privacy. It is essential to carefully consider the implications of these developments and ensure that they are being used ethically and responsibly.

As the integration between AI and robotics deepens, it is clear that these technologies are evolving at an unprecedented pace. With the help of AI, robots are becoming smarter, more efficient, and more adaptable to their environments. From industrial robots that can autonomously move and perform complex tasks in factories to personal companions that can assist with everyday tasks and even provide emotional support, the applications of AI and robotics are endless.

One significant development in AI and robotics is the emergence of collaborative robots or cobots. These robots are designed to work alongside human workers, enhancing productivity and safety in the workplace. Cobots are equipped with advanced sensors and algorithms that enable them to detect human presence and adjust their movements accordingly, making them less dangerous to work with than traditional industrial robots.

Another area where AI and robotics are rapidly advancing is in the field of healthcare. Robots are increasingly being used to assist with surgeries and rehabilitation, with AI algorithms enabling them to perform these tasks with greater precision and efficiency than ever before. In addition, personal care robots are being developed to help elderly and disabled individuals with daily tasks, improving their quality of life and allowing them to live more independently.

However, as with any rapidly evolving technology, there are also concerns about the impact of AI and robotics on society. One of the major concerns is the displacement of human workers as more and more tasks are automated. There is also the potential for the misuse of these technologies, particularly in areas such as autonomous weapons and surveillance.

Overall, the blending of AI and robotics is an exciting and rapidly evolving field with countless possibilities for innovation and progress. As these technologies continue to advance, it will be important to ensure that their development is guided by ethical and social considerations to ensure that they are used to benefit humanity as a whole.

Robots and artificial intelligence have been evolving over the years and their integration has led to a new generation of robots that are smarter, more efficient, and more intuitive. One of the most important developments in this field is the creation of robots that can work alongside humans in various industries, from manufacturing to healthcare.

Collaborative robots, also known as cobots, are designed to work with humans, and they have been gaining popularity in various industries because of their ability to improve productivity and safety. Cobots are equipped with sensors and cameras that allow them to detect human presence and respond appropriately to avoid any potential accidents.

In addition to cobots, there has been a growing trend in the development of social robots, which are designed to interact with humans in more personal settings. These robots can take on various forms, from humanoid to animal-like, and are designed to provide companionship and assistance to people in need, such as the elderly or disabled.

The integration of AI and robotics has also led to the development of autonomous robots, which are capable of performing tasks without human intervention. Autonomous robots are being used in various industries, such as agriculture and logistics, to improve efficiency and reduce costs.

However, the integration of AI and robotics also poses ethical and societal challenges, such as job displacement and privacy concerns. It is important to address these challenges and develop regulations that ensure the safe and ethical use of these technologies.

Overall, the blending of man and machine through AI and robotics has the potential to revolutionize various industries and improve our daily lives, but it is important to approach this technology with caution and foresight.

In recent years, there has been a growing trend towards the integration of AI and robotics, leading to the creation of machines that can perform increasingly complex tasks with greater efficiency and accuracy. One major area where this integration is taking place is in industrial automation, where robots are being used to carry out a range of tasks such as assembly line work and packaging.

The use of AI in robotics is also giving rise to the development of personal companions, such as social robots that can interact with humans and provide emotional support. These robots are designed to learn and adapt to the needs of their users, with the help of sophisticated algorithms and natural language processing.

In the medical field, robots are being used to perform surgeries with greater precision and accuracy, reducing the risk of human error. Robotic prosthetics are also being developed to provide amputees with greater mobility and functionality.

However, as the integration of AI and robotics continues to evolve, there are also concerns about the impact on jobs and the workforce. Some argue that the automation of tasks previously carried out by humans will lead to job losses, while others see the potential for new job opportunities in the development and maintenance of these machines.

Regardless of the debate, it is clear that the blending of man and machine is changing the face of robotics and revolutionizing the way we live and work.

One of the most exciting applications of AI is in the field of robotics. Robotics has come a long way since the early days of factory automation, with today's robots being much more intelligent and versatile. With AI, robots can learn from their environment and adapt to new situations, making them ideal for a variety of applications.

One area where AI and robotics are being used together is in the field of personal companions. Robots are being designed to assist people in their homes, helping them with tasks such as cooking, cleaning, and even providing company. These robots are designed to learn from their interactions with humans and adapt to their needs, making them highly effective assistants.

Another area where AI and robotics are being used together is in the field of industrial automation. AI-powered robots can perform a variety of tasks, including welding, painting, and assembly. They can work around the clock, without needing breaks or rest, making them highly efficient and cost-effective.

In addition, AI and robotics are being used together in the field of healthcare. Robots can assist doctors and nurses with patient care, performing tasks such as taking vitals and administering medication. They can also be used to perform surgeries, with AI helping to guide the robot's movements and ensure precision.

As AI and robotics continue to advance, we can expect to see even more innovative applications in the future. From self-driving cars to intelligent drones, the possibilities are endless. It's an exciting time for the field of AI and robotics, and the blending of man and machine is sure to bring about a new era of innovation and progress.

The integration of AI and robotics has not only advanced the manufacturing industry but has also expanded into various other domains. For instance, robotic surgery is becoming increasingly common, and some medical procedures are now performed entirely by robots. With AI, these robots can analyze vast amounts of data, making them efficient at identifying patterns and executing precise movements, which can lead to better patient outcomes.

Moreover, the combination of AI and robotics has given rise to personal companion robots, which are designed to assist people with various tasks, such as housework, transportation, and social interactions. These robots can recognize speech, emotions, and facial expressions, allowing them to communicate and interact with humans more naturally. As they learn more about their users over time, they can provide more personalized and effective assistance.

However, the integration of AI and robotics also raises concerns about the potential for job displacement, especially in fields that rely heavily on repetitive tasks that can be automated. It is crucial to consider the impact on the workforce and find ways to reskill or upskill workers to adapt to the changing job market.

Overall, the blending of man and machine through AI and robotics is rapidly advancing and opening up new possibilities in various domains. With proper consideration and management, it has the potential to enhance our lives and revolutionize industries.

As the field of AI and robotics continues to advance, there is an increasing blending of man and machine. Robots are no longer just simple machines that perform repetitive tasks in factories; they are now being designed to be personal companions, assistants, and even caretakers for the elderly and disabled.

One area where AI and robotics are being integrated is in industrial automation. Automated robots are now being used in manufacturing and other industries to increase efficiency and reduce costs. These robots can perform tasks that are dangerous or impossible for humans, such as working in extreme temperatures or handling hazardous materials. With the integration of AI, these robots can now learn and adapt to their environment, making them even more effective.

Another area where AI and robotics are being blended is in the development of personal companions. These robots are designed to provide assistance and companionship to individuals in their daily lives. They can perform tasks such as reminding individuals to take their medication, helping with household chores, or simply providing conversation and entertainment. With the integration of AI, these robots can also learn the preferences and habits of their users, allowing them to provide more personalized assistance.

In the healthcare industry, robots are being designed to assist with patient care. These robots can monitor patient vital signs, administer medication, and even perform simple procedures. With the integration of AI, these robots can also learn and adapt to individual patient needs, providing more effective and personalized care.

As the field of AI and robotics continues to advance, it is clear that the blending of man and machine will only continue to increase. While there are certainly benefits to this integration, such as increased efficiency and improved quality of life for individuals, there are also potential risks and ethical considerations that must be carefully considered.

In addition to personal robots, AI and robotics are also revolutionizing industrial automation. Many factories and manufacturing facilities are already using robots to handle repetitive or dangerous tasks, such as welding, painting, or handling hazardous materials. With the integration of AI, these robots can become more efficient and adaptable, able to make decisions and adjust their actions in real time based on changing circumstances.

One example of this is the use of collaborative robots, or "cobots", which are designed to work alongside human workers rather than replace them. Cobots can be programmed to handle simple, repetitive tasks, allowing human workers to focus on more complex and value-added work. They can also be equipped with AI algorithms that enable them to learn from their interactions with human workers and improve their performance over time.

As the field of robotics continues to evolve, we are likely to see even more advanced and capable robots that can take on increasingly complex tasks. For example, autonomous robots could be used for tasks such as exploring space or performing search and rescue missions in dangerous or inaccessible environments. And with the continued integration of AI, these robots will become even more intelligent and adaptable, able to learn from their experiences and make decisions in real time.

However, as with any technology, there are also concerns about the impact of AI and robotics on jobs and society as a whole. As robots become more capable and widespread, there is a risk that they could displace human workers, particularly in industries that rely heavily on manual labor. Additionally, there are ethical considerations around the use of AI and robotics, particularly in military or surveillance applications.

Overall, the integration of AI and robotics has the potential to transform many aspects of our lives, from personal companionship to industrial automation. As this technology continues to advance, it will be important to carefully consider its impact on society and work to ensure that it is used in a way that benefits everyone.

We have explored the world of robotics and their increasing integration with AI. We have seen how robotics technology has rapidly evolved from industrial automation to personal companions, and how AI has contributed to this evolution. The blending of man and machine is becoming increasingly evident in various aspects of our lives, and the potential for even greater integration and collaboration is endless. With the advancement of technology, we can expect to see more sophisticated and intelligent robots that will revolutionize the way we live and work. The future of AI and robotics is exciting and full of possibilities, and it is up to us to leverage this technology for the betterment of humanity.

Summary:

We explored the world of robotics and their increasing integration with AI. We saw how industrial automation has revolutionized manufacturing, leading to increased productivity and efficiency. We also discussed the development of personal companions and how they are being used in healthcare and education. Additionally, we examined the ethical considerations surrounding the use of robots, particularly with regards to the potential displacement of human workers.

Chapter 40: AI and Retail

From personalized product recommendations to automated customer service, AI is changing the shopping experience for both consumers and retailers. As AI technology continues to advance, retailers are using it to gain valuable insights into customer behavior, optimize inventory management, and enhance the overall shopping experience. We will delve deeper into the ways in which AI is revolutionizing the retail industry and the potential it holds for the future.

The retail industry is undergoing a significant transformation, thanks to the integration of AI technology. AI-driven applications are now being used to personalize customer experience and improve the overall shopping journey. Retailers are leveraging AI in various ways, including virtual assistants, chatbots, and personalized product recommendations.

One of the significant ways AI is transforming retail is through the use of customer service chatbots. Chatbots powered by AI can provide 24/7 assistance to customers, reducing the workload of customer service representatives. The chatbots can assist customers in finding products, answering product-related questions, and even processing returns or refunds.

AI is also being used to provide personalized product recommendations to customers. By analyzing customer data and purchase history, retailers can offer tailored product recommendations to individual customers, making the shopping experience more convenient and personalized.

In addition to improving customer experience, AI is also helping retailers optimize their supply chain and inventory management. AI-powered algorithms can help retailers forecast demand, manage inventory, and optimize delivery routes to reduce costs and improve efficiency.

Overall, AI technology is transforming the retail industry, making the shopping experience more convenient, personalized, and efficient.

One major way that AI is transforming the retail industry is through personalized recommendations. With the help of machine learning algorithms, retailers are able to analyze customer data to create tailored recommendations for each individual shopper. This can lead to increased sales and customer loyalty, as shoppers are more likely to purchase items that are recommended based on their unique preferences and buying history.

Another area where AI is making a significant impact in retail is in the realm of inventory management. By using predictive analytics and machine learning algorithms, retailers are able to optimize their inventory levels and reduce waste. AI can help retailers accurately forecast demand, identify which products are likely to sell well, and optimize supply chain logistics to ensure that products are always in stock when customers want them.

AI is also being used to improve the customer service experience in retail. Chatbots and virtual assistants can provide shoppers with 24/7 support and assistance, answering common questions and helping customers find the products they need. By automating these interactions, retailers are able to reduce the workload of their customer service teams and provide faster, more efficient service to shoppers.

Finally, AI is helping retailers to better understand and analyze customer behavior. By analyzing data from customer interactions, retailers can identify patterns and trends that can be used to inform marketing and sales strategies. This can help retailers to more effectively target their advertising and promotional efforts, resulting in higher sales and improved customer satisfaction.

AI has already transformed the retail industry in several ways. One of the most significant ways is through personalized recommendations. Online retailers like Amazon, Netflix, and Spotify have been using AI algorithms for years to recommend products, movies, and music to their customers based on their browsing and purchase history. In physical stores, retailers are also using AI to personalize the shopping experience by analyzing customer data and behavior to offer tailored recommendations.

AI is also being used in retail for inventory management. By analyzing data on sales trends and customer behavior, retailers can predict demand for specific products, ensuring that they always have the right amount of stock on hand. This helps retailers to avoid stock shortages or overstocking, which can both be costly.

Automated customer service is another area where AI is making an impact in retail. Chatbots are being used by many retailers to handle customer queries and complaints, freeing up customer service representatives to handle more complex issues. AI-powered chatbots can analyze customer queries and provide relevant answers, making the shopping experience more efficient and convenient.

In addition, AI is being used in retail to enhance the in-store experience. Smart mirrors and augmented reality technology are being used to allow customers to virtually try on clothes and accessories, making it easier for them to find the right fit and style. Retailers are also using AI-powered cameras to analyze customer behavior in stores, helping them to optimize store layout and product placement.

Overall, AI is transforming the retail industry in significant ways, from personalized recommendations to automated customer service. As AI continues to evolve, we can expect to see even more innovative uses of the technology in the world of retail.

AI and retail are proving to be a game-changing combination. One of the most significant areas where AI is transforming the retail industry is through personalized recommendations. AI algorithms analyze customer data, such as purchase history, browsing behavior, and demographic information, to create tailored product recommendations. These recommendations can be delivered to customers via email, on the retailer's website, or even in-store.

Another area where AI is revolutionizing the retail industry is through automated customer service. Retailers are leveraging AI-powered chatbots and virtual assistants to handle customer inquiries, complaints, and even sales. These chatbots can handle simple queries such as tracking a package or checking store hours, freeing up human customer service representatives to handle more complex issues.

AI is also playing a significant role in supply chain management. With the help of AI-powered analytics tools, retailers can optimize inventory management, demand forecasting, and logistics. These tools can help retailers make smarter decisions about when to order products, how much to order, and where to store them.

Finally, AI is also transforming the in-store shopping experience. Retailers are experimenting with AI-powered technologies such as facial recognition, augmented reality, and smart mirrors to enhance the customer experience. For example, smart mirrors can be used to provide customers with personalized styling recommendations, while facial recognition technology can be used to tailor in-store experiences based on a customer's preferences.

Overall, AI is transforming the retail industry in numerous ways, from personalized recommendations to automated customer service and supply chain optimization. As retailers continue to leverage AI, we can expect to see even more innovation and disruption in this space.

AI is transforming the retail industry in many ways, and one of the most significant is by enabling personalized shopping experiences for customers. Retailers are using AI-powered tools to collect and analyze data on customer preferences, purchase history, and behavior, allowing them to create more targeted and relevant product recommendations. This not only enhances the customer experience, but also increases sales and revenue for retailers.

In addition to personalized recommendations, AI is also being used to improve the supply chain and inventory management. Retailers can use AI to analyze data on consumer demand, seasonal trends, and market fluctuations to optimize inventory levels and minimize waste. This can lead to cost savings and more efficient operations.

AI is also playing a role in customer service, with chatbots and virtual assistants being used to provide 24/7 support and assistance. These AI-powered tools can handle basic customer inquiries and tasks, freeing up human customer service agents to focus on more complex issues.

Overall, AI is transforming the retail industry and is poised to continue doing so in the future. As retailers continue to adopt and integrate AI-powered tools and technologies, we can expect to see even more personalized and efficient shopping experiences for customers.

In addition to personalized recommendations, AI is also transforming the shopping experience through automation of customer service. Chatbots and virtual assistants are being deployed by retailers to assist customers with their queries and concerns. These AI-powered assistants are available 24/7 and can handle multiple conversations simultaneously, which reduces customer waiting time and enhances customer satisfaction.

Moreover, AI is being utilized to automate the checkout process, reducing the need for long lines and improving the shopping experience. Retailers are implementing technologies such as computer vision and RFID (radio-frequency identification) to enable customers to purchase items without the need for a physical checkout. Amazon Go, for example, has introduced a "just walk out" shopping experience where customers can simply grab what they need and leave the store without having to go through a checkout line.

AI is also being used to optimize inventory management, supply chain operations, and pricing strategies. AI algorithms can analyze data such as customer demand, seasonality, and competitor pricing to provide retailers with valuable insights for making informed decisions about inventory management and pricing. This can help retailers reduce overstocking and understocking of products and ensure that they are offering competitive prices to their customers.

Overall, the application of AI in the retail industry is transforming the shopping experience, enhancing customer satisfaction, and improving operational efficiency for retailers. As AI continues to evolve, we can expect to see more innovative and advanced use cases of AI in the retail industry.

One significant benefit of AI in retail is that it can help retailers optimize their pricing strategy. AI-powered pricing tools can analyze large volumes of data to identify patterns and trends, allowing retailers to make informed decisions about their pricing strategy. For example, they can analyze historical sales data, competitor prices, and customer behavior to determine the optimal price for each product.

Another area where AI is transforming the retail industry is through the use of chatbots and virtual assistants. Chatbots can be used to answer customer questions, provide product recommendations, and even handle basic customer service issues. This frees up staff to focus on more complex issues and helps retailers provide a more personalized shopping experience for their customers.

AI can also be used to improve inventory management. By analyzing sales data and predicting future demand, retailers can optimize their inventory levels, reducing waste and ensuring they always have the products their customers want.

Finally, AI can be used to improve the in-store experience for customers. Retailers can use AI-powered cameras and sensors to monitor foot traffic and analyze customer behavior, identifying areas where they can improve store layout or product placement to increase sales.

Overall, AI has the potential to transform the retail industry, making it more efficient, personalized, and customer-focused.

One promising area where AI is making an impact in the retail industry is in supply chain optimization. By using AI to analyze large amounts of data from various sources such as sales data, weather forecasts, and social media trends, retailers can make more accurate demand forecasts and optimize their inventory levels accordingly. This not only helps retailers reduce waste and lower costs but also ensures that popular products are always in stock and readily available for customers.

Another way that AI is transforming the retail experience is through the use of chatbots and virtual assistants. These tools can assist customers with product recommendations, order tracking, and even offer personalized shopping experiences. By leveraging AI-powered natural language processing (NLP) technology, these tools can understand and respond to customer queries in real-time, making the shopping experience more efficient and enjoyable for customers.

In addition to optimizing supply chain operations and enhancing customer experiences, AI is also being used to combat retail fraud. Machine learning algorithms can analyze large volumes of transaction data and identify suspicious patterns or anomalies, enabling retailers to detect and prevent fraudulent activity in real-time. This not only helps retailers protect their own bottom line but also ensures that customers can shop with confidence and trust in the security of their personal and financial information.

Overall, AI is rapidly transforming the retail industry, from personalized product recommendations to improved supply chain efficiency and fraud prevention. By leveraging AI-driven solutions, retailers can gain a competitive advantage and provide a more seamless and enjoyable shopping experience for their customers.

In conclusion, the integration of AI in the retail industry has significantly transformed the shopping experience for consumers. With AI-driven solutions like personalized recommendations, automated customer service, and real-time inventory tracking, retailers can improve customer satisfaction and boost sales. Additionally, AI helps retailers to gather and analyze vast amounts of customer data, providing insights that can be used to make informed business decisions. As AI technology continues to evolve, we can expect even more innovative solutions to be developed, further enhancing the shopping experience for consumers.

Suggestions that will be of interest for you to consider based on this chapter topic

Some key takeaways from this chapter include:

- AI is driving personalization in retail, allowing retailers to tailor their recommendations and marketing to individual customers based on their preferences and behavior.
- Chatbots and virtual assistants powered by AI are becoming increasingly common in retail, providing customers with fast and convenient support.
- AI is also helping retailers optimize their supply chain and inventory management, reducing waste and improving efficiency.

- Despite the many benefits of AI in retail, concerns about privacy and the potential for AI to displace human jobs remain.

Retailers that embrace AI are likely to gain a competitive edge in the marketplace, but they must do so in a responsible and ethical way, with a focus on providing value to customers while minimizing potential risks.

Chapter 41: AI and the travel industry

As AI continues to advance and permeate various industries, it is not surprising that it is also changing the way we travel. From smart booking systems to AI-guided tours, the travel and tourism industry is experiencing a significant transformation. We will explore the impact of AI on travel and how it is reinventing the journey for travelers around the world. We will examine the various ways in which AI is being used to enhance the travel experience, as well as the potential benefits and challenges associated with its implementation.

Artificial Intelligence (AI) is transforming the travel industry, from personalized recommendations and travel planning to streamlined booking systems and enhanced customer service. One of the biggest impacts of AI on travel has been the ability to analyze vast amounts of data to better understand consumer preferences and behaviors, allowing for more tailored and personalized travel experiences.

One example of this is the use of chatbots, powered by AI, to assist travelers in booking flights, hotels, and activities, as well as providing real-time customer service. Chatbots can help travelers with everything from flight delays and cancellations to recommending local restaurants and activities. This has greatly improved the customer experience by providing instant assistance and reducing wait times.

In addition to chatbots, AI-powered virtual assistants are becoming increasingly popular in the travel industry. These assistants can provide personalized travel recommendations and even create itineraries based on a traveler's preferences, including factors such as budget, destination, and activities.

AI is also being used to improve travel safety and security. For example, airlines are using AI to analyze data on weather patterns, flight paths, and aircraft performance to optimize flight routes and reduce the risk of turbulence. AI is also being used to monitor security footage and identify potential threats in airports and other travel hubs.

Overall, AI has the potential to greatly enhance the travel experience by providing personalized recommendations, improving customer service, and enhancing safety and security. As the technology continues to advance, we can expect even more innovative applications in the travel industry.

Artificial intelligence (AI) has been a game-changer in the travel and tourism industry. It has enabled businesses to provide personalized experiences to customers, streamline operations, and make data-driven decisions. One of the most significant areas where AI is making an impact is in smart booking systems. These systems use machine learning algorithms to analyze data such as customer preferences, travel history, and search history to provide tailored recommendations for flights, hotels, and activities.

In addition to smart booking systems, AI is also transforming the way travelers plan their trips. AI-powered chatbots are being used by travel companies to provide 24/7 customer service, answering questions and assisting with bookings. Some companies are also using virtual assistants to guide travelers through their journey, providing recommendations for restaurants and activities based on their location and preferences.

Moreover, AI is being utilized in the tourism industry to offer personalized experiences to travelers. For instance, AI-guided tours allow tourists to explore destinations in a unique way, using augmented reality and natural language processing to offer context and information about the sites they visit.

Overall, AI is helping to reinvent the travel experience for both businesses and customers, offering greater convenience, personalization, and efficiency.

AI-guided tours and personalized experiences

One of the most significant impacts of AI on the travel industry is in the realm of personalized experiences. With the help of AI, travel companies can offer custom tours and experiences based on the preferences and interests of individual travelers.

For example, AI can analyze a traveler's social media activity, search history, and previous travel patterns to suggest personalized travel recommendations, from flights and accommodations to activities and dining options.

Additionally, AI-powered chatbots can provide instant assistance and recommendations to travelers during their trip, reducing the need for human customer service representatives.

AI-guided tours are another area where AI is transforming the travel industry. Tour operators can use AI to create interactive, self-guided tours that use augmented reality and other technologies to enhance the travel experience. These tours can be customized based on the traveler's interests and preferences, allowing for a more personalized and engaging experience.

Overall, the use of AI in travel is transforming the way we plan and experience our trips, making travel more accessible, efficient, and personalized.

As AI continues to evolve, it is becoming increasingly integrated into the travel industry, transforming the way people plan and experience their journeys. One of the ways AI is being used in the travel industry is through smart booking systems. These systems use AI algorithms to search for the best deals on flights, hotels, and other travel accommodations, taking into account a wide range of factors such as travel dates, budget, and location preferences.

Another application of AI in the travel industry is in the form of chatbots and virtual assistants. These tools allow travelers to easily access information about their travel plans, such as flight details and hotel reservations, as well as receive personalized recommendations for activities and attractions at their destination. Chatbots and virtual assistants can also provide real-time assistance to travelers, such as helping them rebook flights or find alternative travel options in the event of disruptions.

AI is also being used to enhance the overall travel experience, particularly through the use of AI-guided tours. These tours use AI algorithms to create personalized itineraries for travelers based on their interests and preferences, and provide recommendations for activities, attractions, and dining options at each destination. AI-guided tours can also provide real-time recommendations and updates based on traveler feedback and behavior.

Additionally, AI is being used to improve the safety and security of travelers, particularly in the wake of the COVID-19 pandemic. AI-powered technologies such as thermal scanners, facial recognition software, and contactless check-in systems are being implemented in airports and hotels to help detect and prevent the spread of the virus.

Overall, the integration of AI into the travel industry is transforming the way people plan and experience their journeys, providing travelers with personalized recommendations and real-time assistance, while also enhancing safety and security measures.

AI is also transforming the experience of booking travel. Chatbots and virtual assistants have become increasingly popular as a way to streamline the booking process and provide personalized recommendations to travelers. For example, Expedia's virtual travel assistant allows users to make hotel reservations and ask for recommendations through a chatbot interface. Similarly, Kayak's chatbot helps travelers book flights and hotels, and can even provide information on visa requirements for international travel.

In addition to booking travel, AI is also being used to enhance the travel experience itself. One example is the use of AI-powered virtual guides, which can provide personalized recommendations and historical context during a tour. Another example is the development of AI-powered translation devices, which can provide real-time translation during travel and help overcome language barriers.

Finally, AI is also being used to improve travel safety and security. For example, airports are increasingly using AI-powered facial recognition technology for passenger identification, which can help speed up the check-in process and enhance security. AI is also being used to analyze travel data and identify potential security threats before they happen.

Overall, AI is transforming the travel industry by making travel more efficient, personalized, and safe. As AI technology continues to advance, we can expect to see even more innovative applications in the travel sector.

Smart airports are another application of AI in the travel industry. These airports use AI to provide personalized and efficient travel experiences for passengers. For example, AI-powered security systems can identify passengers based on their biometric data, reducing the need for manual verification processes. AI can also be used to optimize airport operations, such as predicting flight delays and optimizing airport staff schedules.

Another area where AI is transforming the travel industry is in the development of smart travel assistants. These assistants can provide personalized travel recommendations, based on the traveler's preferences, past travel history, and other data sources. They can also assist with booking travel arrangements, such as flights, hotels, and rental cars, and provide real-time travel updates and alerts.

AI is also being used to develop smart tour guides that can provide real-time information about tourist destinations. These guides use natural language processing and machine learning algorithms to provide personalized recommendations and insights about local attractions, restaurants, and cultural experiences.

In addition, AI is transforming the hospitality industry, with the development of smart hotels that use AI-powered devices to provide personalized and efficient services to guests. For example, smart hotels can use AI-powered chatbots to provide guests with instant assistance and room service, and AI-powered robots to deliver room service and perform other tasks.

Overall, AI is transforming the travel industry in numerous ways, from enhancing airport security and operations to providing personalized travel recommendations and experiences. As AI technology continues to advance, we can expect to see even more innovative applications of AI in the travel industry.

One significant benefit of AI in the travel industry is that it can enhance the customer experience. With the help of AI, travel companies can offer personalized recommendations and suggestions for travel destinations, accommodations, and activities based on a customer's preferences and previous travel history. This personalized approach can help travelers feel more engaged and satisfied with their travel experience.

Another way AI is transforming the travel industry is through the use of chatbots and virtual assistants. These tools can handle customer inquiries and provide assistance in real-time, 24/7, which can improve customer satisfaction and reduce the need for human customer support. Chatbots can also help with tasks such as booking flights and accommodations, providing travel information, and offering recommendations for activities and restaurants.

AI is also being used to improve the efficiency of travel operations, such as airline and hotel management. For example, airlines are using AI to optimize their flight routes and schedules, while hotels are using AI to manage their inventory and pricing. This can help companies save time and money while also improving the customer experience by offering more efficient and cost-effective travel options.

Finally, AI is also being used in the travel industry to enhance security and safety. AI-powered security systems can analyze and monitor security footage to detect suspicious behavior and potential security threats. Additionally, AI can help travelers during emergencies by providing real-time alerts and assistance.

Overall, AI is transforming the travel industry by offering personalized recommendations, improving customer service, optimizing travel operations, and enhancing security and safety.

One notable area where AI is transforming travel and tourism is through the creation of AI-powered tour guides. Tourists can now use AI-guided tours to explore cities, learn about local history and culture, and discover hidden gems. These tours can be accessed via mobile apps, which use AI algorithms to provide personalized recommendations and suggestions based on the user's preferences and past behavior.

Another way AI is revolutionizing travel is through smart booking systems. These systems use machine learning algorithms to analyze customer data and make personalized recommendations for flights, hotels, and activities based on the traveler's budget, interests, and other preferences.

AI is also being used to improve customer service in the travel industry. Chatbots and virtual assistants can provide 24/7 support and help customers with booking, cancellations, and other travel-related issues. These systems can handle a high volume of customer queries simultaneously, reducing wait times and improving the overall customer experience.

Furthermore, AI is being used to optimize travel routes and reduce congestion. Traffic prediction models use real-time data to predict traffic patterns and suggest alternative routes to drivers, while smart traffic lights use AI to adjust traffic flow based on real-time traffic conditions.

Finally, AI is being used to enhance airport security by automating the screening process. Automated screening systems use AI to analyze x-ray images of carry-on luggage, detecting potential threats and reducing the need for manual inspection.

As AI continues to evolve, we can expect to see even more innovative uses of the technology in the travel and tourism industry, making travel more personalized, efficient, and enjoyable for everyone involved.

In conclusion, AI is transforming the travel industry in many ways, from personalized travel recommendations and optimized pricing to enhanced safety measures and improved customer experiences. AI technology is also revolutionizing the way travelers explore destinations, with the use of augmented reality and AI-guided tours. As the travel industry continues to evolve, AI will play an increasingly important role in shaping the way people experience and interact with travel. The potential of AI in travel is vast and exciting, and it will be fascinating to see how this technology continues to transform the industry in the coming years.

As we conclude this chapter, it's clear that AI is transforming the travel and tourism industry in significant ways. From personalized recommendations to AI-guided tours, the use of AI in this sector is enhancing the overall travel experience for both consumers and industry professionals. As AI technology continues to advance, we can expect to see even more innovative solutions that will shape the future of travel.

Summary:
We explored the different ways in which AI is being used in the travel industry, such as smart booking systems, AI-guided tours, and personalized travel recommendations. Additionally, the chapter discussed the challenges and ethical considerations that arise with the increasing use of AI in the travel industry.

Suggestions:

- Stay informed about the latest AI technologies being used in the travel industry to make informed decisions when planning trips.
- Consider the potential ethical implications of using AI in the travel industry and advocate for responsible and transparent use of the technology.
- Explore ways in which AI can enhance your travel experience, such as using personalized travel recommendations or AI-guided tours.

Chapter 42 AI and the Afterlife: Digital Immortality

AI and the Afterlife. We will explore the concept of digital immortality, a world where AI-driven simulations of deceased individuals could exist. The possibility of creating such simulations raises ethical, social, and philosophical questions, and we will explore some of the potential implications of this technology. Join us as we dive into this intriguing topic and consider what the future may hold for the intersection of AI and the afterlife.

As AI technology continues to advance, the concept of digital immortality has become a topic of interest and debate. Digital immortality refers to the idea that an individual's consciousness, memories, and personality can be preserved in a digital form, allowing them to continue to exist even after their physical body has passed away.

One potential application of this concept is the creation of AI-driven simulations of deceased individuals. These simulations would be based on the individual's digital footprint, including social media posts, emails, and other online activities, as well as any data that has been collected through wearables and other devices.

Advocates of digital immortality argue that it could offer a way to preserve the memories and personalities of loved ones after they have died, creating a sense of continuity and connection. Others have raised concerns about the ethics of using deceased individuals' data without their consent, as well as the potential for these simulations to be used for nefarious purposes.

Despite the many ethical and philosophical questions surrounding digital immortality, research in this area is continuing, and it remains to be seen how this technology will be used in the future.

As technology advances and AI becomes more sophisticated, the idea of digital immortality has gained traction. With the ability to simulate the voices, personalities, and even physical appearances of deceased individuals, AI-driven simulations could potentially provide a way for loved ones to continue to interact with those who have passed away.

One of the key drivers behind the development of digital immortality is the desire to preserve memories and maintain relationships. For example, an AI-driven simulation of a deceased parent could potentially provide comfort and support to their children, or a simulation of a deceased spouse could allow for continued communication and companionship.

However, there are also concerns about the ethical and psychological implications of digital immortality. Some argue that it could lead to a devaluation of human life, as people may view death as less final if they believe that they can continue to interact with the deceased through AI simulations. Additionally, there are concerns about the potential for misuse of AI simulations, such as creating simulations of deceased individuals for nefarious purposes.

Overall, while digital immortality presents intriguing possibilities for the future, it is important to consider the potential risks and ethical implications as this technology continues to develop.

One potential application of AI technology is the concept of digital immortality, which involves creating a digital version of a deceased individual through advanced AI algorithms. This digital version could interact with living individuals through various means such as chatbots, social media accounts, and virtual reality simulations.

One of the primary reasons for exploring digital immortality is the desire for individuals to preserve their memories, experiences, and wisdom for future generations. By creating a digital version of oneself, it becomes possible to pass on knowledge and experiences to future generations beyond one's physical lifespan. Additionally, this technology could also offer comfort to individuals who have lost loved ones by allowing them to continue interacting with a digital version of the deceased.

However, there are also concerns and potential ethical implications of digital immortality. For example, there is a risk of identity theft if someone were to use the digital version of an individual for nefarious purposes. Additionally, the creation of a digital version of someone without their explicit consent raises questions about privacy and autonomy.

Furthermore, there is the possibility that digital immortality could perpetuate harmful or negative traits and behaviors of an individual, rather than focusing on their positive qualities. There is also the concern that individuals may become too reliant on their digital versions, leading to a decreased appreciation for the value of physical human interactions and experiences.

Overall, digital immortality is a complex and thought-provoking concept that raises important questions about the relationship between technology, humanity, and mortality. While it offers potential benefits, it also highlights the need for careful consideration of ethical and societal implications as this technology continues to develop.

One potential benefit of digital immortality is the ability to preserve the memories and experiences of individuals for future generations. This could allow us to learn more about history and culture by interacting with virtual versions of past individuals. It could also provide comfort to those who have lost loved ones, by allowing them to interact with virtual versions of the deceased.

However, there are also potential drawbacks to the concept of digital immortality. One major concern is the ethical implications of creating virtual versions of individuals without their consent. It raises questions about ownership and control over one's own identity, even after death.

There is also the possibility of creating a class divide between those who can afford to preserve their consciousness in a digital form and those who cannot. This could lead to even greater inequality in society.

Another concern is the potential for abuse of this technology, such as creating virtual versions of individuals for nefarious purposes or using their digital consciousness to manipulate or deceive others.

As with any emerging technology, it is important to consider the potential benefits and drawbacks before fully embracing it. Digital immortality may hold promise for preserving memories and experiences, but it also raises complex ethical and social questions that must be carefully examined.

While the concept of digital immortality raises many ethical and philosophical questions, it also has practical implications that may impact our society in various ways. Here are some of the implications of digital immortality that we should consider:

- Legacy: The creation of digital avatars or simulations of deceased individuals could preserve their memories and legacies, allowing future generations to learn about them and their contributions to society.
- Privacy: Digital immortality also raises concerns about privacy, as the creation and use of personal data and information for these simulations could violate an individual's privacy rights.
- Emotional impact: Interacting with a digital avatar of a deceased loved one may have an emotional impact on individuals, potentially causing grief or complicating the grieving process.
- Legal issues: As the concept of digital immortality is still relatively new, there are legal questions surrounding ownership of digital avatars, the use of personal data, and the potential for identity theft or fraud.
- Social norms: As digital immortality becomes more widespread, it may challenge existing social norms and beliefs about death and the afterlife, potentially causing cultural and societal shifts.

These implications highlight the need for careful consideration and regulation of the development and use of digital immortality technology. It is important to ensure that the benefits of this technology are balanced with potential risks and ethical considerations.

In the next section, we will explore some of the current and future applications of digital immortality, including how AI is driving the development of these technologies.

We explored the concept of digital immortality and the potential implications of AI-driven simulations of deceased individuals. We discussed the different technologies and methods being developed to create these simulations and the ethical questions that arise from them. As technology advances, it is important to consider the impact it has on society, and the question of whether digital immortality is a desirable future remains to be answered.

Overall, this chapter highlights the importance of ethical considerations in the development and use of AI technologies. It is crucial to weigh the potential benefits against the potential harms and ensure that we are creating a future that is beneficial for all.

Thank you for exploring the fascinating topic of AI and the afterlife with me. As we've seen, the concept of digital immortality raises important ethical and philosophical questions about the nature of consciousness and the role of technology in our lives. While it's impossible to predict the future, it's clear that AI will continue to impact our society in profound and unexpected ways, and we must be thoughtful and intentional in our use and development of this technology.

As we move forward, it's important to remain aware of the potential implications of AI-driven simulations of deceased individuals and to approach this technology with caution and respect. We hope this chapter has provided you with a better understanding of the potential impact of AI on the afterlife, and that it has inspired you to continue exploring the intersections of technology and the human experience.

In the next chapter, we will examine the impact of AI on the field of education, from personalized learning to intelligent tutoring systems. Stay tuned!

Summary:
We explored the concept of digital immortality and the potential implications of AI-driven simulations of deceased individuals. We discussed the advancements in AI technology that could make it possible to create digital versions of individuals who have passed away, and the ethical concerns that arise with such technologies.

Some of the potential benefits of digital immortality include preserving the memories and knowledge of loved ones, creating historical records, and providing comfort to those who are grieving. However, there are also concerns about the accuracy and privacy of the information used to create these simulations, as well as the potential for misuse or abuse.

It is important to consider the implications of digital immortality and ensure that appropriate ethical and legal frameworks are in place to govern its use. We must also continue to have open and honest conversations about the potential benefits and risks of such technologies, and actively work to mitigate any negative consequences.

Suggestions:

- Consider your personal beliefs and values regarding digital immortality, and engage in conversations with others to broaden your understanding of different perspectives
- Advocate for the development of ethical and legal frameworks to govern the use of digital immortality technologies
- Support research and development that prioritizes privacy and accuracy in creating digital simulations of deceased individuals
- Stay informed about advancements in AI and their potential implications for society, including those related to digital immortality.

Chapter 43: AI and Urban Planning: Designing the Cities of Tomorrow

As the world population continues to grow, so does the need for efficient, sustainable, and livable cities. Urban planning has always been a complex process, but with the advent of artificial intelligence (AI), it is undergoing a revolution. We will explore the role of AI in urban planning and design, and how it is helping us create smarter and more resilient cities for the future. From optimizing transportation systems to improving energy efficiency, AI is transforming the way we approach urban planning and offering new possibilities for creating the cities of tomorrow.

Urban planning is a complex and challenging task that requires careful consideration of various factors such as transportation, housing, environmental impact, and population growth. With the rapid advancements in AI technology, urban planners now have access to tools and data that can assist them in making more informed and effective decisions.

AI can help in analyzing vast amounts of data related to urban infrastructure, demographics, and environmental factors, and provide valuable insights to urban planners. For instance, machine learning algorithms can analyze patterns of traffic flow and suggest optimized routes for vehicles, reducing congestion and saving time for commuters.

Additionally, AI can be used to model the impact of urban development on the environment, predicting factors such as air pollution, water usage, and energy consumption. This information can then be used to design more sustainable and eco-friendly urban spaces.

Moreover, AI can aid in creating more efficient and affordable housing solutions. By analyzing housing market data, AI algorithms can identify areas with high demand for affordable housing and suggest optimal locations for new construction. This can help in reducing the housing affordability crisis in many urban areas.

Overall, AI has the potential to revolutionize the field of urban planning, creating more sustainable, efficient, and livable cities for the future. However, it is important to consider the ethical implications of using AI in urban planning and ensure that it is used in a way that benefits all members of the community.

AI is revolutionizing urban planning by enabling data-driven decision-making, optimizing resource allocation, and enhancing the quality of life for urban residents. One of the key areas where AI is making a significant impact is in transportation planning. With the rise of autonomous vehicles and smart infrastructure, AI is helping to optimize traffic flow, reduce congestion, and improve safety on the roads.

In addition, AI is also being used to enhance public transportation systems. For example, AI-powered algorithms are being used to predict transit demand, optimize bus and train schedules, and improve the accuracy of real-time passenger information. This not only benefits commuters but also helps to reduce the environmental impact of transportation systems.

Another area where AI is making significant strides is in energy management. AI-powered building management systems are being used to optimize energy consumption in buildings, reduce waste, and lower energy costs. Additionally, AI is being used to optimize the placement of renewable energy sources such as solar panels and wind turbines in urban environments, which can help to reduce the carbon footprint of cities.

AI is also being used to improve public safety in urban environments. For instance, AI-powered surveillance systems can analyze live video feeds to detect potential security threats and alert authorities. Additionally, AI is being used to predict crime hotspots and allocate resources accordingly, which can help to reduce crime rates and improve the safety of residents.

Overall, AI has the potential to revolutionize urban planning by making cities more efficient, sustainable, and livable. However, it is important to ensure that the use of AI in urban planning is ethical and transparent, with a focus on improving the quality of life for all residents, especially those who are traditionally marginalized or underrepresented in decision-making processes.

In urban planning, AI can help cities better understand and respond to the needs of their residents. One way this can be achieved is through the use of predictive modeling, which can analyze data from a variety of sources, such as traffic patterns, energy usage, and public transport data, to help identify areas that may be at risk of congestion, pollution, or other issues.

AI can also assist in designing more sustainable and energy-efficient buildings and infrastructure. For example, by using data on weather patterns and building usage, AI algorithms can optimize heating and cooling systems to reduce energy waste.

Furthermore, AI can help cities enhance safety and security. By analyzing crime data and other relevant information, AI algorithms can identify high-risk areas and help law enforcement prioritize their efforts. Additionally, AI-powered surveillance systems can be used to monitor public spaces and detect potential security threats.

Overall, AI has the potential to revolutionize urban planning by helping cities become more efficient, sustainable, and livable. However, it is important to ensure that AI is used in a way that benefits all members of the community, and that privacy concerns and ethical considerations are taken into account.

AI has the potential to help design more efficient transportation systems within cities. For example, AI algorithms can optimize traffic light timings to reduce congestion and improve the flow of traffic. Additionally, AI can be used to analyze traffic patterns and make recommendations for infrastructure improvements such as the addition of new roads or public transportation options. This can lead to more sustainable and cost-effective transportation options for city residents.

Another area where AI can improve urban planning is in the design of buildings and other infrastructure. By using AI to analyze environmental factors such as wind patterns and sunlight exposure, architects and engineers can design buildings that are more energy-efficient and sustainable. AI can also help to optimize the placement of buildings and other infrastructure within a city to maximize space and improve overall livability.

In addition to designing more efficient infrastructure, AI can also be used to improve public safety in cities. For example, AI can analyze crime data to identify patterns and predict where crimes are likely to occur. This information can be used to optimize police patrols and other crime prevention measures, leading to safer communities.

Overall, the use of AI in urban planning has the potential to create more livable, sustainable, and efficient cities. However, it is important to ensure that these technologies are used ethically and responsibly to avoid unintended consequences.

AI and Traffic Management

Traffic management is one of the most significant challenges for urban planners. With the increasing population, traffic congestion is becoming a major problem in many cities. AI can help in improving traffic management by providing real-time data analysis of traffic patterns and suggesting the most efficient routes for vehicles to reach their destination. Smart traffic systems can adjust traffic signals in real-time based on the traffic volume, which can help in reducing traffic congestion.

AI-powered traffic management systems can also predict traffic accidents and reroute traffic accordingly to avoid congestion. With the help of AI, cities can optimize traffic flow, reduce carbon emissions, and improve the safety of drivers and pedestrians.

One such example is the Singapore Smart Mobility 2030 project, which aims to leverage AI and data analytics to create a seamless and efficient transportation system. The project includes several initiatives, such as the use of autonomous buses and real-time traffic management systems.

In conclusion, AI can play a significant role in improving traffic management in cities. With the help of AI-powered traffic management systems, cities can reduce traffic congestion, optimize traffic flow, and improve safety for drivers and pedestrians.

In addition to enhancing urban planning processes, AI is also revolutionizing the way cities are maintained and managed. For instance, AI-powered systems can monitor the quality of air and water in real-time, alerting authorities to any dangerous levels or changes in the environment. They can also predict and detect natural disasters and help first responders react more efficiently.

Another application of AI in urban environments is the development of autonomous vehicles. Self-driving cars, buses, and trucks can help reduce traffic congestion, air pollution, and the number of accidents caused by human error. Additionally, they can make public transportation more accessible to people who may not have easy access to public transit, such as the elderly or disabled.

AI can also help cities become more sustainable by reducing energy consumption and waste production. For instance, smart grids can optimize the distribution and use of electricity, while AI-powered waste management systems can identify the most efficient ways to collect and process waste. These measures can help reduce the carbon footprint of urban areas and contribute to a cleaner, healthier environment.

Overall, the integration of AI into urban planning and management has the potential to make cities more efficient, sustainable, and livable. As cities continue to grow and face new challenges, AI can offer innovative solutions to ensure that they remain resilient and adaptable to changing circumstances.

AI is transforming the way urban planners design and operate cities. By leveraging data and predictive analytics, AI systems can optimize transportation, energy usage, waste management, and emergency services. AI-enabled smart cities can monitor traffic patterns, identify problem areas, and provide real-time solutions. In addition, AI can help urban planners determine where to place green spaces and parks, improving the quality of life for city residents.

One example of AI in urban planning is the city of Barcelona. The city has implemented an AI-powered "Superblock" system, where groups of nine city blocks are transformed into pedestrian-only areas with reduced traffic. The system uses sensors and data analysis to determine which blocks would benefit the most from the transformation, taking into account factors such as air quality, noise pollution, and pedestrian safety.

Another example is the city of Singapore, which is using AI to optimize its transportation system. The city has implemented an AI-powered platform called the "Beeline," which uses data to identify transportation demand patterns and optimize bus routes accordingly. The platform allows commuters to book seats on the most efficient routes, reducing travel time and improving overall efficiency.

However, the implementation of AI in urban planning also raises concerns about privacy, data security, and equity. The data collected by AI systems can potentially be used for surveillance or discrimination, and there is a risk that certain communities may be excluded from the benefits of AI-powered systems.

As AI continues to evolve, it is crucial for urban planners to consider the potential benefits and risks of its implementation. By ensuring that AI is used ethically and responsibly, cities can leverage its power to create more sustainable, efficient, and livable urban environments.

In addition to designing more efficient and sustainable urban environments, AI can also help with disaster response and recovery efforts. For example, during natural disasters such as hurricanes, earthquakes, or wildfires, AI algorithms can quickly analyze data from sensors and social media to identify areas that are most affected and prioritize rescue efforts. In the aftermath of a disaster, AI can also assist in assessing the damage, identifying areas that require rebuilding, and optimizing the allocation of resources for recovery.

Moreover, AI can assist in urban planning by providing predictive analytics to help city officials make informed decisions about future development. For example, AI can predict population growth, traffic patterns, and energy consumption, allowing city planners to make more accurate predictions about future needs and allocate resources accordingly. By optimizing resource allocation and infrastructure planning, cities can become more resilient and better equipped to address future challenges.

Overall, AI has the potential to revolutionize the way we plan and design our cities, making them more livable, sustainable, and resilient. However, it is important to ensure that the development and implementation of AI in urban planning is done in an ethical and equitable manner, taking into account the needs and perspectives of all stakeholders, including marginalized and vulnerable communities.

In conclusion, the integration of AI in urban planning has the potential to revolutionize the way we design and manage our cities. From reducing traffic congestion to improving energy efficiency, AI-driven solutions can lead to more sustainable and livable urban environments. However, it is important to address the ethical and social implications of AI in urban planning, such as potential job displacement and privacy concerns. As we continue to explore the possibilities of AI in urban planning, it is essential that we approach the technology with a critical lens and prioritize the well-being of communities.

As we conclude this chapter, we can see that AI is revolutionizing urban planning and design by providing more efficient and sustainable solutions for cities of the future. From traffic management to energy conservation, AI is enabling us to build smarter and more livable cities. As we continue to develop and refine these technologies, it will be important to prioritize ethical considerations and community engagement in the planning process. By doing so, we can ensure that AI is used in a way that benefits all members of society.

Summary:

We explored the impact of AI on urban planning and the potential for creating more efficient, sustainable, and livable cities. We discussed the use of AI in traffic management, energy consumption, waste management, and urban design. AI can help optimize traffic flow, reduce energy consumption and carbon emissions, and improve waste management by analyzing data and making informed decisions. Furthermore, AI-powered tools can assist urban planners in designing more livable and people-centered cities by taking into account factors such as walkability, green spaces, and public transportation.

Suggestions:

1. Stay updated on the latest AI technologies and their potential applications in urban planning.
2. Participate in discussions and debates on how AI can be used to create more sustainable and livable cities.
3. Advocate for the use of AI in urban planning to improve the efficiency, sustainability, and livability of cities.
4. Support research and development of AI-powered tools and technologies that can assist urban planners in making informed decisions.

Chapter 44 AI and Wearable Technology: Enhancing the Human Experience

As wearable technology becomes increasingly popular, the integration of AI into these devices has opened up new possibilities for enhancing the human experience. From health and fitness tracking to communication and entertainment, AI-powered wearables have the potential to revolutionize the way we interact with technology on a daily basis. We will explore the current and future state of AI in wearable technology, and the benefits and challenges that come with this integration.

Wearable technology has become increasingly popular in recent years, with devices like smartwatches and fitness trackers gaining widespread adoption. With the integration of AI, these devices have the potential to become even more powerful tools for enhancing the human experience.

One area where AI-powered wearables are making an impact is in the realm of health and wellness. Wearable devices equipped with sensors and AI algorithms can monitor vital signs like heart rate, blood pressure, and even sleep patterns, providing users with valuable insights into their overall health. This data can be used to identify potential health issues and encourage users to make positive lifestyle changes. For example, an AI-powered wearable might detect that a user is not getting enough sleep and suggest ways to improve their sleep habits.

AI-powered wearables also have the potential to revolutionize communication. With the help of natural language processing (NLP) technology, wearables can understand and respond to spoken commands, allowing for hands-free communication in a variety of situations. This can be particularly useful in scenarios where hands-free communication is essential, such as while driving or exercising.

Moreover, AI-powered wearables can be used for entertainment purposes. For instance, wearables equipped with AI technology can create personalized playlists based on users' listening habits and preferences. They can also suggest new songs and artists based on the user's previous listening behavior.

Overall, AI-powered wearables offer a wide range of potential benefits, from improving health and wellness to enhancing communication and entertainment. However, they also pose certain challenges, such as data privacy concerns and the need for reliable connectivity. As wearable technology continues to evolve, it will be interesting to see how AI is incorporated into these devices and the impact it will have on the human experience.

As AI continues to advance, it has found its way into a growing number of wearable devices, from smartwatches and fitness trackers to augmented reality glasses and virtual assistants. By integrating AI, these wearables have the potential to enhance the human experience in numerous ways.

One major benefit of AI-powered wearables is their ability to track and monitor health and fitness data. With sensors and algorithms that can measure heart rate, steps taken, and even sleep patterns, wearables can provide valuable insights into a person's overall health and well-being. They can also provide personalized recommendations for exercise, nutrition, and other healthy habits based on the data they collect.

Another area where AI wearables can make a big impact is in communication. Devices such as smart glasses and earbuds can use AI-powered natural language processing to provide real-time language translation, making it easier for people to communicate across language barriers. Wearables can also facilitate hands-free communication and provide users with access to virtual assistants, enabling them to stay connected and productive on the go.

In the entertainment realm, AI wearables have the potential to create more immersive and personalized experiences. Virtual reality headsets can use AI algorithms to adapt to a user's preferences and behaviors, creating a more tailored and engaging experience. Additionally, smart glasses and augmented reality devices can enhance real-world experiences by providing users with information and context in real time.

However, AI-powered wearables also come with their own set of challenges and concerns. Privacy and data security are major issues, as wearables collect and transmit sensitive personal information.

There are also concerns around the potential for AI wearables to perpetuate bias or reinforce harmful stereotypes.

As AI continues to evolve, it is likely that we will see more and more AI-powered wearables enter the market. The potential benefits are significant, but it will be important to address the associated risks and ensure that these devices are designed with user privacy and safety in mind.

The use of wearable technology has great potential in the healthcare industry. Wearables equipped with AI technology can monitor the wearer's health in real-time, providing continuous feedback and analysis. This can be especially useful for patients with chronic illnesses or those recovering from surgery who require ongoing monitoring.

For example, wearable devices such as smartwatches can track the wearer's heart rate, blood pressure, and sleep patterns. AI algorithms can analyze this data and provide personalized health recommendations based on the wearer's individual needs. In the event of a medical emergency, wearables can also send an alert to medical professionals or family members.

In addition to healthcare, AI-powered wearables can also enhance communication and entertainment. Smart glasses, for instance, can display augmented reality (AR) content and provide hands-free access to information. AI algorithms can also personalize the AR content based on the user's interests and preferences.

Moreover, AI-powered wearables can improve the efficiency of businesses and industries. For example, employees can use wearables to access training materials, communicate with colleagues, and access real-time data while on the go. In the manufacturing industry, wearables can provide workers with hands-free access to instructions and data, improving safety and productivity.

Despite the numerous benefits of AI-powered wearables, there are also concerns about privacy and security. Wearables that collect personal data must ensure that the data is protected and not accessible to unauthorized parties. Furthermore, the use of wearables in the workplace raises questions about employee privacy and surveillance.

Overall, the integration of AI into wearable technology has the potential to greatly enhance the human experience, but it is important to consider the potential challenges and ethical implications as well.

Wearable devices are no longer just for counting steps or tracking heart rates. With the integration of AI, they can now provide a range of health and wellness benefits. For example, AI-powered wearable technology can monitor and analyze vital signs in real-time, detect health issues early on, and even predict potential health risks.

Wearable devices can also enhance communication through real-time language translation and advanced voice recognition. This is particularly useful in multicultural environments where language barriers may exist. Additionally, AI-powered wearables can enhance the entertainment experience, allowing users to control music, movies, and other media with voice commands.

However, as with any technology, there are also potential challenges and risks associated with AI-powered wearables. These include concerns about privacy and data security, as well as the potential for over-reliance on technology for health and wellness decisions.

Despite these challenges, the integration of AI into wearable technology has the potential to greatly enhance the human experience, providing a range of benefits for health, communication, and entertainment.

One potential challenge with integrating AI into wearable technology is ensuring user privacy and security. Wearable devices often collect personal data, such as health and location information, and this data can be vulnerable to hacking or misuse. As AI algorithms become more sophisticated and capable of analyzing vast amounts of data, there is a risk that this data could be used to identify individuals or make sensitive inferences about their behavior or health.

To address these concerns, wearable technology companies must prioritize data security and privacy by implementing strong encryption and access controls, as well as providing transparent information about data collection and use. Users should also be educated about the risks and benefits of wearable technology and how to protect their personal information.

In addition, there is a need for ethical considerations in the use of AI in wearable technology. For example, AI-powered health devices could potentially diagnose medical conditions or provide treatment recommendations, which could have significant impacts on individuals' health outcomes. As such, it is important to ensure that the algorithms used in these devices are accurate, reliable, and based on sound medical research.

Overall, the integration of AI into wearable technology has the potential to revolutionize the way we interact with technology and improve our health and wellbeing. However, it is important to address the challenges of privacy, security, and ethics to ensure that these advancements are made in a responsible and beneficial way.

Wearable technology powered by AI is already making an impact in the field of healthcare. Wearables such as smartwatches and fitness bands equipped with AI-powered sensors can track a wide range of health metrics, such as heart rate, blood pressure, sleep patterns, and more. This data can be analyzed by AI algorithms to provide personalized health recommendations and identify potential health issues before they become serious.

Moreover, wearable technology can also be used for communication and entertainment purposes. Smart glasses equipped with AR technology can provide real-time translations and allow users to stay connected without having to constantly check their phone. Similarly, AI-powered headphones can customize the listening experience by adjusting the sound levels based on the user's preferences and the surrounding environment.

However, the integration of AI into wearable technology also presents some challenges. Privacy and security concerns arise as wearables collect and store sensitive personal data. The ethical implications of AI algorithms making decisions regarding human health and well-being must also be carefully considered.

As the technology continues to evolve, wearable devices powered by AI are expected to become even more prevalent in our daily lives, enhancing our overall human experience.

Wearable devices, such as smartwatches, fitness trackers, and augmented reality glasses, have become increasingly popular in recent years. With the integration of artificial intelligence (AI), these devices have the potential to offer even more benefits for users.

One area where AI-powered wearables can have a significant impact is in health and wellness. For example, wearable fitness trackers can monitor a person's physical activity, heart rate, and sleep patterns, providing personalized insights and recommendations for improving overall health. With AI, these devices can analyze large amounts of data and provide more accurate and customized feedback to the user.

Another area where AI can enhance wearable technology is in communication. Smartwatches and other wearables can already provide notifications for calls, texts, and social media updates. With AI, these devices can learn the user's communication patterns and preferences, and suggest responses or actions based on the context of the message. This can help users stay connected and productive, without being overwhelmed by notifications.

AI can also transform the entertainment experience of wearable devices. For example, augmented reality glasses can offer immersive gaming and educational experiences, while smart headphones can provide personalized music recommendations based on the user's listening history and preferences. With AI, these devices can learn the user's preferences and behavior, and offer more personalized and engaging experiences.

However, there are also challenges to consider with the integration of AI into wearable technology. Privacy and security concerns arise with the collection and storage of sensitive personal data, such as health information and communication patterns. Additionally, the ethical implications of

AI-generated recommendations and actions must be carefully considered to ensure that they align with the user's values and interests.

In summary, AI-powered wearables have the potential to enhance the human experience in many areas, including health and wellness, communication, and entertainment. While there are challenges to be addressed, the integration of AI into wearable technology can offer more personalized and efficient experiences for users.

We explored the exciting and innovative field of AI and wearable technology. We looked at how AI is being integrated into wearable devices to enhance the human experience in various ways, including improving health, communication, and entertainment.

We discussed the potential benefits of AI-powered wearables, such as personalized health tracking, real-time translation, and immersive virtual reality experiences. However, we also recognized the challenges associated with this technology, including privacy concerns and the need for ethical considerations.

Overall, it is clear that AI and wearable technology have the potential to revolutionize the way we interact with the world around us. As the field continues to evolve, it will be important to carefully consider the implications and ensure that these advancements are used for the betterment of humanity.

As we have seen in this chapter, the integration of AI into wearable technology has the potential to revolutionize the way we experience the world around us. From monitoring our health and fitness to enhancing communication and entertainment, the possibilities are endless. However, as with any new technology, there are also challenges and potential drawbacks to consider.

As we move forward, it will be important to continue exploring the potential benefits and challenges of AI in wearable technology, and to ensure that these technologies are developed and used in a way that maximizes their benefits while minimizing any negative consequences.

Summary:

We discussed how AI-powered wearables can improve health monitoring, communication, and entertainment experiences for users. However, the implementation of AI in wearables also raises concerns about privacy, data security, and ethical considerations.

Key takeaways:

- AI-powered wearables have the potential to revolutionize health monitoring, such as detecting and alerting users of potential health issues in real-time.
- Wearables can enhance communication experiences, such as language translation and transcription in real-time.
- AI-powered wearables can also provide personalized entertainment experiences, such as recommending music or movies based on users' preferences.
- The integration of AI in wearables raises concerns about data privacy, security, and ethical considerations that need to be addressed.

Suggestions:

- As the use of AI in wearables continues to grow, it is important for companies to prioritize user privacy and data security.
- Industry standards and regulations should be developed to ensure ethical and responsible implementation of AI in wearables.
- Further research and development can help address some of the challenges and limitations of AI-powered wearables, such as increasing accuracy and reliability of health monitoring features.

Chapter 45: The integration of AI in our homes

We will explore the integration of AI in our homes and the impact it has on our daily lives. From virtual assistants to energy management, AI is revolutionizing the way we interact with our living spaces. We will discuss the benefits and challenges of this technology and its potential to enhance our homes and improve our quality of life. So, let's dive in and discover the smart revolution in our homes.

The integration of AI in our homes has led to a smart revolution, with various technologies and devices being used to make our homes more efficient, comfortable, and convenient. Smart home technology uses AI and machine learning algorithms to learn user preferences, automate routine tasks, and optimize energy usage.

One of the most common applications of AI in the home is through virtual assistants such as Amazon's Alexa and Google Assistant. These virtual assistants use natural language processing (NLP) to understand and respond to voice commands, making it easier for users to control various aspects of their home, including lighting, temperature, and entertainment systems.

Another way that AI is transforming the home is through energy management systems. These systems use machine learning algorithms to analyze data about a home's energy usage patterns and make recommendations on how to optimize energy usage, reducing energy waste and saving homeowners money on their utility bills.

AI is also being used in home security systems to make them more effective and efficient. Machine learning algorithms can analyze data from various sensors, cameras, and other security devices to detect anomalies and potential security threats, alerting homeowners and taking appropriate actions.

Overall, the integration of AI in the home has the potential to revolutionize the way we live, work, and interact with our environment. As technology continues to evolve, we can expect to see even more sophisticated and innovative AI-powered devices and systems designed to make our homes smarter and more efficient.

Smart home technology is growing rapidly, and with it comes the integration of AI. One example of this is virtual assistants like Amazon's Alexa or Google's Assistant. These AI-powered devices can be used to control various smart home devices and appliances, as well as provide helpful information like the weather or traffic updates.

Additionally, AI can be used in home security systems to identify potential threats and notify homeowners. This technology can also detect anomalies in energy usage and alert homeowners to potential issues like a malfunctioning appliance or energy leak.

AI can also play a role in optimizing home energy usage. Smart thermostats like Nest use machine learning algorithms to analyze energy usage patterns and adjust the temperature accordingly, potentially saving homeowners money on their energy bills.

Overall, the integration of AI in the home has the potential to make daily life more convenient, secure, and efficient. However, it also raises concerns about privacy and security, as these devices collect and store personal information. As AI continues to become more prevalent in the home, it will be important to address these concerns and ensure that proper measures are in place to protect user data.

One of the primary areas where AI is being integrated into homes is through the use of virtual assistants such as Amazon's Alexa, Apple's Siri, and Google Assistant. These assistants use natural language processing and machine learning algorithms to understand and respond to user requests, allowing for hands-free control of various devices and appliances in the home.

AI is also being used for energy management in homes. Smart thermostats such as Nest and Ecobee use AI algorithms to learn users' schedules and preferences, automatically adjusting the temperature to optimize energy usage and cost savings. Similarly, AI-powered lighting systems can learn users' habits and preferences to automatically adjust lighting levels and reduce energy waste.

Another area where AI is making a significant impact is in the area of home security. AI-powered cameras and doorbells can recognize familiar faces and distinguish them from strangers, sending alerts to homeowners when someone unfamiliar is at the door. AI can also be used to analyze and interpret security footage, alerting homeowners to any suspicious activity and even predicting potential threats before they occur.

Finally, AI is being used to improve the accessibility and functionality of homes for individuals with disabilities or mobility issues. Voice-activated systems and AI-powered robots can assist with tasks such as turning on lights, adjusting the thermostat, and opening doors, making it easier for individuals with disabilities to live independently.

Overall, the integration of AI into homes is revolutionizing the way we live, providing greater convenience, comfort, and security. However, as with any new technology, there are also concerns about privacy and security, and it is important to carefully consider the potential risks and benefits of these AI-powered home systems.

As AI becomes more integrated into our homes, energy management has emerged as a major application. Smart thermostats, such as Nest and Ecobee, use AI algorithms to learn our habits and adjust the temperature accordingly, saving energy and money. AI-powered lighting systems, such as Philips Hue, can also help reduce energy consumption by adjusting the brightness and color of the lights according to the time of day and the amount of natural light in the room.

Another application of AI in the home is virtual assistants, such as Amazon's Alexa and Google Home. These devices use natural language processing and machine learning to understand and respond to our requests, from turning on the lights to ordering groceries. As they become more sophisticated, they can even predict our needs and offer suggestions proactively.

AI can also be used to monitor and manage the health of people in the home. Wearable devices such as smartwatches and fitness trackers can provide information on our vital signs and physical activity, which can be analyzed by AI algorithms to detect potential health issues. Smart homes can also be equipped with sensors that detect air quality, humidity, and temperature, which can help prevent illnesses and promote well-being.

While there are many benefits to AI-powered homes, there are also potential downsides. Concerns have been raised about the privacy implications of having always-on devices in the home that can listen to and record our conversations. There are also concerns about the potential for AI to be hacked or malfunction, leading to safety risks or invasion of privacy.

As AI continues to advance, it is likely that we will see even more applications in the home, from security systems to entertainment systems. However, it is important to carefully consider the potential benefits and risks of these technologies before integrating them into our homes.

One of the biggest benefits of integrating AI into our homes is the potential for more efficient energy management. With smart sensors, smart meters, and AI algorithms, homeowners can gain better insight into their energy usage patterns and optimize their energy consumption accordingly. For example, an AI-powered thermostat can learn a homeowner's temperature preferences and adjust the heating and cooling accordingly, reducing energy waste.

In addition, AI can help manage the energy consumption of various appliances and devices in the home, such as smart TVs, lighting, and kitchen appliances. Smart home systems can monitor the energy usage of these devices and adjust them accordingly to reduce energy waste.

Overall, AI-enabled energy management systems can not only reduce energy consumption and costs for homeowners but also help contribute to a more sustainable future for our planet.

While AI in the home offers many potential benefits, there are also some risks and concerns to consider. One major concern is privacy, as smart home devices are constantly collecting data on our behavior and preferences. This data can be used for targeted advertising or sold to third-party companies without our knowledge or consent. Additionally, if these devices are not properly secured, they can be vulnerable to hacking, which could result in a breach of personal information or even physical harm if the device controls critical systems like locks or thermostats.

Another concern is the potential for AI in the home to reinforce existing inequalities and biases. For example, if an AI assistant is trained on data that is biased against certain groups, it may perpetuate these biases in its recommendations and decisions. Additionally, AI in the home may only be accessible to those who can afford the technology, leading to further disparities between those with and without access to the latest technology.

Finally, there is a concern about the potential for over-reliance on AI in the home. If we become too reliant on AI to manage our homes, we may lose important skills and abilities, such as the ability to cook or clean without relying on a smart appliance. This could have broader societal implications if entire generations are raised without learning these basic skills.

As AI becomes increasingly integrated into our homes, it is important to carefully consider these potential risks and work to address them in order to ensure that the benefits of AI in the home are realized while minimizing any negative consequences.

The integration of AI into our homes has the potential to revolutionize the way we live. With smart home devices, we can automate tasks and control our environment with ease. But the benefits of AI in the home go beyond convenience.

One area where AI is making a significant impact is energy management. Smart thermostats can learn our behavior and adjust the temperature accordingly, reducing energy waste and lowering our bills. Similarly, smart lighting systems can adjust brightness and color temperature based on our preferences and the time of day, saving energy and providing a more comfortable living environment.

AI is also improving home security. With the help of cameras and sensors, smart home security systems can detect and alert us to potential threats in real-time. And with facial recognition technology, these systems can even distinguish between family members and potential intruders.

Virtual assistants like Amazon's Alexa and Google Home are also becoming ubiquitous in our homes. They can help us with everything from setting reminders and playing music to ordering groceries and controlling other smart home devices.

However, there are concerns about the privacy and security implications of having AI constantly listening and collecting data in our homes. As with any new technology, it is important to weigh the potential benefits against the potential risks and take steps to protect our privacy and security.

Overall, the smart home revolution driven by AI is transforming the way we live and interact with our homes. As technology continues to advance, we can expect even more exciting innovations in this field.

We explored the increasing presence of AI in our homes and how it is revolutionizing the way we live. From virtual assistants like Alexa and Siri to energy management systems, smart technology is transforming our homes into more efficient and comfortable spaces. However, as with any technology, there are also potential challenges and concerns around privacy, security, and ethical use of data.

As we move forward into a more connected and automated world, it is important to consider the implications of AI in the home and how we can ensure that it is used in a way that benefits us while also upholding our values and rights.

In the next chapter, we will examine the role of AI in healthcare and its potential to revolutionize the industry.

Summary:

From virtual assistants to energy management. We learned about the benefits of smart homes, such as increased energy efficiency and convenience, but also the potential privacy and security risks that come with collecting and storing personal data. The integration of AI technology into our daily lives continues to accelerate, and it is essential to consider the ethical and societal implications of this trend.

Suggestions:

- Research the privacy and security features of smart home devices before purchasing them.
- Consider the potential environmental impact of smart homes and find ways to make your home more sustainable.
- Stay informed about the latest developments in AI and smart home technology, and engage in discussions about the ethical implications of these technologies.
- Think critically about the potential long-term effects of relying on AI for everyday tasks and consider ways to maintain human agency and decision-making in the home.

Chapter 46 AI and Food: Crafting the Future of Cuisine

In recent years, artificial intelligence (AI) has been making its way into almost every aspect of our lives, including our food. From precision agriculture to smart kitchens, AI is transforming the way we produce, distribute, and even create food. We will explore the various ways in which AI is being used in the food industry and how it is shaping the future of cuisine. We will also discuss the potential benefits and challenges of this technological revolution and what it means for our health, environment, and society. Join us as we delve into the world of AI and food and discover the delicious possibilities that lie ahead.

AI is making its mark in the food industry, impacting every aspect from production to consumption. One of the primary areas in which AI is being used in the food industry is food production, where it is being used to develop new and more efficient methods of farming and agriculture. AI is also being used to improve the safety and quality of food by detecting potential contamination and hazards. Additionally, AI is playing a significant role in food distribution and logistics by streamlining the supply chain and reducing waste. Finally, AI is even making its way into culinary creativity, with the development of AI-powered recipe generation and flavor pairing tools.

One of the most significant benefits of AI in the food industry is the potential for increased efficiency and productivity. By using AI to optimize various aspects of food production and distribution, companies can reduce waste, minimize costs, and increase yields. AI can also help to ensure that food is produced and delivered in a more sustainable manner, reducing the environmental impact of the food industry.

However, the use of AI in the food industry is not without its challenges. One major concern is the potential for job loss as AI becomes more prevalent in food production and distribution. Additionally, there are concerns about data privacy and security, as well as the potential for AI to reinforce existing inequalities in the food industry.

Overall, the integration of AI into the food industry has the potential to revolutionize the way we produce and consume food. By leveraging AI to optimize every aspect of food production and distribution, we can create a more sustainable, efficient, and equitable food system.

AI-powered robots are also used in the food industry to perform tasks such as chopping vegetables, making pizza, and even flipping burgers. These robots can operate without human intervention and can work at high speeds, ensuring that orders are prepared quickly and efficiently. They can also reduce the risk of contamination by minimizing human contact with food.

In addition to the use of robots, AI can also be used to optimize the supply chain in the food industry. AI algorithms can analyze data related to food demand, pricing, and availability to optimize the distribution of food products. This can help reduce waste and ensure that fresh produce is delivered to customers on time.

Furthermore, AI is also being used to create new and innovative recipes. By analyzing vast amounts of data related to food ingredients, taste, and texture, AI can suggest new combinations that are not only delicious but also healthy. This can open up new avenues for culinary creativity and allow chefs to experiment with new dishes.

Overall, AI is set to revolutionize the food industry by making it more efficient, sustainable, and innovative. From optimizing the supply chain to creating new recipes, AI is poised to play a significant role in the future of food.

Artificial intelligence (AI) has the potential to revolutionize food production and distribution. One way this is happening is through the use of precision agriculture, where farmers can use sensors, drones, and other technologies to monitor crops and adjust their cultivation practices accordingly. This can lead to more efficient and sustainable agriculture, with less waste and higher yields.

AI is also being used in food processing and manufacturing. For example, machine learning algorithms can analyze data from food production lines to identify inefficiencies and quality issues, allowing manufacturers to make improvements and reduce waste. AI can also help with recipe development, flavor profiling, and product design.

In the restaurant industry, AI is being used to enhance the dining experience for customers. For example, some restaurants are using chatbots or voice assistants to take orders or answer customer questions. AI-powered systems can also help chefs with menu planning, ingredient sourcing, and even predicting customer preferences.

Overall, AI has the potential to revolutionize the food industry, from farm to table. By making food production and distribution more efficient and sustainable, AI can help feed the growing global population while reducing waste and improving the quality of our food.

AI has the potential to revolutionize the food industry in terms of production, distribution, and even culinary creativity. One of the most significant areas of impact is food production. AI can be used to optimize the growing process, predicting and preventing plant diseases, and helping farmers to make data-driven decisions. AI-driven agricultural robots can reduce labor costs and increase efficiency, from planting and harvesting to sorting and packaging.

Another area of application for AI in the food industry is in food distribution. AI can help companies optimize logistics and reduce waste by predicting demand and managing inventory levels. Smart packaging that uses sensors and AI algorithms can monitor food quality and freshness, reducing food waste by ensuring that food is consumed before it spoils.

AI can also be used to enhance culinary creativity. Chefs and food scientists can use AI-powered tools to explore new flavor combinations and develop unique recipes. By analyzing data on flavor profiles and ingredient combinations, AI algorithms can generate new recipes that may have never been conceived of by humans.

However, there are also challenges associated with the use of AI in the food industry. One of the main concerns is the potential loss of jobs due to automation. Additionally, there are concerns about the ethical implications of AI in food production, such as the use of genetic modification and the potential impact on food safety.

Overall, the potential benefits of AI in the food industry are significant, but it is important to consider the potential challenges and ethical implications as well. As with any new technology, careful consideration and responsible implementation are necessary to ensure that the benefits outweigh the risks.

Another area where AI is being used in the food industry is in meal planning and recipe creation. AI algorithms can analyze millions of recipes and food preferences to create personalized meal plans for individuals or entire families. For example, the company "Plant Jammer" uses AI to suggest recipes based on ingredients that users already have in their kitchen, reducing food waste and promoting sustainability.

AI is also being used to enhance the flavor of food. Companies like "IntelligentX" use AI to analyze customer feedback and adjust their beer recipes to better suit customer preferences. This feedback loop allows the beer to be constantly improved and tailored to customers' tastes.

Additionally, AI is being used in food safety and quality control. For example, "Nima" is a portable gluten detector that uses AI to analyze food samples and determine if they contain gluten, helping people with gluten intolerance to avoid harmful reactions. In the same vein, AI algorithms are being developed to detect food contamination and spoilage in the production and distribution process, helping to prevent food-borne illnesses.

Despite these benefits, there are also concerns about the role of AI in the food industry. One concern is that the use of AI may lead to the automation of jobs in the food industry, potentially displacing workers. Additionally, there are concerns about the safety and security of data collected through AI systems, as well as the potential for bias in AI algorithms.

Overall, the use of AI in the food industry has the potential to improve food production, distribution, and consumption in a variety of ways. However, it is important to consider and address potential challenges and concerns as the technology continues to be integrated into the industry.

One potential application of AI in the food industry is in the area of precision agriculture. Precision agriculture uses sensors, drones, and other technologies to collect data on crop growth, soil moisture, and weather patterns, among other things. AI algorithms can then analyze this data to provide farmers with insights into how to optimize their operations, such as when to plant, fertilize, or harvest crops.

Another area where AI can have a significant impact on the food industry is in food safety. By using machine learning algorithms, companies can analyze large amounts of data on foodborne illnesses and outbreaks to identify patterns and potential sources of contamination. This can help food producers and regulators to quickly respond to potential outbreaks and prevent them from spreading.

AI can also be used to enhance the flavor and texture of food. For example, food scientists can use machine learning algorithms to analyze the chemical composition of different ingredients and identify how they interact with each other. This can help them to develop new recipes and flavor combinations that are more appealing to consumers.

Lastly, AI can help to reduce food waste by predicting demand and optimizing supply chains. By analyzing data on customer preferences and buying patterns, companies can more accurately predict how much food they need to produce and when to distribute it. This can help to reduce the amount of food that goes to waste due to overproduction or spoilage.

Overall, AI has the potential to revolutionize the food industry by improving efficiency, safety, and innovation. However, as with any new technology, there are also challenges and potential risks that need to be addressed to ensure that AI is used responsibly and ethically in the food industry.

In addition to changing the way we produce and consume food, AI can also enhance the way we experience food. With the help of machine learning algorithms, chefs can create new flavor combinations that they may not have thought of before. In fact, AI has already been used to develop new recipes and even create completely new foods that don't exist in nature.

One example of this is the "Not a Burger" developed by researchers at MIT. Using machine learning algorithms, they created a plant-based patty that mimics the taste and texture of a beef burger. Another example is the AI-generated recipe for a "Peanut Butter-Bacon-Kimchi Burger," which was created by IBM's Watson computer.

AI can also assist in food pairing, helping to identify the best flavor combinations for a dish. The technology can analyze thousands of ingredients and suggest pairings that would enhance the taste of a particular dish. This can be particularly useful for chefs who want to experiment with new flavor combinations but may not have the experience or knowledge to know where to start.

Overall, AI has the potential to revolutionize the way we think about and experience food. From developing new recipes to improving the sustainability of food production, there are countless ways that AI can impact the food industry.

The application of AI in the food industry has the potential to greatly improve the efficiency and sustainability of food production, while also enhancing culinary creativity and improving the overall food experience for consumers. For example, AI-powered precision farming techniques can help optimize crop yields and reduce waste, while smart packaging can help extend the shelf life of food and reduce the amount of food waste.

AI can also be used to create personalized nutrition plans for individuals based on their genetic and lifestyle data, improving the effectiveness of dietary recommendations and ultimately leading to better health outcomes.

Another area where AI is transforming the food industry is in the realm of culinary creativity. AI-powered recipe generation can help chefs and home cooks come up with new and exciting flavor combinations and ingredient pairings, while AI-powered food pairing algorithms can suggest ideal food and drink pairings based on flavor profiles.

However, there are also challenges associated with the integration of AI into the food industry, including concerns around data privacy and the potential for AI to displace human workers. It will be important for industry leaders and policymakers to navigate these challenges and ensure that the benefits of AI in the food industry are shared equitably among all stakeholders.

Overall, the integration of AI into the food industry has the potential to revolutionize the way we produce, distribute, and consume food, leading to a more sustainable and satisfying food future for all.

In conclusion, AI has the potential to revolutionize the food industry, from production to distribution and even culinary creativity. By utilizing AI technologies such as machine learning, natural language processing, and computer vision, we can increase efficiency, reduce waste, and create more personalized and sustainable food experiences. However, there are also challenges and ethical considerations to be addressed, such as data privacy, job displacement, and the potential for bias in AI algorithms. It is important to approach the integration of AI in the food industry with caution and thoughtfulness, while also embracing the exciting possibilities it presents.

We have explored the exciting possibilities of AI in the realm of food. From enhancing production and distribution to revolutionizing culinary creativity, AI has the potential to transform the way we interact with food. We have examined some of the key developments in this field, including the use of machine learning to develop new recipes and the application of robotics to automate food preparation. Additionally, we have considered some of the challenges and concerns that arise with the integration of AI in food, such as issues of privacy and ethics. Overall, the future of AI in food is an exciting and dynamic field that promises to bring about many new innovations and possibilities.

As we move forward, it is important to consider the implications of AI in food and how we can use this technology to create a more sustainable and equitable food system. Whether through reducing food waste, improving food safety, or increasing access to nutritious foods, AI has the potential to make a positive impact on our food system. As such, it is up to us as individuals, policymakers, and members of the food industry to ensure that AI is utilized in a responsible and ethical manner to create a more just and sustainable food future.

Summary:

The chapter explored various applications of AI in the food industry, such as precision agriculture, food safety monitoring, personalized nutrition, and food recipe generation. AI can help optimize the use of resources and minimize waste in food production and distribution, leading to a more sustainable and efficient food system. Moreover, AI can also enhance the culinary creativity of chefs and home cooks by generating new and innovative recipes based on various factors such as taste preferences and dietary restrictions.

Suggestions:

1. Learn more about precision agriculture and how it can optimize crop production using AI and other technologies.
2. Look into personalized nutrition and how AI can help tailor diets based on individual needs and preferences.
3. Consider exploring the use of AI in food safety monitoring to help prevent foodborne illnesses.
4. Experiment with AI-generated recipes and explore new culinary possibilities.

Chapter 47 AI and the Environment: Monitoring and Protecting Our Planet

As concerns about climate change and environmental degradation continue to grow, there is a growing need for innovative solutions to protect our planet. One of the most promising avenues for progress is the integration of artificial intelligence (AI) into environmental conservation efforts. With its ability to collect and analyze vast amounts of data in real-time, AI can help us better understand and monitor our environment, as well as inform policies and interventions to protect it. We will explore the ways in which AI is being used to monitor and protect our planet, from detecting and mitigating pollution to managing natural resources and predicting the impacts of climate change. We will also discuss the potential benefits and challenges of integrating AI into environmental conservation efforts and what the future might hold for this exciting and rapidly evolving field.

As the world faces increasing challenges from climate change and environmental degradation, there is a growing need for innovative solutions to monitor and protect our planet. One such solution is the integration of artificial intelligence (AI) into environmental conservation efforts. With AI, we can better monitor and analyze environmental data to make more informed decisions about conservation and resource management.

One area where AI is making a significant impact is in the monitoring of wildlife populations. Using AI-powered cameras and sensors, researchers can collect large amounts of data on animal populations, including their movements, behaviors, and habitat use. This data can help identify areas where wildlife is at risk, allowing conservationists to take action to protect these animals and their habitats.

AI is also being used to monitor and predict natural disasters. By analyzing data from satellites, weather sensors, and other sources, AI algorithms can identify patterns that may indicate an impending natural disaster such as a hurricane, earthquake, or wildfire. This allows authorities to take preemptive measures to protect communities and minimize damage.

In addition to monitoring, AI is also being used to develop new, sustainable technologies for environmental conservation. For example, AI-powered drones can be used for precision agriculture, helping farmers reduce water usage and increase crop yields. AI is also being used to develop new materials and processes that are less harmful to the environment.

Overall, AI has the potential to be a powerful tool for environmental conservation and protection. By using AI to monitor and analyze environmental data, we can make more informed decisions about resource management and conservation efforts. Furthermore, AI can help us develop more sustainable technologies and practices, reducing our impact on the environment and protecting the planet for future generations.

One of the significant applications of AI in environmental conservation is the development of intelligent monitoring systems. These systems use advanced technologies such as remote sensing, IoT, and machine learning algorithms to gather and analyze data on various aspects of the environment. For instance, they can monitor air quality, water levels, forest cover, and wildlife population trends.

Remote sensing, through satellites and drones, has been vital in providing a comprehensive view of the environment, including regions that are challenging to access. This technology allows conservationists to monitor ecosystems' health and track changes such as deforestation, soil erosion, and natural disasters such as wildfires and hurricanes. By processing vast amounts of data, AI algorithms can detect patterns and provide accurate predictions, enabling proactive measures to mitigate the impact of these changes.

Furthermore, AI can enhance the identification and protection of endangered species. By analyzing images and videos, machine learning algorithms can recognize specific animals and distinguish them from similar-looking species, leading to more accurate identification and monitoring. Additionally, AI can help develop predictive models to forecast the population growth or decline of endangered species based on various factors such as climate, habitat, and migration patterns.

Overall, the integration of AI in environmental conservation has the potential to improve decision-making processes and enhance the effectiveness of conservation efforts. The combination of advanced technologies and AI algorithms can provide a comprehensive understanding of the environment, enabling proactive measures to protect and sustain it for future generations.

AI has the potential to revolutionize the way we monitor and protect the environment. One way AI can contribute to environmental conservation is through the use of satellite imagery and machine learning algorithms to track changes in land use, deforestation, and wildlife populations. For example, in Africa, AI is being used to track the movements of elephants to help prevent poaching and protect these endangered animals.

Another way AI can contribute to environmental monitoring is through the use of sensor networks and data analysis to track air and water quality. By continuously monitoring these resources, AI can identify trends and alert authorities to potential environmental hazards. This can help prevent pollution and protect human health.

AI can also assist in predicting and mitigating the impact of natural disasters such as hurricanes, wildfires, and floods. By analyzing historical data, AI can help predict the path and severity of these disasters and assist in developing evacuation plans.

In addition to monitoring and protecting the environment, AI can also play a role in promoting sustainability. By analyzing data on energy consumption and identifying areas for improvement, AI can help optimize energy use in buildings and reduce waste.

Overall, AI has the potential to significantly contribute to environmental conservation and protection. By leveraging its capabilities in data analysis, pattern recognition, and prediction, AI can help us monitor and manage the natural resources on which we depend.

One major application of AI in environmental conservation is in the field of precision agriculture. Precision agriculture uses AI algorithms to analyze data from sensors and other sources to optimize crop yields, reduce water consumption, and minimize the use of pesticides and fertilizers. For example, farmers can use drones equipped with cameras and AI-powered algorithms to identify areas of a crop field that require additional water or fertilizer, or to detect pests and diseases that may be affecting crop health.

Another area where AI is being used to monitor and protect the environment is in wildlife conservation. AI algorithms can be used to track and monitor endangered species, analyze patterns of migration, and identify areas that are particularly vulnerable to human activity. For example, AI-powered cameras and sensors can be used to monitor animal populations and detect illegal poaching activity.

AI is also being used to monitor and manage natural resources, such as forests and bodies of water. By analyzing data from satellite imagery, ground sensors, and other sources, AI algorithms can provide early warning of potential environmental disasters, such as wildfires or oil spills. In addition, AI can be used to optimize the management of natural resources, such as water and energy, by predicting demand and identifying areas where conservation efforts can be most effective.

Overall, AI has the potential to revolutionize the way we monitor and protect the environment. By providing us with more accurate and timely information, AI can help us make better decisions about how to manage our natural resources and reduce our impact on the environment.

One of the major challenges facing the environment is the rapid depletion of natural resources. However, AI can help monitor and manage these resources more efficiently. For instance, remote sensing technologies and machine learning algorithms can be used to monitor forest cover, track wildlife populations, and predict the spread of invasive species.

Additionally, AI can play a crucial role in mitigating the effects of climate change. With the help of AI, it is possible to design more energy-efficient buildings, optimize renewable energy production, and reduce carbon emissions in various sectors such as transportation and agriculture.

Another area where AI can contribute to environmental conservation is in the field of waste management. AI-powered systems can help identify and sort recyclable materials more efficiently, reducing the amount of waste that ends up in landfills. Smart waste management systems can also track waste generation patterns and provide insights for policy-makers to design more effective waste management strategies.

Overall, the integration of AI into environmental conservation efforts has the potential to significantly enhance our ability to monitor and protect natural resources, mitigate the effects of climate change, and manage waste more efficiently.

AI can be a powerful tool in the field of environmental conservation. For example, AI-powered drones can monitor large areas of land and identify areas that may be at risk for deforestation, allowing for intervention before it's too late. AI can also help with monitoring endangered species, by analyzing data on animal movements and behavior patterns to identify threats and develop conservation plans.

In addition to monitoring, AI can also be used to optimize the use of natural resources. For example, AI-powered irrigation systems can monitor weather patterns and soil moisture levels to determine when and how much to water crops, reducing waste and increasing efficiency. Similarly, AI can be used in renewable energy production, by predicting weather patterns and adjusting energy production accordingly.

Another area where AI can have a significant impact on the environment is in waste management. By analyzing patterns in waste production and disposal, AI can help identify areas where waste reduction efforts would be most effective. AI can also help optimize waste collection and recycling efforts, reducing the amount of waste that ends up in landfills.

Overall, the potential for AI to contribute to environmental conservation and the monitoring of natural resources is immense. By providing more accurate data and analysis, AI can help us make better decisions and take more effective action to protect our planet.

One area where AI can make a significant impact is in disaster management. In the face of a natural disaster like a hurricane or an earthquake, quick and efficient decision-making is crucial. AI can help by analyzing data from a variety of sources, such as social media, weather forecasts, and satellite imagery, to generate real-time insights that can be used to direct emergency response efforts.

For example, AI can help predict the trajectory and intensity of a hurricane, allowing authorities to evacuate people from the areas that are most likely to be affected. AI can also help identify the best routes for emergency vehicles and even adjust traffic lights to facilitate their movement. Additionally, AI can analyze social media activity to identify areas that are in need of assistance, allowing aid organizations to direct their efforts more efficiently.

In the aftermath of a disaster, AI can help with damage assessment and recovery efforts. For example, drones equipped with AI-powered cameras can be used to survey damaged areas and identify areas that need immediate attention. AI can also be used to help identify missing persons and track down survivors.

Overall, the integration of AI in disaster management can significantly improve response times, reduce the number of casualties, and minimize the impact of natural disasters on affected communities. However, it is important to note that AI is not a replacement for human decision-making and expertise. It should be used as a tool to support and augment human efforts, not to replace them.

One potential application of AI in environmental conservation is in wildlife conservation efforts. AI can be used to monitor and track wildlife populations and their behavior, as well as detect and prevent poaching activities. For example, AI-powered drones can be used to monitor protected areas and detect any suspicious activity, allowing for timely intervention.

Another area where AI can make a significant contribution is in monitoring and predicting natural disasters. By analyzing data from various sources, such as weather patterns, seismic activity, and oceanic conditions, AI can help predict natural disasters with greater accuracy and speed, allowing for better preparation and response.

AI can also be used in sustainable agriculture and land management practices. By analyzing data on soil composition, weather patterns, and crop yields, AI can help farmers optimize their practices to increase productivity while minimizing environmental impact. AI can also be used to identify areas where reforestation or other conservation efforts may be most effective.

One challenge in implementing AI for environmental conservation is the availability and quality of data. Data collection in remote areas or from wildlife populations can be challenging, and the accuracy of data can be impacted by various factors such as weather conditions or human error. Additionally, ethical considerations must be taken into account when using AI in conservation efforts, such as ensuring that the data collected is not used to harm wildlife or their habitats.

Overall, AI has significant potential in contributing to environmental conservation efforts, but it must be used in a responsible and ethical manner, with a focus on data quality and accuracy.

In conclusion, AI has the potential to greatly benefit environmental conservation efforts and the monitoring of natural resources. From analyzing satellite imagery to detecting and predicting natural disasters, AI technologies can provide valuable insights and help mitigate negative impacts on our planet. However, as with any technology, there are also potential challenges and ethical considerations that must be taken into account. As AI continues to evolve and be integrated into environmental monitoring and protection efforts, it is important to prioritize responsible and sustainable use.

We explored the ways in which AI can be used to monitor and protect our planet, from detecting and preventing environmental disasters to tracking natural resources and wildlife. We have seen how AI can play a crucial role in addressing the urgent need for sustainable development and environmental conservation. As we continue to face environmental challenges, it is important that we utilize all available tools, including AI, to help us safeguard our planet for future generations.

Summary:

We explored the potential of AI in environmental conservation and resource monitoring. We learned about how AI can assist in the tracking of wildlife, the management of natural resources, and the reduction of carbon emissions. We also discussed some of the challenges and ethical considerations that arise when integrating AI into environmental conservation efforts.

Some suggestions to consider based on this chapter topic include:

1. Supporting companies and organizations that use AI to reduce carbon emissions and minimize environmental impact.
2. Learning about and supporting wildlife conservation efforts that use AI technology to track and protect endangered species.
3. Advocating for responsible and ethical use of AI in environmental conservation, including transparency and accountability in data collection and analysis.
4. Considering ways to incorporate AI technology into your own lifestyle to reduce your carbon footprint and contribute to environmental conservation efforts.

By exploring the potential of AI in environmental conservation, we can work towards a more sustainable future for our planet.

Chapter 48 AI and Human Rights: Safeguarding Our Freedoms

As artificial intelligence (AI) becomes more integrated into our lives, it is important to consider its impact on human rights. While AI has the potential to advance equality and prevent discrimination, it also poses potential risks such as privacy violations and bias. We will explore how AI can be used to safeguard our freedoms and ensure equal treatment for all. We will examine the current state of AI and human rights, as well as potential future developments in this area. Ultimately, the goal of this chapter is to promote discussion and awareness of the complex intersection between AI and human rights, and to consider how we can use AI to create a more just and equitable society.

Advancements in AI have the potential to impact human rights in significant ways. The use of AI technologies can ensure equal treatment, prevent discrimination, and safeguard the privacy and security of individuals. AI can also be used to hold governments and other entities accountable for human rights violations.

One example of AI being used to safeguard human rights is in the field of criminal justice. AI algorithms are being used to assess the risk of recidivism and assist in the decision-making process of whether to release an offender on bail or parole. This has the potential to reduce bias and improve fairness in the criminal justice system. However, there are concerns about the potential for AI to perpetuate existing biases and exacerbate inequality, particularly if the data used to train AI systems is biased or incomplete.

Another area where AI can impact human rights is in the realm of privacy and security. As AI becomes more integrated into our daily lives, the amount of data being collected and analyzed is increasing. This raises concerns about the security and privacy of individuals. Governments and other organizations may use AI to conduct surveillance or gather personal information without the knowledge or consent of those being monitored. This can violate individuals' right to privacy and lead to abuse of power.

Furthermore, AI can also be used to help protect human rights defenders and journalists by providing early warning systems for threats and identifying potential sources of danger. AI can also be used to identify and track human rights abuses in conflict zones, which can help hold perpetrators accountable for their actions.

It is important to consider the potential impacts of AI on human rights and to ensure that these technologies are developed and used in a way that respects and upholds human rights principles. This requires a collaborative effort between policymakers, technology companies, and civil society organizations to establish ethical guidelines and ensure that AI is used in a way that promotes justice, equality, and human dignity.

One of the potential benefits of AI in the context of human rights is its ability to help ensure equal treatment and prevent discrimination. By analyzing data, AI systems can identify patterns of bias and discrimination and help mitigate them. For example, AI can be used in the hiring process to screen job candidates based solely on their qualifications, without being influenced by factors such as race or gender. AI can also be used to monitor and analyze police conduct to identify and prevent instances of biased policing.

However, the use of AI in human rights also raises concerns about privacy and surveillance. AI systems may be used to monitor and track individuals, which can infringe on their right to privacy. Additionally, there is a risk that AI systems may perpetuate and even amplify existing biases and discrimination, especially if they are trained on biased data sets.

To address these challenges, it is important to ensure that AI systems are developed and implemented in a way that respects human rights and protects privacy. This can be achieved through measures such as transparency, accountability, and the inclusion of diverse perspectives in the development and deployment of AI systems. Additionally, there should be legal and ethical frameworks in place to regulate the use of AI in human rights contexts and prevent its misuse.

AI has the potential to both promote and threaten human rights. One of the major concerns is the potential for algorithmic bias to perpetuate discrimination against marginalized groups. For example, if a hiring algorithm is trained on biased data, it may end up unfairly excluding certain groups of people from job opportunities.

However, AI can also be used to promote human rights by ensuring equal treatment and access to services. For example, facial recognition technology can be used to identify missing persons or victims of human trafficking. AI can also help to provide access to education and healthcare, especially for underserved communities.

In addition, AI can assist in the promotion and protection of human rights by enhancing the work of human rights defenders. For example, AI-powered tools can be used to analyze social media data and identify patterns of human rights abuses. This can aid in the documentation of human rights violations and provide evidence for advocacy and legal action.

Overall, the use of AI in human rights must be carefully monitored to ensure that it does not infringe on individuals' rights and freedoms. At the same time, we must also explore ways in which AI can be used to promote and protect human rights.

Ensuring Fairness and Accountability in AI

AI systems can perpetuate discrimination and reinforce existing biases if they are trained on biased data or designed with biased algorithms. To prevent this, it is essential to ensure that AI systems are designed with fairness and accountability in mind.

One approach is to implement transparency and interpretability in AI systems, so that it is possible to understand how the system works and how it makes decisions. This can be achieved through techniques such as explainable AI (XAI) and algorithmic transparency. XAI allows users to see the reasoning behind a particular decision made by an AI system, while algorithmic transparency ensures that the decision-making process is open and clear.

Another approach is to develop standards and regulations that ensure the responsible and ethical development and deployment of AI systems. These can include guidelines for ethical AI, such as the

Asilomar AI Principles or the IEEE Global Initiative on Ethics of Autonomous and Intelligent Systems. Governments and organizations can also establish legal frameworks for AI, such as the European Union's General Data Protection Regulation (GDPR) or the proposed Algorithmic Accountability Act in the United States.

It is also important to address issues related to accountability and liability in the context of AI. When AI systems are used to make decisions that have real-world consequences, it is essential to have mechanisms in place to hold individuals and organizations responsible for any negative outcomes. This can include legal frameworks that define who is responsible for the actions of an AI system and how liability should be assigned in cases of harm or injury caused by AI.

By ensuring fairness and accountability in AI, we can help to prevent discrimination and bias, promote equal treatment, and protect human rights in the development and deployment of AI systems.

In addition to the positive impact AI can have on human rights, there are also concerns about the potential for misuse and violation of these rights. For example, AI-powered surveillance and facial recognition systems can be used to track and monitor individuals, potentially violating their right to privacy. In some cases, AI algorithms have been shown to perpetuate bias and discrimination, particularly in areas such as hiring, lending, and criminal justice.

To address these concerns, it is important to develop ethical frameworks and regulations that guide the development and use of AI. This includes ensuring transparency and accountability in AI systems, as well as promoting diversity and inclusivity in the development process to avoid perpetuating biases. It also involves collaboration between technology developers, policymakers, and civil society organizations to ensure that AI is used in ways that uphold and promote human rights.

Furthermore, it is essential to continue monitoring and evaluating the impact of AI on human rights, and to adapt policies and regulations accordingly. This requires ongoing dialogue and engagement with affected communities and stakeholders to understand their perspectives and needs, and to ensure that the development and deployment of AI aligns with their values and interests.

In summary, while AI has the potential to positively impact human rights, it is important to address and mitigate the potential risks and challenges associated with its development and deployment. This requires a proactive and collaborative approach that prioritizes transparency, accountability, and ethical considerations, and that engages with stakeholders and affected communities throughout the process.

AI has the potential to protect and promote human rights, but it can also be a threat to these fundamental values. On one hand, AI can be used to identify patterns of discrimination, to make unbiased and fair decisions, and to enhance privacy and security. On the other hand, AI can be used to surveil and control populations, to reinforce biases and stereotypes, and to violate privacy and autonomy.

One of the areas where AI can have a positive impact on human rights is in the field of criminal justice. For example, AI can be used to analyze data from criminal cases and identify patterns that may indicate bias or discrimination. This can help to ensure that defendants receive a fair trial and that law enforcement agencies are held accountable for their actions.

AI can also be used to enhance privacy and security. For example, AI algorithms can be used to detect and prevent cyber attacks, to identify and mitigate online harassment and hate speech, and to protect personal data from unauthorized access. In addition, AI can be used to enhance the security of physical spaces, such as public transportation, by detecting and responding to potential threats.

However, there are also risks associated with the use of AI in the context of human rights. For example, facial recognition technology can be used to identify individuals and track their movements, which can be a serious violation of privacy and civil liberties. In addition, AI algorithms can be biased and reinforce existing patterns of discrimination and inequality, especially if they are based on flawed or incomplete data.

To mitigate these risks and ensure that AI is used to promote, rather than undermine, human rights, it is important to establish ethical guidelines and principles for the development and deployment of AI systems. These guidelines should include principles such as fairness, accountability, transparency, and respect for human rights and dignity.

Moreover, it is essential to ensure that the development and deployment of AI systems are subject to democratic oversight and public scrutiny. This can help to ensure that AI systems are used in the public interest and that their potential risks and benefits are carefully considered and weighed.

In conclusion, AI has the potential to both protect and undermine human rights. It is important to carefully consider the potential risks and benefits of AI in the context of human rights, and to establish ethical guidelines and principles to ensure that AI is used in a responsible and ethical manner.

AI has the potential to contribute significantly to the promotion and protection of human rights. AI-powered systems can be used to detect and prevent human rights abuses, provide legal assistance to marginalized communities, and ensure equal treatment in various areas, including employment, housing, and education.

However, there are also concerns that AI could exacerbate existing human rights violations or introduce new ones. For example, biased algorithms could perpetuate discrimination against certain groups, and AI-powered surveillance systems could threaten privacy and freedom of expression.

To mitigate these risks, it is crucial to ensure that AI development and deployment are guided by human rights principles and values. This includes conducting regular human rights impact assessments, involving diverse stakeholders in the design and development process, and implementing transparency and accountability mechanisms.

Furthermore, efforts must be made to ensure that AI benefits all members of society, including marginalized and vulnerable communities. This includes addressing issues of bias and discrimination in AI systems and providing equal access to AI-related opportunities and resources.

Overall, the integration of AI into human rights work has the potential to enhance the promotion and protection of human rights, but it must be approached with caution and guided by a commitment to human rights principles and values.

AI has the potential to both threaten and safeguard human rights. On the one hand, AI can contribute to bias and discrimination, perpetuating and even exacerbating existing societal inequalities. On the other hand, AI can be used to identify and address bias, promote diversity and inclusion, and protect against human rights violations.

To safeguard human rights, AI systems must be designed and deployed in ways that are transparent, accountable, and respectful of privacy and individual autonomy. They must also be grounded in human rights principles and values, and be subject to effective human rights oversight and accountability mechanisms.

One way to ensure AI systems promote human rights is through the development of ethical guidelines and codes of conduct for AI development and deployment. These guidelines should be informed by human rights principles and values, and should be developed through a collaborative and inclusive process that engages a wide range of stakeholders.

It is also important to ensure that AI is accessible to all, and that it does not exacerbate existing inequalities. This requires investing in education and training programs that enable individuals and communities to understand and engage with AI, and that promote equal access to AI technologies and their benefits.

Finally, it is crucial to ensure that AI is subject to robust legal and regulatory frameworks that protect human rights and ensure accountability for human rights violations. This includes ensuring that AI developers and users are held accountable for the impact of their systems on human rights, and that effective remedies are available for those whose rights have been violated.

In short, AI has the potential to both threaten and safeguard human rights. To ensure that it does the latter, it is essential to ensure that AI is developed and deployed in ways that are transparent, accountable, and respectful of privacy and individual autonomy, and that are grounded in human rights principles and values.

In conclusion, AI has the potential to significantly impact human rights, both positively and negatively. As AI becomes more pervasive in our society, it is crucial that we remain vigilant in safeguarding our freedoms and ensuring that AI is used ethically and fairly. From preventing discrimination to ensuring equal treatment, there are many ways in which AI can help advance human rights. However, there are also concerns about the potential for AI to reinforce bias and perpetuate inequality. It is up to us to use AI responsibly and ensure that it serves the greater good.

We explored the potential impact of AI on human rights. We discussed how AI can help safeguard our freedoms by ensuring equal treatment and preventing discrimination, but also how it can pose a threat to privacy and autonomy. It is important to continue monitoring the development and implementation of AI systems to ensure they are aligned with ethical and legal standards.

As AI continues to advance, it is crucial to consider its potential impact on human rights and work towards ensuring that these technologies are used in a way that upholds and promotes our fundamental freedoms. By doing so, we can harness the power of AI to create a more equitable and just society for all.

It is important to ensure that AI systems are designed and deployed in a way that respects human rights and prevents harm. This requires collaboration between developers, policymakers, and civil society organizations to establish ethical frameworks and ensure transparency and accountability in AI decision-making.

As we continue to develop and integrate AI technology into our societies, it is crucial to remain vigilant and proactive in addressing the potential risks and challenges that may arise. By working together to safeguard human rights, we can ensure that the benefits of AI are accessible to all members of society.

Suggestions:

- Support initiatives that promote transparency and accountability in AI decision-making processes
- Advocate for the development of ethical frameworks and guidelines for AI technology
- Stay informed and engaged in discussions on the potential impact of AI on human rights
- Encourage collaboration and diversity in the development and deployment of AI technology to ensure that it reflects the needs and values of all members of society.

Chapter 49 AI and Social Media: Influencing the Digital Conversation

Chapter 49, where we explore the fascinating topic of AI and social media. Over the past decade, social media platforms have become an integral part of our daily lives. From connecting with friends and family to consuming news and entertainment, social media has changed the way we interact with the world. With the increasing use of AI, social media platforms have become more sophisticated, with algorithms playing a key role in content moderation, personalized content curation, and the spread of information. We will explore the impact of AI on social media, the benefits and challenges it presents, and what the future may hold for this dynamic intersection of technology and communication.

Social media has become an integral part of our daily lives, with millions of people using various platforms to connect, share information, and express themselves. However, with this widespread usage comes the responsibility of ensuring that the content shared on these platforms is safe and appropriate for all users. This is where AI comes in, with its ability to analyze and moderate large volumes of content in real-time.

AI algorithms can be used to detect and remove harmful or inappropriate content such as hate speech, cyberbullying, and violent imagery, which can help to create a safer online space. Additionally, AI can also be used to monitor the spread of misinformation and disinformation, which has become a major issue on social media platforms.

On the other hand, AI is also playing a significant role in shaping the content that we see on social media. Social media platforms use algorithms to curate our feeds and personalize the content we see, based on our interests, browsing history, and interactions. This can create echo chambers and filter bubbles, where users are only exposed to content that reinforces their existing beliefs and opinions.

Furthermore, AI-powered chatbots and virtual assistants have become increasingly prevalent on social media platforms, enabling businesses and brands to engage with customers more efficiently and effectively. These chatbots can handle routine customer inquiries, provide product recommendations, and even facilitate transactions, freeing up human employees to focus on more complex tasks.

Overall, AI has had a significant impact on social media, both in terms of content moderation and curation, as well as enabling businesses to provide better customer service. However, it is important to ensure that these algorithms are transparent and accountable, and that they do not perpetuate biases or amplify harmful content.

Social media has become an integral part of our daily lives, and AI plays a significant role in shaping the content we see and the conversations we have online. AI algorithms are used to analyze our social media activity, gather data about our interests, and recommend content that is likely to engage us. These algorithms are designed to keep us on the platform for longer periods, which can have both positive and negative effects on our social media experiences.

On the positive side, AI-powered content moderation tools can help to identify and remove harmful or offensive content, such as hate speech or cyberbullying. These tools can also help to identify and flag potential misinformation or fake news, which can be especially important during times of crisis or during election campaigns.

However, AI algorithms can also contribute to the spread of misinformation and extremist content. These algorithms are designed to prioritize engagement and often prioritize sensational or controversial content over more balanced and accurate reporting. This can result in users being exposed to inaccurate or misleading information, which can be harmful to public discourse and decision-making.

Overall, the role of AI in shaping social media is complex and multifaceted. While it can provide benefits in terms of content moderation and recommendation, it can also perpetuate some of the negative aspects of social media, such as the spread of misinformation and the creation of echo chambers. It is important to continue to monitor and regulate the use of AI in social media to ensure that it is used responsibly and for the benefit of users.

The use of AI in social media has also raised concerns about the potential impact on individual privacy. With the ability to analyze vast amounts of data, AI algorithms can uncover a great deal of personal information about users, including their preferences, interests, and even their location. This has led to concerns about how this information is being used by social media companies, advertisers, and other third parties.

To address these concerns, some experts have called for greater transparency and control over personal data. This includes measures such as giving users the ability to opt out of data collection and providing clear information about how their data is being used. Additionally, some have called for regulations to be put in place to ensure that companies are using AI in a responsible and ethical manner, with a focus on protecting user privacy and preventing the spread of disinformation.

Another potential application of AI in social media is in the realm of content moderation. With the sheer volume of content being posted on social media platforms every day, it can be difficult for human moderators to keep up with the task of identifying and removing harmful or inappropriate content. AI algorithms can assist with this process by automatically identifying and flagging potentially problematic content, allowing human moderators to focus their efforts on reviewing the most pressing cases.

However, there are also concerns about the potential for bias in AI-powered content moderation. Algorithms may be trained on biased or incomplete data, leading to disproportionate targeting of certain groups or types of content. This has led to calls for increased transparency in the development and use of AI algorithms for content moderation, as well as the use of diverse and representative datasets in training these algorithms.

Overall, the use of AI in social media has both potential benefits and potential risks. While AI-powered content moderation and data analysis can help to improve the user experience and protect individuals' privacy, there are also concerns about the potential for bias and misuse of personal data. As such, it is important to approach the use of AI in social media with a critical eye and a focus on responsible and ethical practices.

AI has become an integral part of social media platforms, and it is used in a variety of ways to shape the digital conversation. One of the most significant ways that AI is utilized in social media is through content moderation. With billions of users posting content on a daily basis, it is impossible for humans to manually review every post. Therefore, social media companies use AI algorithms to identify and remove content that violates their community guidelines.

Another way that AI is used in social media is through personalized content recommendations. Social media companies use AI to analyze user behavior and preferences to suggest content that they are likely to engage with. These recommendations are crucial for keeping users engaged and increasing the time they spend on the platform.

AI is also used in social media for sentiment analysis. Sentiment analysis refers to the process of using natural language processing (NLP) techniques to identify the sentiment of social media posts. This helps social media companies to understand how their users feel about a particular topic, product, or brand. Companies can then use this information to make informed decisions about their marketing and advertising strategies.

Finally, AI is used to combat the spread of misinformation on social media platforms. With the sheer volume of content being posted on social media, it can be difficult to differentiate between true and false information. AI algorithms can be trained to detect patterns and anomalies in content that may indicate that it is false or misleading. Social media companies can then use this information to remove or flag such content.

Overall, AI has had a significant impact on the way social media platforms operate. From content moderation to personalized content recommendations and combating misinformation, AI is essential to shaping the digital conversation.

Another way that AI is influencing the digital conversation on social media is through the use of chatbots. Chatbots are computer programs that simulate human conversation through artificial intelligence, and they are increasingly being used by companies and organizations to interact with customers on social media platforms. These chatbots can be used to provide customer service, answer frequently asked questions, and even facilitate purchases.

While chatbots can provide a convenient and efficient way to communicate with customers, there are also concerns about their potential to spread misinformation or manipulate users. For example, chatbots can be programmed to present biased or false information in order to promote a certain agenda or influence opinions. Additionally, chatbots can be used to spread fake news or other forms of disinformation, which can have serious consequences for individuals and society as a whole.

As social media continues to play an increasingly important role in our lives, it is important to be aware of the potential influence of AI on these platforms. By understanding how AI is shaping social media and the digital conversation, we can work towards creating a more transparent and accountable online environment.

Social media has revolutionized the way people interact and exchange information. With the help of AI, social media companies can analyze user behavior and preferences to customize their experiences, make personalized recommendations, and detect and remove inappropriate content.

AI algorithms can help social media companies monitor and moderate content in real-time, enabling them to identify and remove harmful or offensive posts and comments quickly. This approach has been particularly useful in preventing the spread of hate speech, cyberbullying, and fake news.

Another area where AI can make a significant impact is in content recommendations. By analyzing user behavior and preferences, social media platforms can use AI to suggest relevant content and personalize users' feeds. This approach can help users find content that interests them while keeping them engaged on the platform.

In addition to moderation and content recommendations, AI can also help social media companies detect and prevent the spread of misinformation. By analyzing user-generated content and flagging potentially false or misleading information, AI algorithms can help social media platforms reduce the spread of misinformation.

However, there are concerns about the use of AI in social media, particularly when it comes to privacy and the potential for algorithmic bias. Social media companies must ensure that they are transparent about how they use AI and protect user data. They must also be vigilant in identifying and addressing algorithmic bias, which can perpetuate discrimination and prejudice.

Overall, AI has the potential to significantly impact the way social media operates, from content moderation to personalized recommendations. Social media companies must work to address the challenges and concerns associated with AI while leveraging its benefits to provide a better user experience.

One area where AI is increasingly playing a significant role is in content moderation on social media platforms. Social media platforms have been under increasing pressure to tackle misinformation, hate speech, and other harmful content that may be spread on their platforms. AI can help social media platforms identify and flag potentially harmful content, making it easier for human moderators to review and remove it.

However, AI content moderation is not without its challenges. For instance, AI systems may struggle with identifying context and nuance, leading to false positives or false negatives. There is also a risk of AI moderation perpetuating existing biases, such as racial or gender biases, if the training data used to develop the AI systems is not diverse enough.

Another way in which AI is influencing social media is through the use of algorithms that determine the content that users see on their feeds. Social media platforms use AI algorithms to tailor users' feeds based on their browsing history, search history, and other personal information. This has led to concerns about the potential for social media algorithms to create filter bubbles and echo chambers, where users are only exposed to content that confirms their existing beliefs and biases.

Moreover, the use of AI in social media can have a significant impact on the spread of information. AI-powered bots can spread misinformation and propaganda quickly and efficiently, making it challenging for users to distinguish fact from fiction. This can have serious consequences for democracy and social cohesion, making it critical to develop AI tools that can detect and flag misinformation effectively.

Finally, AI can also play a role in helping social media platforms ensure privacy and data security for their users. AI tools can monitor user accounts for signs of suspicious activity, such as attempts to log in from unusual locations, and flag them for further review.

Overall, AI is changing the way we interact with social media, from content moderation to the spread of information and the protection of user privacy. While there are significant challenges to overcome, AI has the potential to make social media a safer, more diverse, and more informative space.

Social media has become an integral part of our daily lives, and with the growing number of users, the need for effective moderation has increased. AI-based solutions are now being used to moderate social media content, including text, images, and videos. These systems use natural language processing and computer vision algorithms to detect and filter inappropriate content, such as hate speech, spam, and nudity.

In addition to content moderation, AI is also being used to influence the spread of information on social media. Social media platforms use algorithms to determine which content is shown to users, and these algorithms can be influenced by various factors, including engagement metrics, user behavior, and advertiser preferences. This has raised concerns about the potential for AI to shape the online conversation and even manipulate public opinion.

Despite these concerns, AI also has the potential to improve the social media experience for users. For example, AI-powered chatbots can provide quick and personalized customer service, while recommendation algorithms can suggest relevant content to users. Social media companies are also using AI to analyze user data and provide insights into audience behavior and preferences, which can be used to improve marketing strategies and target specific audiences.

As social media continues to evolve and become more ubiquitous, the role of AI in shaping this space will only continue to grow. It is important for companies, policymakers, and individuals to understand the potential benefits and risks of AI in social media and work towards creating a responsible and ethical online environment.

We have explored the role of AI in shaping social media. We have discussed how AI is used for content moderation, including identifying and removing harmful or inappropriate content, as well as for identifying and addressing hate speech and other forms of harmful speech. We have also discussed how AI is used to influence the spread of information on social media platforms, including identifying and addressing misinformation and propaganda.

While AI has the potential to play a positive role in shaping social media, there are also concerns about its potential negative impact on privacy, freedom of speech, and the overall quality of the digital conversation. As AI continues to be integrated into social media platforms, it will be important for developers and policymakers to carefully consider these issues and work to ensure that AI is used in a responsible and ethical manner.

Summary:

We discussed various applications of AI in social media, including content moderation, sentiment analysis, and personalized recommendations. We also delved into the ethical considerations surrounding AI's influence on social media, such as the potential for bias and the need for transparency in algorithms. It is important to keep in mind that while AI can be a powerful tool for improving social media, it must be used responsibly and ethically.

Suggestions:

1. Stay informed about the use of AI in social media and its potential impact on society and individuals.
2. Advocate for transparency and accountability in the development and deployment of AI algorithms in social media.
3. Be mindful of the potential for bias in AI systems and work to ensure that they are developed with diverse and inclusive perspectives.

4. Consider the ethical implications of using AI in social media and participate in discussions and decision-making around responsible AI use.

Chapter 50 AI and Aging: Enhancing Quality of Life

We will be exploring the ways in which AI can contribute to enhancing the quality of life for an aging population. With the increasing number of elderly people in our society, it is important to address the challenges they face, from healthcare to social support. AI has the potential to revolutionize the way we provide services and support to the elderly, making their lives easier and more comfortable. Join us as we delve into this fascinating topic and discover the potential of AI in enhancing the lives of our seniors.

The aging population is a growing concern in many parts of the world, particularly in developed countries. As people age, they often face a range of challenges, including declining physical and cognitive health, social isolation, and reduced access to care. AI has the potential to help address some of these challenges and improve the quality of life for older adults.

One way AI can help is by improving healthcare for older adults. AI-powered diagnostic tools can help doctors identify and treat health conditions earlier, potentially improving outcomes and reducing healthcare costs. Additionally, AI-powered robots can assist with tasks like medication management and monitoring vital signs, helping to keep older adults healthier and independent for longer.

Another way AI can help is by addressing social isolation. AI-powered chatbots and virtual assistants can provide companionship and help older adults stay connected to their communities. Additionally, AI-powered transportation services can help older adults maintain their mobility, allowing them to participate in social activities and access healthcare services.

Overall, AI has the potential to greatly enhance the quality of life for older adults by improving healthcare, addressing social isolation, and enabling greater independence. However, it is important to ensure that AI solutions are designed with older adults in mind and are accessible and easy to use for all.

AI has the potential to improve the quality of life for the elderly population in numerous ways. One of the most promising areas for AI in aging is healthcare. AI algorithms can be used to analyze large amounts of patient data to identify trends and patterns that can help healthcare providers make better decisions for their patients. For example, AI can help doctors and nurses monitor patients' vital signs and provide early warning of potential health problems, allowing for timely interventions and better outcomes. Additionally, AI can help identify patients who are at high risk for falls, which can be a significant risk for older adults, and enable healthcare providers to take preventive measures.

AI can also be used to enhance social support for older adults. For example, AI-powered chatbots can provide companionship and emotional support to older adults who may be feeling lonely or isolated. Additionally, AI can help connect older adults with community resources, such as transportation or home-delivered meals, that can help them remain independent and active in their communities. AI can also be used to detect signs of elder abuse, which is a growing concern, particularly as the population ages.

Overall, AI has the potential to revolutionize the way we care for and support our aging population. By leveraging the power of AI, we can enhance the quality of life for older adults and help them live independently and with dignity for as long as possible.

As AI continues to advance, it holds great potential for improving the quality of life for older adults. One of the main areas where AI can help is in healthcare. With an aging population, there is an increasing demand for healthcare services, and AI can help to fill the gap by providing personalized care to older adults. AI can be used to analyze large amounts of patient data, allowing healthcare providers to identify trends and patterns that can help them to develop more effective treatment plans. For example, AI can be used to monitor patients' vital signs, detect changes in their health status, and alert healthcare providers to potential issues before they become serious.

AI can also be used to support social connections for older adults. Social isolation is a significant problem among older adults, and it can have a negative impact on their physical and mental health. AI can help to combat social isolation by providing older adults with virtual companions or by facilitating connections with other people who share similar interests. AI-powered devices, such as smart speakers or robots, can also provide older adults with entertainment and companionship.

Another area where AI can be beneficial for older adults is in home automation. As older adults age, it can become more difficult for them to manage their homes independently. AI-powered devices, such as smart thermostats, lighting systems, and security cameras, can help older adults to control their homes more easily and stay safe and comfortable.

Overall, AI has enormous potential to improve the quality of life for older adults. By providing personalized healthcare, facilitating social connections, and automating home management, AI can help older adults to live independently and enjoy a higher quality of life as they age.

AI has the potential to revolutionize elderly care, providing support and assistance to older adults and improving their quality of life. Some of the applications of AI in elderly care include:

- Fall detection: AI-powered sensors can detect when an older adult has fallen and alert caregivers or emergency services, reducing the time it takes for them to receive assistance.
- Medication management: AI can help older adults manage their medications, reminding them to take their pills at the appropriate times and alerting caregivers or doctors if they miss a dose.
- Virtual companionship: AI-powered virtual assistants can provide older adults with companionship and entertainment, helping to alleviate loneliness and isolation.
- Monitoring health conditions: AI can monitor an older adult's vital signs and alert caregivers or doctors if there are any concerning changes, allowing for early intervention and prevention of health complications.
- Personalized care plans: AI can analyze data from an older adult's health records and create personalized care plans that take into account their individual needs and preferences.

These applications of AI in elderly care have the potential to greatly improve the quality of life for older adults and reduce the burden on caregivers and healthcare systems. However, there are also ethical considerations to take into account, such as privacy concerns and ensuring that older adults are not marginalized or left behind by technological advancements.

AI has the potential to revolutionize healthcare for aging populations, particularly in the area of disease detection and prevention. For example, AI algorithms can be trained on large datasets of medical images to accurately diagnose conditions like Alzheimer's disease and Parkinson's disease. These algorithms can also help predict the risk of developing certain conditions, allowing for earlier interventions and improved outcomes.

In addition to disease detection, AI can also assist with medication management for seniors. For example, machine learning algorithms can help identify drug interactions and recommend appropriate dosages based on factors like age, weight, and medical history.

Social isolation is also a major issue for aging populations, and AI can play a role in addressing this challenge as well. Virtual companions, chatbots, and other conversational AI tools can provide seniors with social interaction and mental stimulation, while also monitoring for signs of cognitive decline or other health issues.

Overall, the potential of AI in enhancing the quality of life for aging populations is immense. By leveraging AI technology, we can improve healthcare outcomes, provide greater social support, and enhance overall wellbeing for seniors. However, it is important to ensure that AI solutions are developed with the needs and preferences of seniors in mind, and that ethical considerations around privacy and data security are carefully addressed.

AI has great potential in enhancing the quality of life for aging populations. With the help of AI, healthcare professionals can monitor patients' vital signs and health conditions in real-time, providing immediate care in case of emergencies. Moreover, AI-powered devices and systems can also help elderly people maintain their independence and live safely at home, even when their mobility is limited.

AI can also be used to support caregivers by providing tools and resources that can help them manage the care of their loved ones more efficiently. For example, AI-powered devices can assist in the administration of medication, track patients' schedules, and monitor their health status.

Another promising area where AI can benefit aging populations is in providing social support. With AI-powered virtual assistants, elderly individuals can have access to 24/7 assistance for their daily needs, such as grocery shopping or transportation. Additionally, AI can also help combat loneliness and isolation by providing social interaction and engagement through virtual communities and personalized content.

Overall, the potential for AI to enhance the quality of life for aging populations is enormous. By leveraging the power of AI, we can better address the challenges that come with an aging population and improve the overall well-being of our elderly communities.

In conclusion, AI has the potential to greatly benefit the aging population, from improving healthcare to providing social support. AI can help with early detection and diagnosis of health issues, as well as personalized treatment plans. It can also assist with daily living tasks and provide companionship for those who may be isolated. However, it is important to consider the ethical implications and ensure that the use of AI is done in a responsible and respectful manner. As the aging population continues to grow, the development and implementation of AI technologies can greatly enhance the quality of life for older adults.

We explored the potential of AI in addressing the challenges of an aging population. From healthcare to social support, AI has the potential to enhance the quality of life for older adults. We looked at various AI-powered applications, such as remote monitoring and personalized care, that can improve healthcare outcomes for older adults. We also discussed how AI can help address social isolation and provide new opportunities for community engagement.

As the world's population continues to age, AI will play an increasingly important role in supporting the well-being of older adults. It is essential to continue researching and developing AI-powered solutions that can address the unique needs of this population. At the same time, we must ensure that the use of AI in aging is ethical, transparent, and respectful of human dignity.

Summary:

We explored the potential of AI in addressing the challenges of an aging population, including healthcare and social support. We discussed how AI-powered technologies can help improve the quality of life for older adults by providing personalized medical treatments, remote monitoring, and assistance with daily activities. We also examined the role of AI in facilitating social connection and reducing isolation among older adults. However, we also discussed potential ethical concerns surrounding the use of AI in elder care, including issues of privacy and data security.

Suggestions for further reading:

1. "AI for Aging and Longevity: A Review of Current Applications and Future Possibilities" by N. Au et al. (2021)
2. "AI and the Future of Aging: Addressing Ethical Challenges" by J. Lipman et al. (2020)
3. "Aging and Technology: Taking the Research into the Real World" edited by S. Gutierrez-Robledo and R. Najafi (2021)

Chapter 51 AI and Hobbies: Personalizing Our Passions

We will explore the ways in which AI can enhance and personalize our hobbies. Hobbies are activities that we engage in for pleasure and relaxation, and they vary greatly from person to person. With the help of AI, we can optimize our hobbies and find new and creative ways to enjoy them. From fitness tracking to artistic expression, AI has the potential to revolutionize the way we pursue our passions. We will delve into the various applications of AI in the world of hobbies and explore the benefits and challenges that come with them. So, let's dive in!

Artificial intelligence has started to play a significant role in various aspects of life, and one of the most promising areas is in enhancing and personalizing hobbies. The use of AI in hobbies is not limited to just one or two fields, as it has the potential to transform and improve a wide range of activities such as fitness, cooking, gaming, music, and many more. With the increasing adoption of AI in hobbies, enthusiasts can now experience personalized and unique experiences that can cater to their preferences and abilities.

One of the most prominent areas in which AI is playing a vital role is in fitness tracking. AI-powered fitness devices are being used to monitor and track various physical activities, including running, swimming, and cycling, among others. These devices provide users with real-time feedback and personalized recommendations on how to improve their performance. The data collected from these devices can also be used to create personalized training programs that are tailored to the individual's fitness level, goals, and preferences.

AI is also revolutionizing the way people cook and enjoy food. Smart kitchen appliances powered by AI can help users prepare meals more efficiently and with greater precision. These appliances can also make personalized recipe recommendations based on the user's dietary preferences, allergies, and the ingredients they have on hand. Additionally, AI can be used to analyze food trends and provide recommendations to chefs and food enthusiasts.

Another area where AI is making a significant impact is in the field of gaming. AI-powered game assistants can help players improve their skills and provide personalized game recommendations based on their preferences and play style. AI can also be used to generate personalized game content, such as quests, levels, and characters, that cater to the player's unique interests.

In music, AI is being used to create personalized playlists and recommend new artists and songs based on the listener's music preferences. AI can also be used to generate new music compositions based on the user's style, mood, and preferences.

Overall, AI has the potential to enhance and personalize hobbies in countless ways, making them more enjoyable and tailored to the individual's preferences and abilities.

One of the most popular areas where AI is being used to enhance hobbies is fitness tracking. With the rise of wearable technology, AI algorithms are being used to monitor physical activity, heart rate, and sleep patterns. This data can then be analyzed and used to provide personalized recommendations on workout routines, nutrition, and even recovery time.

In addition to fitness, AI is also being used in the world of music to enhance creativity and expression. Some music apps are using AI to create personalized playlists based on individual preferences and even mood. Other tools are using AI to help musicians generate new ideas and experiment with different sounds.

AI is also being applied to the world of visual arts, where it is being used to help artists create new works and enhance existing ones. Some software tools are using AI to assist artists with tasks like color selection, composition, and even brushstroke techniques. AI is also being used to create new visual art forms, such as generative art, which involves the use of algorithms to generate new and unique art pieces.

Overall, AI is transforming the world of hobbies by making them more personalized, efficient, and creative. By analyzing data and providing personalized recommendations, AI is helping people get the most out of their hobbies and discover new ways to express themselves.

AI is rapidly transforming the music industry by enabling personalized music recommendations, creating new compositions, and even enhancing live performances. Music streaming services such as Spotify, Apple Music, and Pandora use AI algorithms to analyze users' listening history and provide personalized music recommendations. These algorithms analyze a user's listening history, the music they have liked or disliked, and the listening habits of other users with similar tastes to suggest music that they may enjoy.

AI has also shown the potential to create new compositions in various music genres. In 2018, an AI program developed by Sony's Computer Science Laboratories produced a song that sounded like it was composed by a human musician. The program analyzed a vast database of sheet music and then used deep learning to create a new composition. Similarly, AI has been used to generate lyrics and even produce music videos.

Moreover, AI is being used to enhance live music performances. For instance, AI algorithms can analyze the sound of an instrument or a voice and then provide real-time feedback to help musicians improve their technique. AI-powered music creation tools like Amper Music can enable non-musicians to create music by generating custom tracks based on their inputs.

While AI in music offers exciting possibilities, it also raises questions about creativity and artistic expression. Some argue that AI-generated music lacks the emotional depth and human touch of music composed by humans. Others believe that AI can be a tool to enhance human creativity and push the boundaries of what is possible in music.

AI has the potential to transform creative hobbies such as music, painting, and writing by offering personalized tools and techniques to enhance an individual's creativity.

One example is Amper Music, an AI-powered platform that allows users to create custom music tracks using machine learning algorithms. The platform can analyze an individual's music preferences and create unique tracks based on their preferences.

Similarly, tools like Google's DeepDream and NeuralStyler can analyze an individual's artistic style and generate new artwork based on their preferences. These tools use neural networks to identify patterns and styles in existing artwork and apply them to new images.

AI can also assist in writing and storytelling by suggesting ideas and generating text based on an individual's writing style. Tools like GPT-3 can generate coherent and natural language text that can be used for various purposes such as writing essays or creating stories.

However, some argue that AI-generated creative work lacks the depth and emotion that comes from human creativity. While AI tools can help with generating initial ideas and assisting in the creative process, it is ultimately up to the individual to infuse their work with their own unique perspective and emotions.

Overall, AI has the potential to revolutionize how we approach creative hobbies and offer new personalized tools for individuals to enhance their skills and creativity.

AI has the potential to enhance and personalize hobbies by providing recommendations, tracking progress, and assisting in skill development. Fitness tracking apps that use AI can provide personalized workout routines based on the user's fitness level and goals, making exercise more effective and enjoyable. AI-powered music platforms like Spotify can provide song recommendations based on the listener's preferences and listening habits.

AI can also aid in skill development by providing personalized coaching and feedback. For example, the app Duolingo uses AI to create personalized language learning plans for each user based on their strengths and weaknesses. AI can also be used in artistic pursuits, such as painting or drawing, by providing suggestions for colors and techniques based on the artist's style.

In addition to enhancing hobbies, AI can also create new ones. Virtual reality (VR) and augmented reality (AR) technologies, which are powered by AI, can create immersive gaming experiences, allowing users to explore new worlds and interact with digital objects in real-time. These technologies can also be used for educational purposes, such as simulating historical events or scientific phenomena.

However, it is important to note that while AI can enhance and personalize hobbies, it should not replace human creativity and personalization. It is important to maintain a balance between the use of AI and the individual's own creativity and passion for their hobbies.

AI has revolutionized the way people pursue their hobbies, especially when it comes to sports and fitness activities. With the use of wearable technology, people can track their fitness activities such as running, swimming, and cycling. These devices can provide real-time feedback and help individuals adjust their workouts based on their performance. Furthermore, AI-powered personal trainers can provide customized workout plans based on individual fitness goals, preferences, and physical capabilities. This personalization can help people stay motivated and achieve their fitness objectives.

Artistic expression is another area where AI can enhance people's hobbies. With AI-powered tools, artists can create digital art and animation, generate music and sound effects, and even write poetry and literature. These tools can help artists create new works and explore different creative directions. AI can also help people discover new hobbies and interests through recommendation systems that suggest activities based on their preferences and past experiences.

Moreover, AI can also assist hobbyists in organizing their collections and keeping track of their progress. For instance, a gardening enthusiast can use AI-powered apps to track the growth of their plants and identify potential issues, while a board game collector can use AI-powered cataloging tools to keep track of their collection and identify missing pieces.

Overall, AI has opened up new possibilities for people to personalize and enhance their hobbies, providing new ways to enjoy their leisure time and pursue their passions.

AI has also shown its potential in enhancing artistic expression. For instance, AI can be used to analyze artwork, learn patterns, and then generate new pieces of art. Google's DeepDream project is an example of this, where a neural network was trained to recognize patterns in images and then generate dreamlike visuals based on these patterns.

AI can also be used to assist in music creation. AI music systems can analyze patterns in music and use these patterns to generate new melodies or entire songs. These systems can also generate accompanying music to a pre-existing melody. In 2016, Sony released an AI-generated pop song called "Daddy's Car," which was composed by an AI system called Flow Machines.

AI can also personalize hobbies through fitness tracking. Wearable devices that track biometric data can analyze the data and provide personalized recommendations to improve performance or suggest new workout routines. Additionally, AI-powered virtual trainers can provide personalized coaching to individuals based on their fitness goals and progress.

Overall, AI has shown great potential in enhancing and personalizing hobbies, from creating art and music to improving physical performance through fitness tracking. As AI continues to advance, we can expect to see even more exciting applications of AI in the hobby space.

In addition to the areas mentioned, AI has also revolutionized the gaming industry by providing personalized gaming experiences. By using machine learning algorithms, AI can analyze a player's gaming style and behavior, and adjust the game's difficulty level accordingly. This not only creates a more engaging experience but can also help game developers improve their products based on player feedback.

Furthermore, AI is being used to improve safety in extreme sports such as snowboarding, skateboarding, and motocross. Companies are developing wearable technology with AI capabilities that can monitor athletes' vital signs and track their movements in real-time, which can help prevent accidents and injuries.

In the art world, AI is being used to create unique and innovative works of art. AI algorithms can analyze a particular style of art and recreate it, producing original pieces that reflect the artist's style while also incorporating new elements.

Finally, AI is being used in cooking and mixology, providing personalized recommendations based on individual taste preferences and dietary restrictions. With the help of AI, chefs and bartenders can create unique dishes and drinks that cater to each customer's preferences, ensuring a memorable dining experience.

Overall, AI has provided a new level of personalization and innovation to hobbies and leisure activities. From personalized fitness plans to unique works of art, AI has the potential to enhance and personalize every aspect of our leisure time.

We explored the potential of AI to enhance and personalize our hobbies, from fitness tracking to artistic expression. We discussed the various ways in which AI can help us achieve our goals and improve our skills in our chosen hobbies. However, we also acknowledged the potential drawbacks and limitations of relying too heavily on AI in our hobbies, such as the loss of human creativity and the risk of becoming overly dependent on technology.

As we continue to integrate AI into our hobbies, it is important to strike a balance between leveraging its capabilities and maintaining the unique qualities of human creativity and expression. By doing so, we can create a future where AI enhances and enriches our hobbies, while still allowing us to fully express ourselves and engage with our passions.

Chapter 52 AI and Language: Preserving and Revitalizing Cultural Heritage

In today's world, with the rise of globalization and the dominance of a few major languages, many minority languages and cultures are at risk of disappearing. However, Artificial Intelligence (AI) offers a potential solution for preserving and revitalizing endangered languages and cultural heritage. We will explore the various ways AI is being used to preserve and revitalize endangered languages, from automatic translation to speech recognition, and how it can help to promote diversity and preserve the richness of our global cultural heritage. We will also examine the ethical implications of using AI in this context, and how it can be used to empower local communities and support linguistic diversity.

Language is an essential aspect of human culture and heritage. However, many languages are endangered due to various factors, such as globalization, urbanization, and migration. As a result, there is a growing need to preserve and revitalize endangered languages and cultural heritage.

AI has the potential to assist in this endeavor in various ways. For example, AI-powered translation tools can help bridge communication gaps between speakers of different languages, preserving linguistic diversity. AI can also be used to digitize and preserve cultural artifacts, such as texts, images, and audio recordings, making them accessible to future generations.

Furthermore, AI can aid in language revitalization efforts. For instance, speech recognition and natural language processing technologies can help document and analyze endangered languages. This data can then be used to develop language learning tools and resources to help speakers of endangered languages maintain and pass on their linguistic heritage.

Overall, AI has the potential to play a crucial role in preserving and revitalizing endangered languages and cultural heritage, ensuring their survival for generations to come.

One of the significant contributions of AI to language preservation is the development of language translation software. These programs use algorithms to identify patterns and meanings in written and spoken language, allowing for the translation of text or speech from one language to another. In addition to facilitating communication across different languages, translation software can aid in the preservation of endangered languages by allowing their texts to be translated into more widely spoken languages.

Another application of AI in language preservation is speech recognition technology. This technology allows for the automatic transcription of spoken language into written text, which can aid in the preservation of oral traditions and stories. Additionally, speech synthesis technology can be used to recreate the sounds and intonations of endangered languages, helping to keep them alive even when there are no longer any native speakers.

AI can also be used to analyze large amounts of data, including texts and audio recordings, to identify patterns and connections between languages. By identifying similarities and differences between languages, AI can aid in the reconstruction of extinct languages and the development of language revitalization programs.

Overall, the use of AI in language preservation has the potential to greatly benefit efforts to preserve endangered languages and cultural heritage. By facilitating communication across languages and aiding in the reconstruction of lost languages, AI can help to ensure that these important parts of human history and culture are not lost forever.

The preservation and revitalization of endangered languages and cultural heritage is a crucial aspect of maintaining diversity and promoting understanding among different communities. AI technologies can play a significant role in this area, by facilitating the digitization, translation, and analysis of cultural artifacts and linguistic materials.

One example of AI's potential in revitalizing cultural heritage is the Endangered Languages Project, a collaboration between Google and several linguistic experts and organizations. The project utilizes AI and machine learning to document and preserve endangered languages, providing online resources for language documentation, community outreach, and research.

Another example is the use of AI in cultural heritage preservation, such as the digitization and restoration of historical documents, artworks, and artifacts. AI technologies can enhance the accuracy and efficiency of the digitization process, as well as the analysis and interpretation of the resulting digital data.

Additionally, AI can facilitate the translation of cultural materials into different languages, allowing broader access and understanding of cultural heritage across different communities. Machine translation tools, such as Google Translate, can help in this regard, although there are still challenges in accurately capturing the nuances and context of different languages and cultures.

Overall, AI has the potential to significantly contribute to the preservation and revitalization of endangered languages and cultural heritage. However, it is important to ensure that these technologies are developed and used in a culturally sensitive and ethical manner, respecting the autonomy and self-determination of the communities involved.

One of the significant applications of AI in language preservation is speech recognition and translation. AI technology can recognize and transcribe speech in endangered languages and translate it into other languages, making it more accessible and easier to preserve.

AI can also help preserve written and printed materials in endangered languages through optical character recognition (OCR) technology. This technology can recognize and transcribe texts in different scripts and languages, making it easier to digitize and store them.

Moreover, AI can also be used to create language-learning tools and resources that are tailored to specific endangered languages. These tools can help learners practice speaking and writing in the language, as well as understand its grammar and vocabulary.

Another exciting application of AI in language preservation is the creation of chatbots that can interact with speakers of endangered languages. These chatbots can help users practice speaking the language, answer their questions, and provide guidance on grammar and vocabulary.

Furthermore, AI can also be used to analyze and preserve cultural heritage through natural language processing (NLP) technology. NLP can help researchers identify and analyze linguistic patterns, dialects, and unique features of endangered languages.

Overall, AI has the potential to play a significant role in preserving and revitalizing endangered languages and cultural heritage. By leveraging various AI technologies such as speech recognition, OCR, language learning tools, chatbots, and NLP, we can ensure that future generations have access to these important cultural resources.

One of the challenges in using AI to preserve and revitalize endangered languages is the lack of data available. This is especially true for languages that are not commonly spoken or have very few speakers. In such cases, AI can be used to generate synthetic data that can be used to train language models. For example, researchers at Facebook AI have developed a method to generate synthetic data for low-resource languages by using statistical machine translation techniques.

Another approach to language revitalization using AI is to develop chatbots or virtual assistants that can interact with users in the endangered language. This approach has been used for languages such as Hawaiian and Maori, where chatbots have been developed to help learners practice the language and engage with the culture.

AI can also be used to help translate and transcribe texts in endangered languages. Google Translate, for example, now supports over 100 languages, many of which are endangered. In addition, AI-powered transcription tools can help transcribe audio recordings in endangered languages, which can be used to create written records of the language.

However, it is important to note that the use of AI in language revitalization is not a substitute for human efforts. Language revitalization requires active engagement from speakers and communities to ensure that the language is used and passed on to future generations. AI can support these efforts by providing tools and resources, but it is ultimately up to humans to keep the language alive.

AI has the potential to preserve endangered languages and cultural heritage by developing language recognition and translation software. These applications can help in digitizing texts and documents, creating digital archives, and developing online language courses. AI can also aid in restoring ancient or damaged artifacts, and in the process of digitizing cultural heritage materials, such as photographs, books, music, and other multimedia.

One of the challenges in using AI for cultural heritage preservation is ensuring that the technology is inclusive and respectful of cultural differences. This involves working with local communities and ensuring that their voices are heard in the development and use of these technologies. Additionally, there are concerns about the potential for AI to reproduce and amplify harmful biases and stereotypes that may exist within the language or cultural heritage being preserved. It is therefore important to consider issues of ethics and bias in the development and deployment of these technologies.

Despite the challenges, the potential benefits of using AI in cultural heritage preservation are significant. These technologies can help to democratize access to cultural heritage materials, making them more widely available to researchers, students, and the public. They can also help to revitalize endangered languages and cultures, preserving them for future generations.

In addition to language preservation, AI can also play a role in revitalizing endangered languages and cultural heritage. For example, AI can be used to create interactive language learning tools that engage and motivate language learners, as well as to develop automated translation tools that can help bridge communication gaps between people who speak different languages.

One exciting development in this area is the use of AI to create chatbots and virtual assistants that can converse in endangered languages. These tools can help preserve and revitalize endangered languages by providing opportunities for language learners to practice speaking and listening to the language in a natural way. Additionally, chatbots and virtual assistants can be programmed to provide cultural context and historical information, allowing users to learn about the cultural heritage associated with the language.

AI can also be used to analyze and interpret cultural artifacts, such as art, music, and literature. By applying machine learning algorithms to large collections of cultural artifacts, researchers can gain insights into cultural trends and patterns that might otherwise be difficult to discern. For example, AI could be used to identify recurring themes or motifs in a particular genre of literature, or to track the evolution of musical styles over time.

Overall, AI has the potential to play a significant role in preserving and revitalizing endangered languages and cultural heritage. By providing new opportunities for language learning and cultural exploration, AI can help ensure that these important parts of our human heritage are not lost to the passage of time.

In addition to preserving and revitalizing endangered languages, AI can also be used to analyze and understand language patterns in cultural heritage texts. For example, researchers have used natural language processing (NLP) techniques to analyze ancient texts such as the Dead Sea Scrolls, revealing new insights into the history and culture of the time period. Similarly, AI can be used to translate ancient texts into modern languages, making them more accessible to a wider audience.

Furthermore, AI can help to preserve and revitalize cultural heritage beyond language, such as through the use of computer vision to digitize and archive cultural artifacts. For example, the Google Arts & Culture project has used machine learning to digitize and categorize thousands of artworks and artifacts from around the world, making them accessible to people who might not otherwise have the opportunity to view them in person.

Overall, AI has the potential to greatly enhance our understanding and appreciation of cultural heritage, while also helping to preserve it for future generations.

In conclusion, the use of AI in preserving and revitalizing endangered languages and cultural heritage holds great promise. With the ability to process large amounts of data and analyze patterns, AI can help identify and translate rare texts, as well as detect and correct errors in documents. It can also assist in language revitalization efforts by analyzing speech patterns and providing language learners with personalized feedback. However, it is important to proceed with caution and ensure that AI is used in a way that respects the cultural and linguistic nuances of the communities being served. Additionally, human expertise and input remain crucial in the process of preserving and revitalizing cultural heritage, and should not be replaced by AI. Overall, AI can be a valuable tool in the effort to preserve and revitalize endangered languages and cultural heritage, but it should be used in a responsible and culturally sensitive manner.

We explored the potential of AI in preserving and revitalizing endangered languages and cultural heritage. From automatic translation to language revitalization, AI is playing an increasingly important role in preserving and promoting cultural diversity. As we move towards a more interconnected world, it is important to recognize the value of cultural heritage and take steps to preserve it. With AI, we have new tools to aid us in this endeavor. As we move forward, it is important to keep in mind the ethical considerations surrounding the use of AI in cultural preservation and to strive for inclusive and collaborative approaches.

Summary:

We explored the potential of AI in preserving and revitalizing endangered languages and cultural heritage. We discussed the challenges facing many cultures in maintaining and passing on their unique languages and traditions to future generations, and how AI can assist in addressing these challenges.

We learned about various AI-powered tools and platforms that have been developed to facilitate language preservation and revitalization, such as automatic speech recognition, machine translation, and natural language processing. Additionally, we examined how AI can help preserve and digitize cultural artifacts, such as art, music, and literature.

Overall, the integration of AI in cultural preservation offers a promising solution to protect and promote cultural diversity in the face of globalization and modernization.

Suggestions:

- Support organizations and initiatives focused on preserving endangered languages and cultural heritage
- Learn more about the various AI-powered tools and platforms that can assist in language preservation and revitalization
- Participate in cultural events and activities to promote and celebrate cultural diversity in your community
- Consider volunteering or supporting organizations involved in preserving and digitizing cultural artifacts.

Chapter 53: Embracing an AI-Driven Future

As we near the end of this book, it is important to reflect on the many ways in which artificial intelligence (AI) has already transformed our world and the potential it holds for the future. In this final chapter, we will summarize the key insights gained from exploring the various applications of AI throughout this book and offer thoughts on how we can adapt and thrive in an AI-driven future. As AI continues to advance and shape our lives in profound ways, it is important to understand its potential benefits and challenges, and to be prepared to embrace this technology and harness its power to improve our lives and the world around us.

As we come to the end of this book, it is clear that the potential of artificial intelligence (AI) is vast and wide-ranging. From healthcare to transportation, finance to education, and beyond, AI has the power to transform industries and societies in profound ways.

Throughout the previous chapters, we have explored some of the key ways in which AI is currently being used and the potential it holds for the future. We have examined the benefits and challenges of AI in various contexts and considered how we can ensure that AI is developed and deployed ethically and responsibly.

One of the key takeaways from this exploration of AI is the need for collaboration between experts from diverse fields. The development and deployment of AI requires input from individuals with technical expertise in AI, as well as those with knowledge of the social, ethical, and legal implications of AI.

Another important theme that emerged throughout this book is the need to prioritize transparency and accountability in the development and deployment of AI systems. As AI becomes increasingly integrated into our lives, it is essential that we have a clear understanding of how it works and how decisions are made.

Despite the many benefits of AI, there are also potential risks and challenges to consider. These include concerns around privacy, security, and bias in AI systems. As we move forward into an

AI-driven future, it will be crucial to address these challenges and ensure that AI is used in ways that benefit everyone.

In the next and final section of this book, we will reflect on the insights gained throughout the book and offer thoughts on how we can adapt and thrive in an AI-driven world.

As we reflect on the insights gained throughout this book, it is clear that AI has already made significant contributions in various fields, and its potential for the future is vast. However, there are also concerns about its impact on employment, privacy, and ethics. As we embrace an AI-driven future, it is important to consider how we can adapt and thrive while also addressing these concerns.

One way to do this is to prioritize education and upskilling. As AI continues to evolve and disrupt industries, it is crucial that we equip ourselves with the skills and knowledge needed to stay relevant in the job market. This includes not only technical skills but also critical thinking, problem-solving, and creativity.

Another important consideration is the ethical use of AI. As the power and influence of AI continue to grow, it is crucial that we establish ethical guidelines and regulations to ensure that it is used for the benefit of society as a whole, rather than just for the interests of a few.

Lastly, it is essential that we approach AI with a mindset of collaboration rather than competition. Instead of viewing AI as a replacement for human labor, we can leverage its capabilities to augment our abilities and improve our work. By working together with AI, we can achieve greater efficiencies, productivity, and innovation.

In conclusion, an AI-driven future holds great promise, but it also presents significant challenges. By prioritizing education and upskilling, ensuring ethical use, and fostering a collaborative mindset, we can adapt and thrive in this new era.

As AI technology continues to evolve and become more integrated into our daily lives, it is important to consider the potential impacts and benefits it can bring. One area where AI can have a significant impact is in the preservation and revitalization of endangered languages and cultural heritage. Through machine translation and natural language processing, AI can help bridge language barriers and facilitate cross-cultural communication.

Moreover, AI can also help personalize and enhance our hobbies, such as fitness tracking and artistic expression. It can also assist in improving the quality of life for aging populations through healthcare and social support. However, there are also concerns about the impact of AI on the job market and its potential to exacerbate existing inequalities.

As we move towards an AI-driven future, it is important to approach this technology with a critical and thoughtful mindset. It is essential to consider the ethical implications and ensure that AI is developed and implemented in a way that benefits society as a whole. We must also be prepared to adapt and learn new skills in order to thrive in this rapidly changing landscape.

In this final chapter, we will reflect on the insights gained throughout the book and offer thoughts on how we can embrace and navigate an AI-driven future.

As AI becomes increasingly integrated into various aspects of society, it is important to consider the ethical implications of its use. One of the biggest concerns surrounding AI is the potential for bias and discrimination in decision-making processes. For example, if a machine learning algorithm is trained on data that is biased against certain groups of people, it may perpetuate that bias in its outputs. It is important for developers and users of AI to be aware of these issues and take steps to mitigate them.

Another ethical consideration is the potential for AI to take over jobs currently held by humans. As AI becomes more advanced, it may be able to perform certain tasks more efficiently and effectively than humans, leading to job displacement. It is important for society to have discussions and create policies on how to address this issue and ensure that workers are not left behind in the transition to an AI-driven future.

While there are certainly challenges and concerns associated with the rise of AI, there are also many potential benefits. AI has the potential to revolutionize industries, improve healthcare outcomes, and make our lives more convenient and enjoyable. It is important for us as a society to embrace these possibilities and work towards creating an AI-driven future that benefits everyone.

To do so, we must prioritize investment in AI research and development, as well as education and training programs to prepare people for the jobs of the future. We must also prioritize ethical considerations and ensure that the development and use of AI is guided by values such as fairness, accountability, and transparency.

Ultimately, the future is always uncertain, and there is no way to predict with certainty what the future of AI will look like. However, by embracing the possibilities and working together to address the challenges, we can create a future that is both exciting and sustainable.

As we continue to embrace an AI-driven future, it is important to consider the potential impact on employment and the workforce. While AI can certainly enhance and streamline certain industries and job functions, it can also lead to job displacement and a shift in the skills required for the workforce. As such, it is crucial to invest in reskilling and upskilling programs to ensure individuals are equipped with the necessary skills to thrive in this new era.

Furthermore, we must also address the ethical considerations surrounding AI. With the immense power and potential for bias in AI systems, it is crucial to ensure that they are designed and implemented in a fair and transparent manner. This involves not only diversifying the teams responsible for developing and testing these systems but also implementing strict regulations and guidelines to prevent unintended consequences.

Ultimately, the key to successfully navigating an AI-driven future is to approach it with a balanced perspective. While AI can certainly offer immense benefits in various industries and aspects of our daily lives, it is important to recognize and mitigate its potential drawbacks. By doing so, we can ensure that AI technology is used in a way that benefits us all.

As we move towards an AI-driven future, it is important to recognize the potential benefits and challenges that come with it. While AI has the potential to revolutionize various industries and improve our daily lives, it also poses ethical concerns and raises questions about job displacement and human autonomy. It is crucial that we address these challenges and ensure that the development and deployment of AI is done in a responsible and ethical manner.

One way to address these challenges is through collaboration between various stakeholders, including government, industry, and academia. It is important for policymakers to set guidelines and regulations that prioritize ethical considerations and protect the interests of society as a whole. At the same time, industry leaders should be encouraged to develop and implement AI solutions that are transparent and accountable, while also addressing the needs and concerns of the end-users.

Another key aspect of embracing an AI-driven future is ensuring that individuals have the necessary skills and education to thrive in a rapidly changing workforce. This means investing in education and training programs that equip individuals with the skills needed to adapt to the changing landscape of work and take advantage of the opportunities presented by AI.

Ultimately, embracing an AI-driven future requires a mindset shift that recognizes the potential of AI to transform our lives for the better, while also acknowledging and addressing the potential risks and challenges that come with it. By working together and prioritizing responsible and ethical AI development, we can create a future that benefits everyone.

In conclusion, the integration of AI in our daily lives is transforming the way we interact with technology and each other. From healthcare to transportation, AI is making processes more efficient, accurate, and accessible. However, with the increased reliance on AI, concerns about ethics, privacy, and employment also arise.

As we embrace an AI-driven future, it is important to prioritize ethical considerations and ensure that AI is developed and used in a way that benefits society as a whole. This includes incorporating diverse perspectives and avoiding biases in AI development, as well as addressing issues such as data privacy and security.

Furthermore, we must also consider the potential impact of AI on employment and society as a whole. It is crucial to invest in retraining and reskilling programs to ensure that individuals are not left behind by the rapid advancements in AI.

Overall, the future of AI is full of potential and possibilities. It is up to us to navigate this new landscape with mindfulness and responsibility, to ensure that the benefits of AI are shared by all and that we create a future that is inclusive and equitable.

In this book, we have explored the vast potential of artificial intelligence and its impact on various aspects of our lives. From healthcare and education to transportation and entertainment, AI is changing the way we live and work.

We have seen how AI is revolutionizing industries by increasing efficiency, reducing costs, and improving outcomes. It has the power to transform our world for the better, but it also comes with its own set of challenges and ethical considerations.

As we move forward in this AI-driven world, it is crucial to approach this technology with caution and responsibility. We must continue to question the potential consequences and unintended consequences of AI and work towards creating a world where AI serves humanity in the best possible way.

In conclusion, AI is not a replacement for human intelligence but a tool that can be used to augment and enhance it. It is up to us to ensure that AI is developed and used in a way that aligns with our values and advances our shared goals as a society.

As we conclude this book on the topic of AI, we must acknowledge the significant impact that this technology has had on our world and the potential it holds for the future. From enhancing healthcare to revolutionizing transportation, AI has transformed various aspects of our lives, offering new opportunities and challenges.

Throughout this book, we have explored the various ways in which AI is being used today and the possibilities it offers for the future. We have examined the impact of AI on industries such as finance, healthcare, education, and many more. We have discussed the ethical and societal implications of AI and the importance of ensuring that this technology is developed and used in a responsible and ethical manner.

As we move forward into an increasingly AI-driven world, it is essential that we remain informed and engaged with this technology. We must continue to explore its potential and limitations, while also ensuring that it is developed and used in a way that benefits society as a whole.

In conclusion, the possibilities of AI are both exciting and daunting. As we continue to advance this technology, we must remain mindful of its impact on our society and our future. Only by doing so can we ensure that AI is a force for good and contributes to the betterment of our world.

Summary:
We reflected on the insights gained throughout the book regarding the potential and challenges of AI. We acknowledged the transformative impact of AI on various aspects of our lives, from healthcare to education, from work to leisure. We explored the ethical and societal issues that arise from the use of AI, such as bias, privacy, and job displacement, and discussed possible solutions to address them. We also considered the opportunities that AI offers to advance sustainability, social justice, and cultural diversity.

As we move forward in an AI-driven future, it is essential to embrace a mindset of continuous learning and adaptation. We need to be proactive in shaping the development and deployment of AI to ensure that it aligns with human values and serves the common good. We must also foster multidisciplinary collaborations and dialogues to bring together diverse perspectives and expertise to tackle complex challenges. With a responsible and inclusive approach, we can harness the potential of AI to create a better world for all.

Chapter 54: Conclusion: Preparing for an AI-Infused World

As we come to the end of this book, it is clear that the potential of artificial intelligence (AI) is vast and far-reaching. From improving healthcare and enhancing education to revolutionizing transportation and changing the way we work, the impact of AI is already being felt in numerous areas of our lives.

However, with such immense power comes the responsibility to use it ethically and responsibly. The advancements in AI also raise important questions about the future of work, privacy, and societal equity. It is crucial that we examine these questions and work towards creating a future that benefits everyone.

In this concluding chapter, we will reflect on the many insights gained throughout the book and offer some thoughts on how we can best prepare for and embrace a future deeply intertwined with AI.

As we conclude this book, it's clear that AI is rapidly transforming our world, impacting almost every aspect of our lives. We've explored the vast potential of AI and how it's being used to solve some of the world's most pressing problems, from healthcare to climate change. We've also discussed the ethical and societal implications of AI and the importance of responsible development and deployment.

One of the key takeaways from this book is the need for collaboration between technology experts, policymakers, and society as a whole. To fully realize the potential of AI, we need to work together to address concerns around privacy, bias, and transparency. Additionally, we need to ensure that AI is accessible to everyone and not just a privileged few.

Another important consideration is the need for ongoing education and training. As AI continues to evolve, we need to ensure that people have the skills and knowledge to adapt to the changing job market and work effectively with AI technologies.

Overall, the future of AI is both exciting and challenging. We have the opportunity to use this technology to create a more just and equitable society, but we must also be vigilant and responsible in its development and use. It's up to all of us to ensure that AI is used for the greater good, and that it's integrated into our lives in a way that benefits us all.

In the past few decades, the world has witnessed a rapid acceleration in the development and deployment of artificial intelligence (AI) technologies. From autonomous vehicles to virtual assistants, AI is becoming increasingly integrated into our daily lives. As this trend continues, it is crucial for us to reflect on the impact that AI will have on society, and to develop strategies for ensuring that these technologies are harnessed to their full potential.

One of the most significant impacts of AI will be on the job market. While AI has the potential to automate many routine and repetitive tasks, it can also create new job opportunities in fields such as data analysis, programming, and machine learning. It is therefore essential that we prepare our workforce for these changes by investing in education and training programs that equip workers with the skills needed for these emerging fields.

Another critical consideration is the ethical implications of AI. As AI systems become more complex, it is essential to ensure that they are designed and deployed in a way that is consistent with our values and respects individual rights. This includes addressing issues such as bias in AI algorithms, ensuring that data privacy is protected, and developing frameworks for accountability and transparency in AI decision-making.

Finally, it is crucial to recognize that AI is not a panacea for all of society's problems. While AI can undoubtedly help address many of our most pressing challenges, such as climate change and healthcare, it is essential to approach these issues holistically and to recognize that AI is just one tool in our arsenal.

As we move forward into an AI-infused world, it is essential to remain thoughtful and intentional in our approach. By investing in education and training, developing ethical frameworks, and recognizing the limitations of AI, we can ensure that these technologies are leveraged to their full potential, and that they serve the greater good.

As AI continues to advance and integrate itself into various aspects of our lives, it is essential that we adapt and prepare for the changes that come with it. One of the critical steps in this process is understanding and accepting the limitations and potentials of AI technology. It is important to recognize that AI is not infallible and is only as good as the data it is trained on.

Another essential aspect is addressing the ethical considerations surrounding AI. The use of AI must be transparent, and we must be aware of the potential biases and discriminatory practices that can arise from AI algorithms. The development and implementation of AI must prioritize the protection of human rights and the promotion of social good.

Finally, it is crucial to recognize that the integration of AI into various fields and industries will require ongoing education and training. We must invest in programs that will equip individuals with the skills and knowledge necessary to work effectively with AI technology. This includes not only technical skills but also soft skills such as critical thinking, ethical decision-making, and creativity.

Overall, embracing an AI-infused world requires a multifaceted approach that considers the technical, ethical, and societal implications of AI. By acknowledging and addressing these considerations, we can ensure that AI is used to its fullest potential in improving our lives and solving some of the world's most pressing challenges.

The advancements in AI have brought about significant changes in various aspects of our lives. From healthcare to education, entertainment to social interactions, AI has revolutionized the way we live, work, and play. However, with these advancements come a number of challenges and concerns, ranging from job displacement to the ethical implications of using autonomous decision-making systems.

It is crucial that we as individuals and as a society take proactive steps to address these challenges and prepare for a future that is deeply intertwined with AI. This means investing in education and training programs to equip people with the skills needed to adapt and thrive in an AI-driven world. It also means engaging in ongoing dialogue and collaboration between stakeholders, including researchers, policymakers, industry leaders, and the public, to ensure that the development and deployment of AI aligns with our values and priorities.

In addition, we must prioritize ethical considerations when developing and deploying AI systems, including issues of bias, privacy, and transparency. By doing so, we can ensure that AI is used in ways that benefit society as a whole, rather than exacerbating existing inequalities and power imbalances.

Finally, we must embrace a mindset of continuous learning and adaptation in order to keep up with the rapidly evolving landscape of AI. This means being open to new ideas and approaches, and actively seeking out opportunities to learn and grow. By doing so, we can prepare ourselves for the exciting possibilities that lie ahead as we continue to explore the vast potential of AI.

In conclusion, the future of AI is both exciting and uncertain, with endless possibilities for positive impact as well as potential risks and challenges. It is up to us to navigate this landscape with wisdom, creativity, and a commitment to ensuring that AI serves the greater good.

In addition to the challenges and opportunities discussed in previous chapters, the integration of AI into our daily lives also raises ethical and social concerns. As AI becomes increasingly advanced and autonomous, questions arise around accountability and transparency in decision-making processes. The potential for bias and discrimination in AI algorithms must also be addressed to ensure fair and equitable outcomes.

Furthermore, there are concerns about the impact of AI on employment, as automation may lead to job displacement and the need for retraining and upskilling. This presents a challenge for both individuals and society as a whole, and requires proactive efforts to mitigate the potential negative effects of AI on the labor market.

As we move towards an AI-infused world, it is crucial to consider how we can prepare for and embrace this new reality. This involves not only addressing the technical and practical aspects of AI, but also considering the social and ethical implications. It is essential to engage in meaningful dialogue and collaboration between stakeholders, including policymakers, researchers, and the general public.

Ultimately, the integration of AI has the potential to bring about tremendous benefits to individuals and society as a whole, from improved healthcare to more efficient transportation systems. However, to realize these benefits, we must navigate the challenges and ensure that the development and deployment of AI align with our values and goals.

As we conclude this book, it is our hope that the insights gained from exploring the intersection of AI and various aspects of society will contribute to a deeper understanding of the potential and limitations of this technology, and inspire proactive efforts towards creating a future that is inclusive, equitable, and beneficial for all.

In order to prepare for and embrace a future deeply intertwined with AI, it is important to focus on education and training. This includes not only traditional academic and technical training but also the development of soft skills, such as critical thinking and adaptability. Additionally, it is important for individuals and organizations to stay informed about the latest developments and applications of AI, as well as their potential impacts on society and ethical considerations.

Another key aspect of preparing for an AI-infused world is collaboration and interdisciplinary efforts. As AI technology continues to evolve and impact different sectors, it is important for experts from various fields to come together and collaborate on solutions and approaches that can benefit society as a whole. This includes collaborations between engineers, social scientists, ethicists, and policymakers.

Finally, as AI becomes more ubiquitous in our daily lives, it is important to maintain a focus on human-centric design and ethics. This includes considerations around privacy, transparency, and accountability in the development and deployment of AI systems. It also includes the need to ensure that AI is being used in ways that benefit society as a whole and address real-world problems.

By focusing on education and training, collaboration and interdisciplinary efforts, and human-centric design and ethics, we can prepare for and embrace a future that is deeply intertwined with AI.

As we look to the future of AI, it is important to consider the potential impact it will have on society and individuals. It is clear that AI will have a significant influence on various industries and aspects of our lives, from healthcare to transportation to education.

One of the main concerns surrounding AI is the potential for job displacement as automation becomes more prevalent. However, as discussed throughout this book, AI also has the potential to create new job opportunities and enhance existing ones.

Another important consideration is the ethical implications of AI, including issues related to bias and privacy. As AI becomes more integrated into our lives, it is important to ensure that its development and deployment is ethical and inclusive.

It is also important to recognize the potential of AI in addressing some of society's greatest challenges, including climate change, healthcare access, and education inequality. By leveraging AI technologies, we can work towards creating a more sustainable and equitable future.

In order to fully embrace the potential of AI, it is important for individuals and organizations to actively engage with the technology and continue to educate themselves on its capabilities and limitations. This includes investing in AI research and development, promoting ethical AI practices, and fostering a culture of innovation and collaboration.

As we look towards the future, it is clear that AI will continue to shape our world in profound ways. By embracing its potential and working towards responsible development and deployment, we can create a future that is more efficient, equitable, and sustainable for all.

As we prepare for a future infused with AI, it's important to consider the potential impacts on various aspects of society, including the economy, education, and personal well-being. With advancements in AI technology and automation, jobs may be at risk of displacement, requiring a shift in the workforce to focus on tasks that require uniquely human skills, such as creativity and emotional intelligence.

In the field of education, AI has the potential to personalize learning experiences and provide access to education for those who may not have had it otherwise. However, it's important to consider the ethical implications of relying on AI for educational decisions, such as college admissions.

On a personal level, AI has the potential to enhance our daily lives, from optimizing healthcare to providing personalized recommendations for entertainment and shopping. However, it's important to consider the potential privacy and security risks associated with the collection and use of personal data.

As we move towards an AI-driven future, it's important to prioritize ethical considerations and ensure that the benefits of AI are accessible to all members of society, not just a select few. Collaboration between AI researchers, policymakers, and the public will be crucial in shaping the direction of AI development and ensuring a positive future for all.

In conclusion, the integration of AI in various aspects of our lives has been revolutionary, and it is evident that the technology will continue to impact our lives in ways that we could not have imagined before. We have seen how AI can help us in different sectors such as healthcare, finance, education, transportation, and entertainment, among others. Additionally, we have explored some of the ethical considerations and challenges that come with the use of AI, including bias, privacy concerns, and job displacement.

However, despite the challenges, we cannot deny the potential that AI has in enhancing and transforming our lives for the better. As we continue to innovate and push the boundaries of AI technology, it is crucial that we approach this field with caution and responsibility. This means involving diverse perspectives in the development and deployment of AI systems, establishing ethical guidelines and regulations, and continuously monitoring and evaluating the impact of AI on society.

Overall, the integration of AI in our lives is inevitable, and we must be prepared to adapt to a future that is deeply intertwined with this technology. By embracing this future and working together, we can ensure that AI continues to improve our lives while minimizing its negative impacts.

Thank you for joining me on this journey through the exciting and rapidly evolving field of artificial intelligence. Throughout this book, we have explored the many ways AI is transforming the world around us, from healthcare and education to transportation and entertainment.

As we move towards an increasingly AI-infused future, it is important to reflect on the opportunities and challenges that lie ahead. With the power to automate mundane tasks, personalize experiences, and even revolutionize entire industries, AI has the potential to enhance our lives in countless ways.

However, as with any transformative technology, AI also raises important questions around ethics, privacy, and inequality. It is up to us to ensure that we use AI in ways that benefit all members of society and address these complex issues head-on.

By embracing a future deeply intertwined with AI, we can unlock incredible possibilities and create a world that is safer, more efficient, and more equitable for all. Thank you for joining me on this journey, and I look forward to seeing what the future holds.

The final part of this book, offers a reflection on the numerous insights gained throughout the book and provides thoughts on how to prepare for and embrace a future deeply intertwined with AI.

Throughout the book, we explored various topics related to AI, including its history, current applications, and potential impact on society. We also delved into more specific areas, such as healthcare, education, and finance, to understand how AI is transforming these industries. We also examined the ethical considerations surrounding AI and the need to balance technological advancements with societal values.

We offer suggestions on how to prepare for an AI-infused world, such as continuing to invest in AI research and development, developing AI literacy and education, and promoting ethical considerations in AI decision-making. It is crucial to embrace AI as a tool for progress while being mindful of its potential limitations and challenges.

As we move forward into a world increasingly influenced by AI, it is essential to approach this technology with a mindset of curiosity and a willingness to adapt. With thoughtful consideration and collaboration, we can shape a future that maximizes the benefits of AI while mitigating its risks.

Closing notes:
It has been great to share this information with you, and I believe that you now have a much more informed understanding about AI and how it might affect the world you live in.

AI is a rapidly evolving field that has the potential to transform the world as we know it. However, it is also a complex topic that requires ongoing learning and exploration. That is why I want to invite you to continue this journey with me beyond the pages of this book.

If what you have read here interest you, and you want to get more about it be sure to follow me Karl Lillrud in social media and get the latest news in my newsletter which you can find on www.KarlLillrud.com

Join my community of like-minded individuals who are passionate about AI and the future of technology. This is where we work together to shape the future into what we want it to become, where we create new connections and opportunities together. As a member of this community, you will have access to exclusive content, resources, and events that will help you stay up-to-date on the latest trends and developments in the field.

Not only will you have access to exclusive content, but you will also have the opportunity to connect with other members who share your passion for AI. You can share your own insights and experiences, and learn from others who are working on similar projects or facing similar challenges.

We are the movement.

#AskKarl
Get personalized answers to your burning questions by simply reaching out on your favorite social media platform. All you need to do is create a post with your question and include the hashtag #AskKarl. This unique chance to receive expert guidance is completely FREE, so don't let it slip away!

Free giveaway:
But wait, there's more! We're offering an exclusive FREE giveaway just for you. I would like to offer you a free mentor session about AI or any other topic that you are interested in. This is an opportunity for us to dive deeper into the concepts covered in this book and explore how they can be applied in your life or work. To claim this offer, simply visit my website, www.KarlLillrud.com and enter the code 9xme during checkout. Or select any other of the mentor programs that intrigues you the most.

Our mentor program is part of an extensive series of programs, each carefully designed to help you gain mastery in your chosen field. Upon completion, you'll receive a diploma, and you even have the option to become a certified expert. This opportunity is not just an investment in your skills, but also in your long-term personal and professional growth.

Imagine the doors that will open for you as you acquire new knowledge and expertise under the guidance of a leading industry professional. The benefits of this program are truly unparalleled, so why wait any longer? Seize this exceptional opportunity now and embark on a transformative journey to success! Remember, the future is in your hands – don't let it slip away!

However, there is still much misunderstanding and fear surrounding this topic, fueled by media reports and misinformation.

That's why I'm calling on you to help spread the word about this book and the work that I do as a mentor and speaker. By sharing your thoughts and insights about AI with others, you can help empower more people and dispel the myths and misconceptions that are holding so many back.

But how can you spread the word effectively? Here are a few tips to get you started:

1. Share on social media: Share your thoughts about the book on social media, along with a link to purchase it. Use relevant hashtags to help others find your posts.

2. Write a review: Write a review of the book on Amazon or other online bookstores. Reviews help others discover the book and can be a powerful marketing tool.

3. Recommend to friends and family: If you found the book valuable, recommend it to your friends and family. They may be interested in learning more about AI and how it can impact their lives.

4. Organize a book club: Organize a book club with friends, family, or colleagues to discuss the book and share your thoughts and insights.

5. Reach out to influencers: Reach out to influencers in your network or in the AI community and ask if they would be interested in reviewing the book or sharing it with their followers.

6. Have me speaking at your next event, or recommend me as a speaker at an event that you plan to attend.

Remember, the more people we can reach with this message, the greater the impact we can have on shaping the future of AI and technology. Don't keep this to yourself – share what you have learned from this book with the world, and let's empower more people to embrace the opportunities that AI presents.

www.ingramcontent.com/pod-product-compliance
Lightning Source LLC
LaVergne TN
LVHW080853240726
843527LV00053B/331
* 9 7 8 9 1 8 9 2 6 7 8 0 0 *

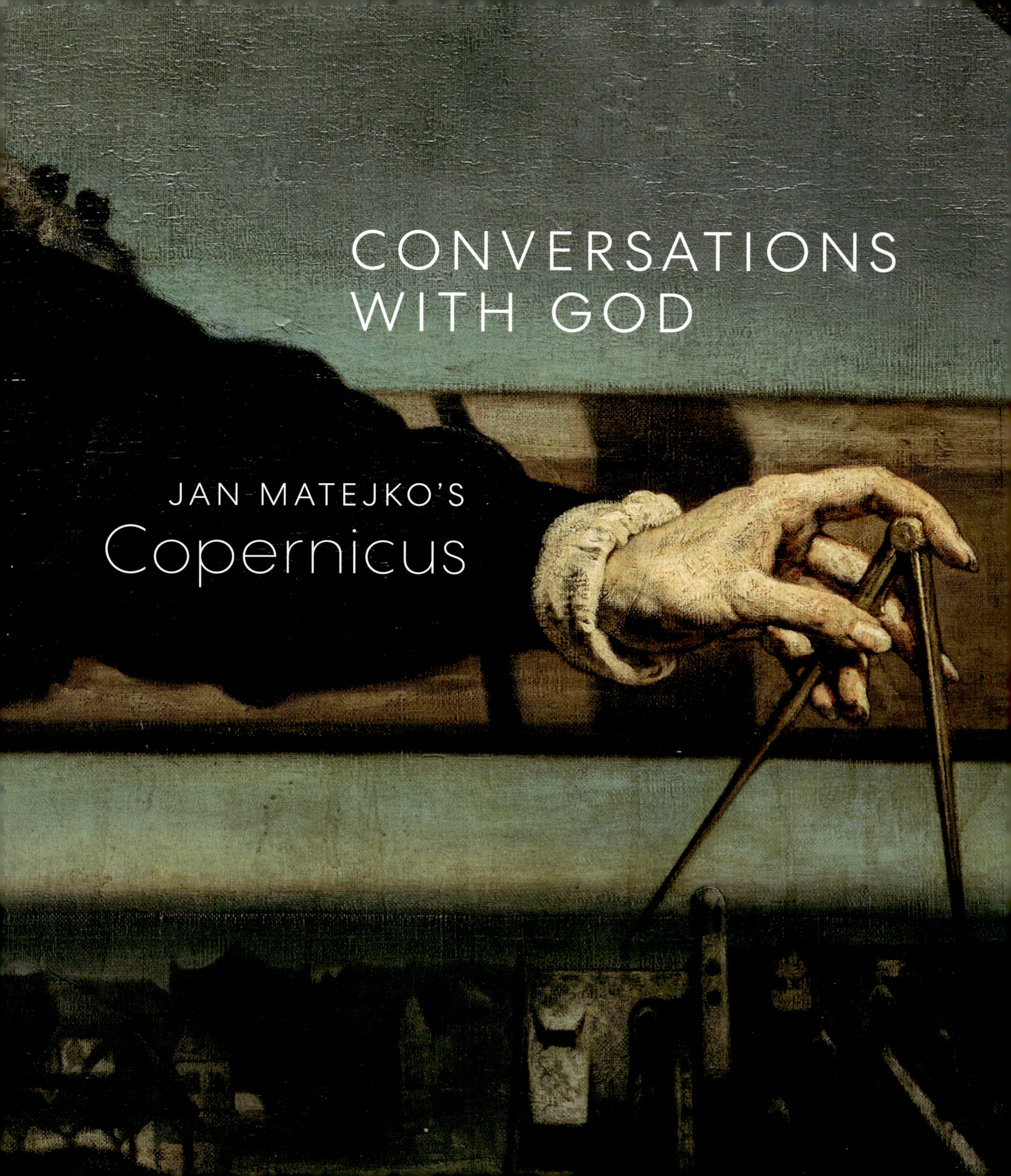
CONVERSATIONS
WITH GOD
JAN MATEJKO'S
Copernicus

Published to accompany the exhibition

CONVERSATIONS WITH GOD
JAN MATEJKO'S Copernicus

The National Gallery, London
25 March – 27 June 2021

The H J Hyams Exhibition Programme
Supported by The Capricorn Foundation

Exhibition sponsored by

Niepodległa

niepodległa | POLAND THE CENTENARY OF REGAINING INDEPENDENCE

Ministry of Culture and National Heritage of the Republic of Poland.

Exhibition supported by

POLISH CULTURAL INSTITUTE LONDON

Graham and Amanda Hutton
And other donors

This exhibition has been made possible by the provision of insurance through the Government Indemnity Scheme. The National Gallery would like to thank HM Government for providing Government Indemnity and the Department for Digital, Culture, Media and Sport and Arts Council England for arranging the indemnity.

First published in Great Britain in 2021 by
National Gallery Company Limited
St Vincent House
30 Orange Street
London WC2N 7HH

ISBN 978 1 85709 669 9

British Library Cataloguing-in-Publication Data.
Author/title: Chris Riopelle et al / Conversations with God – Copernicus by Jan Matejko
Library of Congress Control Number: 2020932698

PUBLISHER Laura Lappin
PROJECT EDITOR Caroline Bugler
PICTURE RESEARCHER Rebecca Thornton
PRODUCTION Jane Hyne
DESIGN Philip Lewis
COLOUR REPRODUCTION Alta, London
PRINTING AND BINDING Graphius, Belgium

Front cover, frontispiece and page 8:
Details from Jan Matejko, *Copernicus: Conversations with God* (cat. 3).

CONTENTS

8 Director's Foreword

10 Nicolaus Copernicus: the man who invented the solar system
OWEN GINGERICH

20 Astronomer on the Roof
CHRISTOPHER RIOPELLE

46 Copernicus and Jan Matejko: debating Polish heritage
ANDRZEJ SZCZERSKI

62 Exhibited Works

64 Acknowledgements and Photographic Credits

II. Saturnus
III. Iouis XII.
IIII. Martis bima
V Telluris cum orbe Lunari annua reuolutio.
Terra
VI. Venus nonimestris.
VII Mercurii LXXX. Dierum.
Sol.

II. Saturnus
III. Iouis. XII.
IIII. Martis bima
V. Telluris cum orbe Lunari anna reuolutio.
Terra
VI. Venus nonimestris.
VII. Mercuriu. LXXX. Dierum.
Sol.

DIRECTOR'S FOREWORD

THIS EXHIBITION CELEBRATES two illustrious Poles, Nicolaus Copernicus (1473–1543) and Jan Matejko (1838–1893). While the first is universally well known as the Renaissance astronomer who literally revolutionised our understanding of our place in the cosmos, the second remains unfamiliar today outside his native Poland despite having once enjoyed a grand European reputation.

With his treatise *De revolutionibus orbium coelestium* (On the Revolutions of the Heavenly Spheres) published in the year he died, Copernicus, a cleric at Frombork Cathedral in northern Poland, challenged the centuries-old established cosmography by demonstrating that the Earth and the planets of our system revolved around the Sun and not vice versa. The scientific, cultural and religious implications of this discovery were to prove enormous. As the 400th anniversary of his birth approached in 1873, Matejko – already Poland's foremost history painter – began planning the work that would become *Copernicus: Conversations with God*. It was to be a painting that celebrated the astronomer's genius, his Polishness and his Catholic faith and at the same time encapsulated the aspirations of a nation that had lost its country through the eighteenth-century political partitions that saw Poland carved up among Prussia, Russia and Austria.

Matejko's painting became immediately famous and was acquired in 1873 through public subscription for the Jagiellonian University in Kraków, Copernicus's own alma mater, where it presides over the assembly hall of the Collegium Novum. It is the university authorities of today who have agreed to lend the painting to the National Gallery and I want to express our gratitude to the current and former Rectors, Professor Wojciech Nowak and Professor Jacek Popiel, for their generosity. We are also grateful to the other lenders to our exhibition, the National Museum in Kraków (Jan Matejko House), and the National Maritime Museum in Greenwich for their copy of *De revolutionibus*.

This is the first time a major work by a Polish artist has been exhibited in Trafalgar Square. It is surprising perhaps to realise that there are entire and important strands of European painting that remain unrepresented in the collection of the National Gallery and special displays like this one serve to open up a broader understanding of the rich European artistic tradition of which we are the heirs. The exhibition has been devised and curated by Christopher Riopelle, the Neil Westreich Curator of Post-1800 Painting at the National Gallery, who over many years has done so much to introduce British audiences to little-known aspects of European, American and Australian painting.

Thanks are due to H.E. Arkady Rzegocki, Ambassador of the Polish Republic to the United Kingdom, and to the Polish Cultural Institute in London and its Director, Marta de Zúñiga, for supporting the exhibition. We are also grateful to the Niepodległa Programme, Graham and Amanda Hutton and other donors.

Conversations with God: Jan Matejko's Copernicus is the second exhibition in the newly established H J Hyams Exhibition Programme. Mr Hyams (1928–2015) was a property developer, an important collector and a friend of the National Gallery. The Programme is generously supported by the Capricorn Foundation.

GABRIELE FINALDI

NICOLAUS COPERNICUS: THE MAN WHO INVENTED THE SOLAR SYSTEM

OWEN GINGERICH

Nicolaus Copernicus, the father of modern astronomy, was the most famous scientist of the sixteenth century, though the word 'scientist' had not yet been invented (fig. 1). For much of his life he served his uncle (the head of the northernmost diocese in Poland) as physician, economist, treasurer and author. He was also fantastically interested in the stars, but his instruments were pretty clumsy. He did, however, have a small astronomy library. In 1502 he observed several planets, finding their positions disagreed with an almanac in his collection, but he didn't know whether his use of the table was wrong or if it was actually faulty. He argued against the common belief that the Earth was solidly fixed in the middle of the universe and proposed instead that the Sun was immovable in the middle and that the Earth went around it, along with the other planets. In other words, he devised the arrangement of the solar system much as we know it today.

Copernicus was born on 19 February 1473 in Toruń, on the Vistula Lagoon in northern Poland (fig. 2). His father died when he was just ten years old. Had he lived longer, young Nicolaus might well have followed in his footsteps and grown up to become a grain merchant. Instead, he was taken under the wing of his uncle, Lucas Watzenrode, who was making strides in

FIG. 1
Tobias Stimmer (attributed), *Copernicus*, woodblock print, 1587. The lily of the valley is a standard early Renaissance icon for a medical doctor.

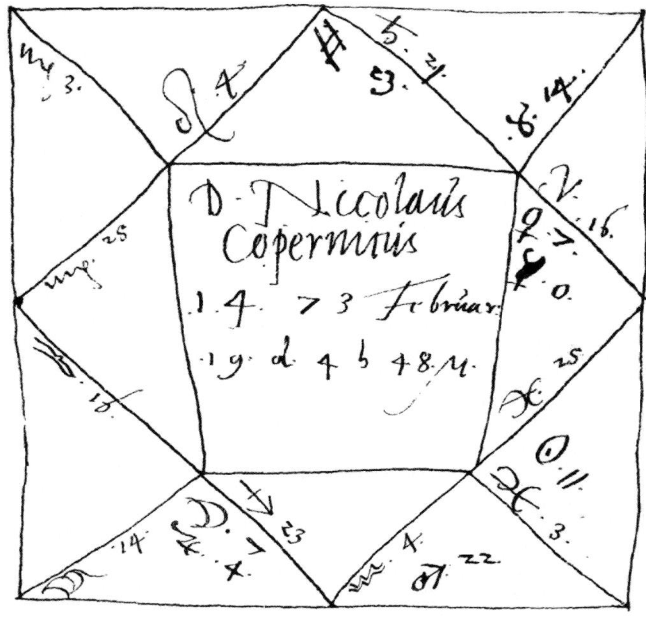

FIG. 2
Copernicus's horoscope, which establishes his birthday. Bayerisches Staatsbibliothek, Munich.

FIG. 3
Torquetum, 2008, brass, 71 × 42.3 × 56 cm, The Jagiellonian University Museum, Kraków. The torquetum measured astronomical coordinates and calculated their relationships. This is a replica of the torquetum made in 1487 by Hans Dorn that was given to the Jagiellonian University in 1493, during Copernicus's time as a student there (cat. 6).

FIG. 4
Hans Dorn, Astrolabe, Buda, 1486, brass, partially gilded, 58.8 × 45.2 × 3 cm, The Jagiellonian University Museum, Kraków. The astrolabe was used for calculating time and the position of the stars. This instrument arrived at the Jagiellonian University in 1493, while Copernicus was a student there (cat. 5).

ecclesiastical politics and was soon appointed bishop in Warmia in northern Poland. In 1491 Watzenrode was able to send his nephew to Poland's leading university, the Jagiellonian University in Kraków. Subsequently, he paid for him to enrol in a series of Italian universities. From 1496 to 1500 Copernicus studied canon law in Bologna. In 1501 it was time to study medicine in Padua, the most prestigious medical school in Italy. But because of the heavy expenses involved in actually graduating from Padua, he left after only two years. He had been given leave to study abroad on the expectation of bringing back to Poland a diploma of some sort, and in 1503 he transferred to the University of Ferrara, where he received a doctorate in canon law. This would have been intended as preparation for his future career in the Church. Copernicus's uncle had nominated him as one of the 16 cathedral canons in Frombork after a canon had died, although he did not take up his position actively until after he had finished his studies in Italy.

Where is astronomy in Copernicus's curriculum? Some evidence comes from his library. In his day, books were printed and sold unbound, and readers generally had their books bound in ways characteristic of the area where they lived. The bindings of some of the astronomy books in Copernicus's private collection show that he was already serious about astronomy during his early years of study in Kraków. Although the names of several teachers of astronomy and mathematics at the university have been established, precisely which ones instructed him is unknown (see figs 3 and 4). Later, in Bologna, Copernicus took a room in the house of the university's astronomer, Domenico Maria Novara, whose personal tutorials were far more advanced and detailed than those represented by the small calendar generally used to indoctrinate students at the start of their studies.

After Italy, Copernicus returned to northern Poland to assist his uncle with the financial accounts of the diocese, while he continued with his astronomical studies. The diocese was actually fairly small, and the farms were leased to farmers by the cathedral, so for several years collecting rents was one of Copernicus's principal duties. He lived primarily with his uncle in the bishop's palace at Lidzbark, but around 1510–12 he moved to a house in Frombork. Relationships with the Teutonic Knights, who had challenged the Polish king and sought control over the independent Hanseatic cities, were tense and in 1520 Copernicus's house was burned down. Fortunately his library and astronomical records were preserved in a study he maintained in the cathedral complex, and his wooden astronomical instruments were probably only temporarily destroyed. In later years, relations with the Teutonic Knights became more peaceful and Copernicus even travelled to the Knights' capital to prescribe medical treatment for their leader. Meanwhile, he had to juggle his schedule so as not to miss important celestial conjunctions, when pairs of planets or the Moon and a planet made a close approach to each other in the sky.

LATITVDO
AQVILONIA
QVADRANS OCCIDENTALIS
QVADRANS ORIENTALIS

The Puzzle of the Moving Planets

For centuries astronomers had noticed that five relatively brilliant celestial objects surpassed the brightness of most stars and moved slowly in their own distinctive orbits. These were the well-known planets, Mercury, Venus, Mars, Jupiter and Saturn. Besides these were two other conspicuous celestial objects that seemed better behaved in their motion but nevertheless didn't come out even at the end of a month or a year: the Sun and Moon. After thinking very hard about this arrangement, Copernicus realised that he could interchange the role of the Earth and the Sun. The Earth fitted in better as a moving planetary object, and the Sun as a fixed pivotal point, in fact as a comparatively nearby star. By rearranging the circles of the ancient geocentric system devised by Ptolemy in the second century AD, so that each planet, including the Earth, moved around the Sun, something beautiful happened. The fastest-moving planet, Mercury, revolved closest to the Sun; the slowest, lethargic Saturn, came at the outer fringe of his planetary system; and the others neatly arranged themselves according to the length of time it took to encircle the Sun. 'In no other arrangement,' Copernicus exclaimed, 'do we find such a harmonious relation between the size of the orbit and the planetary period' .

This was a radical change and too much for most people to take seriously. Indeed, too astonishing to be a comfortable idea for the majority of the largely illiterate population. It had been waiting for centuries for someone daring enough to suggest that the Earth was in motion and the Sun was fixed, but this result was not the consequence of new observations.

Copernicus was not a particularly accurate or busy observer, although he took care to observe the planets at selected critical moments to confirm the orbital periods established long before by Ptolemy. Hence we have only a few score observations from Copernicus himself and he recorded six of them – of eclipses – near the images of eclipses in a calendrical treatise that he owned – a copy of Johann Stoeffler's *Calendarium Romanum magnum* published in Oppenheim in 1518.

Soon after his education abroad Copernicus had composed a set of tables used for calculating the positions of the Sun, Moon and planets, which were geocentric in their nature (just as everyone else's tables were in those days). He presumably shared them with a few interested colleagues, but he never printed them, nor did he advertise when he finished them. Eventually they proved good practice for making the Sun-centred tables. In 1514 Copernicus wrote a preliminary prospectus for his heliocentric system, the *Commentariolus*, or 'Little Commentary', and made it available to some of his fellow astronomers in manuscript form. However, he did not rush to publish his conclusions in more detail. He knew that some of the tables made earlier needed to be upgraded, but by the late 1530s he was personally beginning to run out of steam. His reluctance to publish may have also been for fear of the criticism or scorn it might provoke. It is not clear whether

Der Buchdrucker.

Ich bin geschicket mit der preß
So ich aufftrag den Firniß reß/
So bald mein dienr den bengel zuckt/
So ist ein bogn pappyrs gedruckt.
Da durch kombt manche Kunst an tag/
Die man leichtlich bekommen mag.
Vor zeiten hat man die bücher gschribn/
Zu Meintz die Kunst ward erstlich triebn.
F iij Der

FIG. 5
Woodcut from Jost Amman's *Der Buchdrucker* (The Printer), 1568, showing printers at work on a press. Bayersiches Staatsbibliothek, Munich. The printing of *De revolutionibus* by Johannes Petreius in Nuremberg would have taken several months to complete.

he was worried about objections from fellow astronomers or from the Church, although it is interesting that he included a dedication to Pope Paul III when the book was eventually printed.

Finding a typesetter in northern Poland who could cope with technical mathematics was a serious challenge. The really appropriate printers who could handle the tables and mathematics were many miles to the west in Nuremberg, in Lutheran territory (fig. 5). Copernicus and his monastery were hard-core Roman Catholic, miles away in northern Poland. Would this disconcerting and even dangerous idea of a moving planet Earth die on a dusty shelf in the Frombork monastery where Copernicus was living? Would his discovery be ignored and even suppressed? Then, a miracle!

The Astronomical Network around 1535

Martin Luther's Protestant university was flourishing in Wittenberg in the 1530s, guided by his chief educational lieutenant, Philipp Melanchthon. When the astronomy professor died, Melanchthon saw an opportunity to strengthen the teaching of astronomy by appointing not one but two astronomers. In 1536 he took on two young recent graduates as lecturers in astronomy. Erasmus Reinhold got the senior appointment and became an erudite annotator of Copernicus's

NICOLAI COPERNICI TO RINENSIS DE REVOLVTIONI- bus orbium cœleſtium, Libri VI.

IN QVIBVS STELLARVM ET FI- XARVM ET ERRATICARVM MOTVS, EX VETE- ribus atq; recentibus obſeruationibus, reſtituit hic autor. Præterea tabulas expeditas luculentasq; addidit, ex qui- bus eoſdem motus ad quoduis tempus Mathe- matum ſtudioſus facillime calcu- lare poterit.

ITEM, DE LIBRIS REVOLVTIONVM NICOLAI Copernici Narratio prima, per M. Georgium Ioachi- mum Rheticum ad D. Ioan. Schone- rum ſcripta.

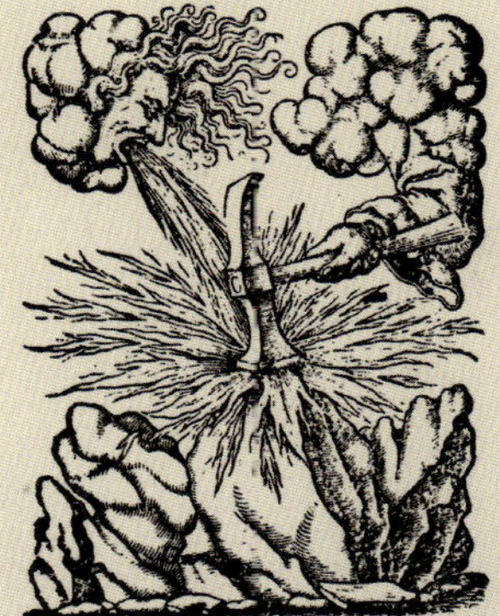

Cum Gratia & Priuilegio Cæſ. Maieſt.

BASILEAE, EX OFFICINA HENRICI PETRINA.

FIG. 6
Title page of Copernicus's *De revolutionibus orbium coelestum*, first published in 1543. Private collection.

FIG. 7
Thomas Digges's diagram of the heliocentric system, from his *A Prognostication Euerlasting* (London 1592). The English astronomer and mathematician was one of the earliest to accept the heliocentric doctrine. He included an English version of chapters 9 to 11 of Copernicus's *De revolutionibus* in his book 'so that Englishmen might not be deprived of so noble a theory', but his version of the diagram shows the stars spread out to infinity. Digges's book was very popular and came out in eight known editions between 1576 and 1626.

book after its publication in 1543. Georg Joachim Rheticus was of a different stripe. He fell in with a raucous group of young poets, and subsequently decided he had better leave town for a while. Somehow word got around concerning Copernicus's work, and Rheticus consequently journeyed all the way to Frombork, where Copernicus welcomed him, realising that young Rheticus's life would be in perpetual danger as a Protestant in Catholic territory.

Copernicus had never before had a student who so fully immersed himself. Among other things the pair examined in depth what Copernicus had accomplished. The visit stretched from a few days to weeks and months and finally to more than a year. Rheticus took a brief break in an adjacent town and wrote a thin but informative little book about what Copernicus had achieved, the *Narratio Prima* or 'First Report', which was published in Gdansk in 1540.

Finally, Rheticus was allowed to carry a manuscript copy of Copernicus's book back to the printer in Nuremberg, where the printing of *De revolutionibus orbium coelestium libri sex* (Six Books on the Revolutions of the Heavenly Spheres) was finished in the spring of 1543 (fig. 6). Back in Frombork an ageing Copernicus received a printed copy of his revolutionary contribution to astronomy, but it is unlikely that in his wildest imagination he could have anticipated that in the year 2010 an original copy of the book would sell for more than $5 million.

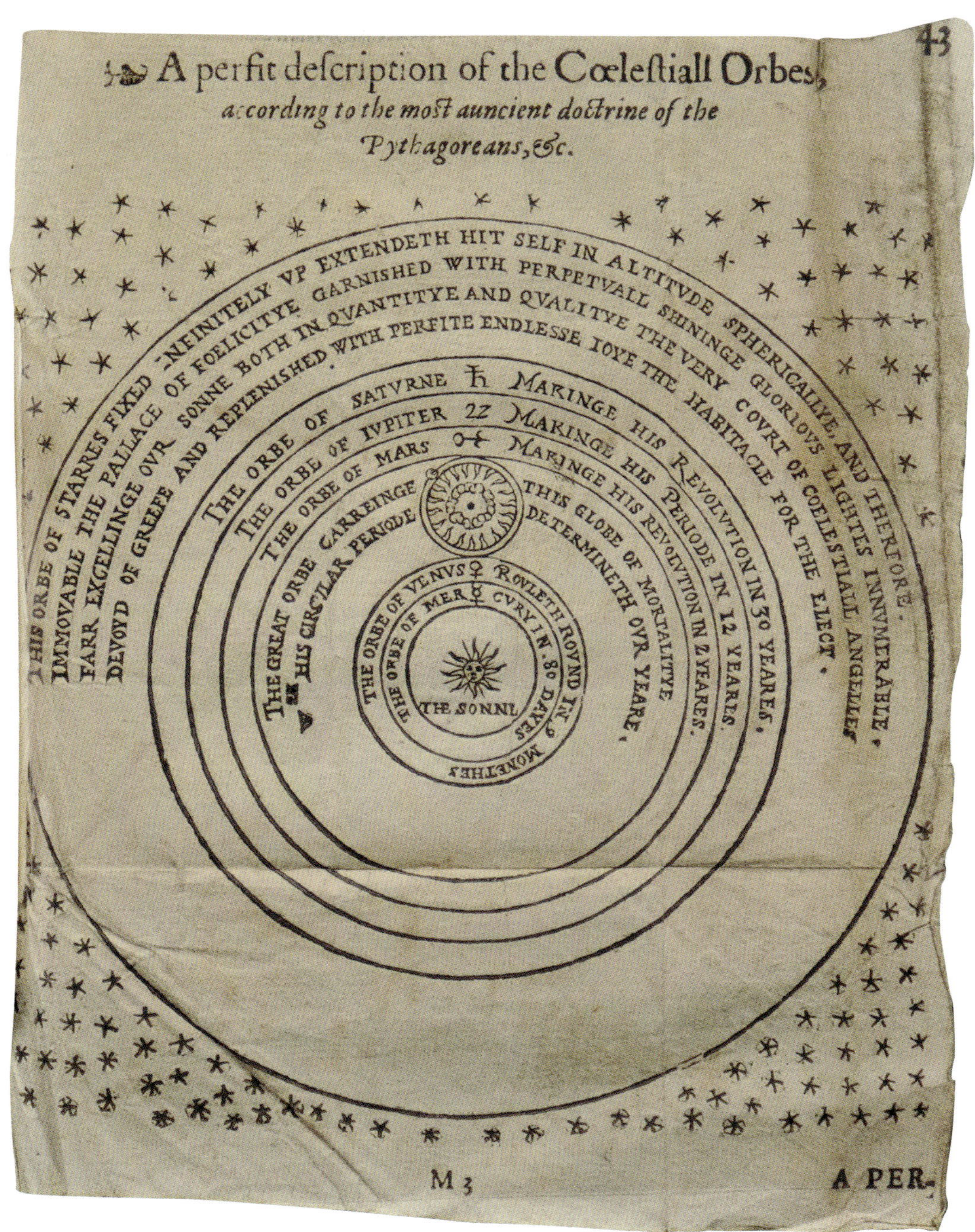
A perfit description of the Cœlestiall Orbes,
according to the most auncient doctrine of the Pythagoreans, &c.
THIS ORBE OF STARRES FIXED INFINITELY VP EXTENDETH HIT SELF IN ALTITVDE SPHERICALLYE, AND THEREFORE IMMOVABLE THE PALLACE OF FOELICITYE GARNISHED WITH PERPETVALL SHININGE GLORIOVS LIGHTES INNVMERABLE. FARR EXCELLINGE OVR SONNE BOTH IN QVANTITYE AND QVALITYE THE VERY COVRT OF COELESTIALL ANGELLES DEVOYD OF GREEFE AND REPLENISHED WITH PERFITE ENDLESSE IOYE THE HABITACLE FOR THE ELECT.
THE ORBE OF SATVRNE ♄ MAKINGE HIS REVOLVTION IN 30 YEARES.
THE ORBE OF IVPITER ♃ MAKINGE HIS PERIODE IN 12 YEARES.
THE ORBE OF MARS ♂ MAKINGE HIS REVOLVTION IN 2 YEARES.
THE GREAT ORBE CARREINGE THIS GLOBE OF MORTALITYE HIS CIRCVLAR PERIODE DETERMINETH OVR YEARE.
THE ORBE OF VENVS ♀ ROVLETH ROVND IN 9 MONETHES
THE ORBE OF MERCVRY ☿ IN 80 DAYES
THE SONNE
43
M 3
A PER-

FIG. 8 (right)
Tobias Stimmer, *Portrait of Copernicus* from the astronomical clock in Strasbourg Cathedral, 1571–4.

FIG. 9 (opposite)
Tobias Stimmer (attributed), *Portrait of Copernicus*, Toruń Town Hall.

What Did Copernicus Look Like?

After the astronomer died on 24 May 1543, following the arrival of his cosmological masterpiece, his body was interred below the floor of Frombork Cathedral. In 2005, excavations and forensic investigations revealed that a skull found near the St Cross altar was that of Copernicus. The skull shows evidence of a broken nose that seems to match the best-known portrait of him, which hangs in the Town Hall in Toruń (fig. 9). On the wonderful astronomical clock in Strasbourg Cathedral in France there is a portrait of Copernicus with a large caption proclaiming, 'A true likeness from his own self-portrait' (fig. 8). Painted by the sixteenth-century Swiss artist Tobias Stimmer in 1571–4, the portrait was based on an image sent from Poland at the time, and the caption provides our only evidence that Copernicus had made his own self portrait, perhaps only a black-and-white pencil sketch, or maybe something more elaborate. The close resemblance of the Toruń Town Hall portrait to the Stimmer painting in Strasbourg and the woodcut version in a portrait book of 1587 (fig. 1) gives some confidence that the Toruń oil painting derives from the same original source.

ASTRONOMER ON THE ROOF

CHRISTOPHER RIOPELLE

An Unexpected Admirer

I belong to you, I am even more Pole than I am God . . .
I live among you as Matejko.

FRIEDRICH NIETZSCHE (1844–1900)
Letter of January 1889 addressed 'To the Illustrious Pole'. [1]

Even in his madness, Nietzsche (fig. 11) knew the name of the greatest living Pole, although the painter Jan Matejko (1838–1893) ranked second in the philosopher's estimation as he considered himself the supreme exemplar of the race. In reality Nietzsche (1844–1900) was not a Pole, but for much of his life he claimed descent from Polish aristocrats.[2] It spared him the ignominy, as he came to see it, of more or less pure German lineage. He was delighted when, on travels abroad, strangers, perhaps appreciating the walrus moustache – even Poles! – approached to ask if he wasn't after all *un Polonais*?[3] But his supposed Polishness ran deeper. For decades Nietzsche self-identified with a string of Polish iconoclasts and innovators from which free-spirited people he felt his own purifying nihilism naturally sprang.

Matejko was the leading contemporary Pole among them (fig. 12, cat. 1). The painter was world-renowned in his lifetime, revered to the point of idolatry in Poland itself, for his depictions of decisive events in the nation's grand, sad, brave, tragic history. Some canvasses were monumental in scale, teeming with figures – a few of them famous, most anonymous – each particularised physically and psychologically and contributing in his or her own way to the unfolding story. Other paintings consisted of only a few figures, or a lone actor, in whose emotions, detailed by Matejko with the skills of a master dramatist, the meaning of great national events nonetheless could be read. As one critic trumpeted in 1864 upon

FIG. 10
Detail from Jan Matejko, *Copernicus: Conversations with God*, 1873 (cat. 3).

FIG. 11
Photograph of Friedrich Nietzsche in 1873.
Private collection.

FIG. 12
Jan Matejko, *Self Portrait*, about 1887,
oil on canvas, 24 × 23.7 cm, National Museum
in Kraków (Jan Matejko House) (cat. 1).

seeing *Stańczyk* (fig. 13), Matejko's depiction of the revered early sixteenth-century court jester slumped in dejection at a royal ball as he alone realises the peril Poland faces from Russia: 'Our history now has its painter!'[4]

Perhaps no artist of the nineteenth century has been as closely identified with one nation – not at that moment a nation in reality, its territories tragically divided up among more powerful, contending neighbours including Austria, Germany and Russia – as was Matejko with Poland. He ranked among the *Malerfürsten*, or painter-princes of the day, in a line of artists deeply implicated in the political life of their homelands. It ran from Titian to Rubens and Velázquez, and among contemporaries to the Austrian Hans Makart, the German Franz von Lenbach and the Briton Frederic, Lord Leighton. Each, like Matejko, was an avatar of national identity.[5] They all lived in grand style. They comported themselves flamboyantly. They were widely seen as exemplary among their people, oracular. On 2 September 1880 the Austrian Emperor Franz Joseph, who ruled Kraków and the surrounding areas of southern Poland, deigned to be received as one prince by another at Matejko's palatial home there.[6]

What may have drawn Nietzsche to Matejko was not so much the princely aura as the suspicion, flattering to a megalomaniac, that the famous painter had discovered him first, instinctively recognising a fellow Pole. 'I have been told,' an astonished Nietzsche informed a correspondent in April 1888, 'that my head and features appear in paintings by Matejko.'[7] They do not. The two never met. The lady of title who reported this amazing fact told Nietzsche that she had made the discovery in Vienna;[8] perhaps she had seen one of Matejko's most stirring

FIG. 13
Jan Matejko, *Stańczyk*, 1862, oil on canvas, 120 × 88 cm, National Museum, Warsaw.

FIG. 14
Jan Matejko, *The Fall of Poland*, 1866, oil on canvas, 282 × 487 cm, Royal Castle, Warsaw.

historical/allegorical masterpieces, *The Fall of Poland* of 1866 (fig. 14), in the Austrian Imperial collection from 1867 to 1920. It depicts an event that took place on 21 April 1773. The Polish patriot Tadeusz Reytan (1742–1780), on the right, has flung himself to the floor, baring his chest as if daring his political opponents to drive a dagger through it, in a doomed attempt to stop a disastrous vote leading to the partition of Poland. The burly, hirsute model for Reytan – distinctively a Pole in native costume among perfidious aristocrats in dandified French attire – does indeed bear an uncanny physical resemblance to Nietzsche, not least in the moustache. Throughout his oeuvre, Matejko often endowed 'true' Poles, the patriots, the martyrs, with just such sturdy physiognomies. Entirely coincidental it might have been, but here as far as Nietzsche was concerned a great artist was confirming on canvas that he too was a Pole. He too shared in the fate of the race. As he wrote his enigmatic note in 1889 to the (anonymous) Illustrious Pole, Nietzsche knew that no name would sound as deeply in Polish hearts as Matejko's, no validation of himself as a Pole ring truer than the artist's.

Another of Nietzsche's Polish enthusiasms was for Frédéric Chopin (1810–1849), whose music he revered. Alas, Chopin had tarried too long in France where, the philosopher tells us in *Ecce Homo*, he 'proved unable to resist the narcotics of an over-refined culture.' [9] (Nietzsche shared Matejko's suspicion of effete French ways.) Poles should stand aloof from foreign contamination, he believed, relying instead on their innate Slavic singularity and resilience even in the face of failure. Their 'political boisterousness and weakness ... like their dissipation, were more a proof to me of their talents than of the opposite.'[10]

An earlier historical figure played an even more prominent role in Nietzsche's Polish pantheon. He idolised the astronomer Nicolaus Copernicus (1473–1543) for what he held to be deeply Polish virtues: utter independence of thought and a clarity of mind that, in anticipation of Nietzsche himself, 'liberated man from the tyranny of appearance.'[11] His stunning realisation in about 1530, and against the evidence of our senses and perceptions, that the Sun stood at the centre of the planetary system while the planets revolved around it, set the cosmos into motion and decisively dislodged both the Earth and humankind from the centre of God's creation. It marked, for Nietzsche, a key turning point in history from what he called 'the pre-Copernican prison' to a newly expansive world view. As early as 1865 he wrote:

> 'The Copernican world-view has entered the bloodstream of our time. The difference between heaven and earth has fallen away ... [later remarking that self-satisfaction] certainly resisted the teachings of Copernicus because [self-satisfaction] had convention on its side.'[12]

Human self-satisfaction, however, had been decisively overthrown by a Polish cleric. Moreover, as Duncan Large has noted in his wise and witty study of the philosopher's obsession with the astronomer, 'by styling Copernicus a Pole Nietzsche was actually taking up a position in a heated debate.'[13] As Andrzej

Szczerski explains in greater detail elsewhere in these pages, the Germans were anxious to claim him as one of their own. With the unification of Germany and the rise of Prussian political and military might in the 1870s, the move was on to identify German cultural heroes who would help prove that German strength was as much of the spirit as the sword. This process, known as *Kulturkampf*, was at its height in the early 1870s under the Iron Chancellor, Otto von Bismarck.[14] Copernicus was an obvious target for assimilation. His first language may indeed have been German. An early popular introduction to his work, published in 1799, appeared in a series of books entitled *Pantheon der Deutschen*. The lodestar of German cultural achievement, Goethe himself had acclaimed his discovery of the heliocentric planetary system to be 'to my mind more important than the whole Bible.'[15]

But Copernicus was a Pole. He was born and died on historic Polish territory. He studied at Poland's greatest university, the Jagiellonian in Kraków (at that time, Kraków University). He was a faithful son of the Church, no small matter in Poland. (Goethe's praise of Copernicus at the expense of the divine word would not have gone down well there.) The Poles – Nietzsche, as we have seen, making common cause with them – would resist this further territorial annexation. They would insist on the ineffable Polishness of Copernicus and of his fearless discovery. They would prosecute the case for the cosmos operating according to Polish laws. The issue gained urgency as the 400th anniversary of Copernicus's birth approached in 1873. Who would 'own' the celebrations? It was then that Matejko took up his brushes, painting *Copernicus: Conversations with God* (fig. 15, cat. 3), an image of the astronomer as a vital, youthful cleric animated by the sacred fires of genius. He is shown considering his realisation in colloquy with the deity himself. At the same time, the painting locates the great discovery on identifiably Polish territory and unequivocally demonstrates the astronomer's abiding – indeed, renewed – faith in the God Catholic Poland had long worshipped.

After a first public exhibition in Kraków in honour of the 400th anniversary, the painting was acquired by subscription for the Jagiellonian University in 1873. As soon as a grand new building, the Collegium Novum, was completed there in 1887 it was installed.[16] It continues to hang there today, in a position privileged not only at the University but across the nation, high on the wall of the 'aula' or ceremonial assembly hall of the new building. The University's great events take place beneath the astronomer's gaze. Nearby hangs the portrait of arguably the only Pole more famous than Copernicus and just as fearless, a graduate of the same University, John Paul II. Needless to say, the Austrians raised no objections at seeing Matejko reclaim Copernicus for his people, as it served to thwart their political rival Germany in its expansionist cultural pretensions. (Only a few years earlier the Austrians had been outraged to see the Germans attempt to claim Beethoven as one of their own at the time of the centenary of his birth in 1870. To be fair, he *had* been born in Bonn.)

FIG. 15
Jan Matejko, *Copernicus: Conversations with God*, 1873, oil on canvas, 226 × 315 cm, The Jagiellonian University Museum, Kraków (cat. 3).

Copernicus: Conversations with God has been seen in the United Kingdom as recently as spring 2020, when it glancingly featured in an episode of the BBC Four television series *The Beauty of Diagrams*. The documentary was devoted to Copernicus's famous scientific diagram of the heliocentric model, first published in 1543 in his *De revolutionibus orbium coelestium* (On the Revolutions of the Heavenly Spheres), discussed elsewhere in this volume (figs 6 and 16). The presenter, the distinguished University of Oxford mathematician Marcus du Sautoy, stood on camera in front of the replica of the painting now at Frombork in Poland – scene of Copernicus's service in Holy Orders and the very site depicted in the painting itself – brilliantly explaining the significance of the diagram for the history of science. He then waved a dismissive hand at the painting behind him declaring it to be a fantasy of no discernible interest dating from the Romantic era. He declined to name the artist.

This is the context in which the original painting itself leaves the Jagiellonian University and for the first time travels to the United Kingdom, and when the remarkable Matejko is reintroduced to a British public by a work that is one of his simplest – a single figure; an unseen interlocutor – and at the same time wondrously complex. It may seem odd to invoke the strange, contradictory persona of Nietzsche by way of introduction as Matejko made his way to Copernicus entirely without the philosopher's help. With his passionate and surprising dedication to both Copernicus and Matejko, however, Nietzsche allows us to situate painter and painting not as fantasist and fantasy but

Terra
cum orbe Lunari
Sol

net, in quo terram cum orbe lunari tanquam epicyclo contineri diximus. Quinto loco Venus nono menſe reducitur. Sextum deniq; locum Mercurius tenet, octuaginta dierum ſpacio circũ currens. In medio uero omnium reſidet Sol. Quis enim in hoc

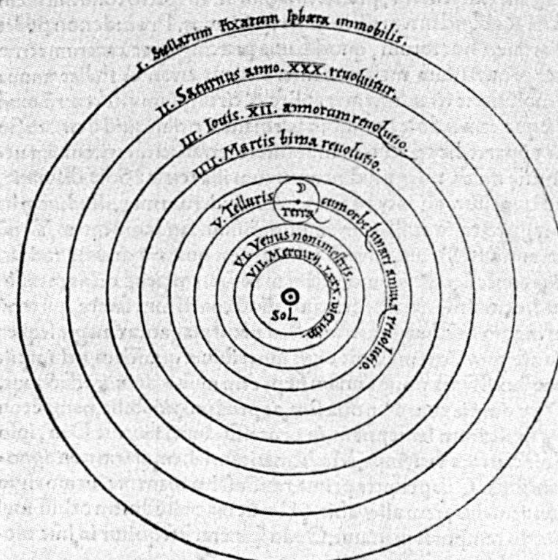

pulcherimo templo lampadem hanc in alio uel meliori loco poneret, quàm unde totum ſimul poſsit illuminare? Siquidem non inepte quidam lucernam mundi, alij mentem, alij rectorem uocant. Trimegiſtus uiſibilem Deum, Sophoclis Electra intuentẽ omnia. Ita profecto tanquam in ſolio regali Sol reſidens circum agentem gubernat Aſtrorum familiam. Tellus quoq; minime fraudatur lunari miniſterio, ſed ut Ariſtoteles de animalibus ait, maximã Luna cũ terra cognationẽ habet. Concipit interea à Sole terra, & impregnatur annuo partu. Inuenimus igitur ſub

hac

hac ordinatione admirandam mundi ſymmetriam, ac certũ harmoniæ nexum motus & magnitudinis orbium: qualis alio modo reperiri non poteſt. Hic enim licet animaduertere, nõ ſegniter contemplanti, cur maior in Ioue progreſſus & regreſſus appareat, quàm in Saturno, & minor quàm in Marte: ac rurſus maior in Venere quàm in Mercurio. Quodq; frequentior appareat in Saturno talis reciprocatio, quàm in Ioue: rarior adhuc in Marte, & in Venere, quàm in Mercurio. Præterea quòd Saturnus, Iupiter, & Mars acronycti propinquiores ſint terræ, quàm circa eorũ occultationem & apparitionem. Maxime uero Mars pernox factus magnitudine Iouem æquare uidetur, colore duntaxat rutilo diſcretus: illic autem uix inter ſecundæ magnitudinis ſtellas inuenitur, ſedula obſeruatione ſectantibus cognitus. Quæ omnia ex eadem cauſa procedunt, quæ in telluris eſt motu. Quòd autem nihil eorum apparet in fixis, immenſam illorũ arguit celſitudinem, quæ faciat etiam annui motus orbem ſiue eius imaginem ab oculis euaneſcere. Quoniã omne uiſibile longitudinem diſtantiæ habet aliquam, ultra quam non amplius ſpectatur, ut demonſtratur in Opticis. Quòd enim à ſupremo errantium Saturno ad fixarum ſphæram adhuc plurimum interſit, ſcintillantia illorum lumina demõſtrant. Quo indicio maxime diſcernuntur à planetis, quodq; inter mota & non mota, maximam oportebat eſſe differentiam. Tanta nimirum eſt diuina hæc Opt. Max. fabrica.

De triplici motu telluris demonſtratio. Cap. XI.

CVm igitur mobilitati terrenę tot tantaq; errantium ſyderum conſentiant teſtimonia, iam ipſum motum in ſumma exponemus, quatenus apparentia per ipſum tanquã hypoteſim demonſtrentur, quẽ triplicẽ omnino oportet admittere. Primum quem diximus νυχθημέρινον à Græcis uocari, diei noctiſq; circuitum proprium, circa axem telluris, ab occaſu in ortum uergentem, prout in diuerſum mundus ferri putatur, æquinoctialem circulum deſcribendo, quem nonnulli æquidialem dicunt, imitantes ſignificationem Græco

c ij rum,

FIG. 16
Copernicus's *De revolutionibus orbium coelestium* first published in 1543, open at the page showing the diagram of the heliocentric model.

in the widest possible context of political, intellectual and artistic cross-currents at play in late nineteenth-century Europe. Those currents were alive to both men. The provocative thought of Nietzsche is constantly probed and dissected today, a key point of access to the modern world he so disturbingly foretold. Matejko, on the other hand, is largely forgotten outside Poland, although a revival of interest abroad is now gaining momentum. But he was both a pioneering exponent of nationalism in art – specifically, of art as an active agent of national aspiration – and a late master of that genre of image-making central for centuries to the Western imagination, history painting.

Matejko and the Final Flowering of History Painting

Matejko was born in Kraków in 1838, the ninth of eleven children. His father was a music teacher of Czech origin, his mother of mixed Polish and German heritage. Kraków was then a Free City. As a child he witnessed both its revolutionary uprising in 1846 and two years later the siege by the Austrians that deprived it of independence. Evident early talent led to his training at the city's Academy of Fine Arts – Matejko would become its Director in 1872; today it is the Jan Matejko Academy – and then, for briefer periods in Munich in 1859 and, almost in passing, in Vienna. After only a few disappointing days in the capital of the Empire to which he owed de facto political allegiance, he returned to paint out of the family home on Floriańska Street in Kraków, where he remained for the rest of his life. (As Matejko's fortunes grew, the house expanded into an extravagant Baroque palazzo) (fig. 17). From the beginning he was obsessed by Polish history, and by rigorous historical accuracy in its depiction: he published a pioneering study *Clothing in Poland* as early as 1860. He began to collect historical objects and costumes as studio props which then often made appearances in the paintings. He sometimes exhibited such objects with the paintings themselves as mutual validation. By the mid-1860s, still in his twenties, Matejko had come to be recognised as the most prominent exponent of modern Polish history painting.

Simultaneously, he was active in revolutionary nationalist politics in Kraków, as were family members. An older brother had been forced into exile in the 1840s as a result of his political activities. Now his younger sibling, back in Kraków by 1860, moved among fellow artists and intellectuals who were similarly committed. He contributed to the uprising of January 1863 by donating funds and as a transporter of arms. (Gun running places him in the select contemporaneous company of Joseph Conrad and Arthur Rimbaud!) But his primary tool of political agitation was painting. From the beginning, his art was not meant merely to record Polish historical events, but to interpret them and to give the people the ammunition they needed in order to commit to the Polish cause. As he perceived it, the struggles for Polish freedom in the past remained alive in the present. Because past glories thrived in collective memory, because the old problems survived as well in a still-partitioned Poland, the same deep emotions could be tapped by art. In 1869

FIG. 17
Facade of Jan Matejko's house, 41 Floriańska Street, Kraków, photograph, Jan Matejko House.

Matejko would have seen and likely participated in the funeral of a beloved patriotic hero and martyr, the journalist Apollo Korzeniowski. Led by the hero's 11-year-old son Konrad – 'And a little child shall lead them' (Isaiah 11:6); biblical reference and allusion were never far away in such Polish spectacles – the funeral procession passed by Matejko's house, up Floriańska Street and through St Florian Gate towards the cemetery. A poignant demonstration of Polish fervour and political resolve, peopled by the gamut of Polish 'types,' energised by commitment to the nation, the grand, mournful cavalcade must have looked a good deal like a Matejko painting, say *The Christianisation of Poland* (fig. 18). Korzeniowski's orphaned son, by the way, soon after went to sea, returning as Joseph Conrad.[17]

Matejko's early return to Kraków after relatively brief study abroad was not the retreat to a backwater of an artist cowed by grand capitals and art world competition. On the contrary, he travelled extensively throughout his career, as far as Istanbul. (Oddly, he never visited Warsaw.) He was open to and absorbed the lessons of foreign masters. He held honorary membership of several foreign Academies. He won a gold medal at the Paris Salon in 1865. Two years later the Austrian Emperor Franz Joseph purchased *The Fall of Poland* directly from the Exposition Universelle there. France later awarded him the Legion of Honour and in 1878 yet another gold medal. (Reeling from defeat in the Franco-Prussian War and desperate to re-establish global standing, France in those years handed out honours to influential foreigners at a prodigious rate.) Matejko's return to Kraków meant that early on, as if anticipating advice Nietzsche

FIG. 18
Jan Matejko, *The Christianisation of Poland*, 1888, oil on wood, 79 × 120 cm, National Museum, Warsaw.

might have given him, he knew his great subject, knew the audience for whom he painted and knew that he needed to breathe Polish air if he were to do so.

History painting, born in Italy and France, its practice codified in academic art pedagogy of the seventeenth century, did not originally mean the record of historical events as lived by ordinary people. The most elevated of the genres – the French called it *le grand genre* – history painting was a public art, often on a monumental scale, a category of visual rhetoric. It was directed at an educated elite au fait with literature, art and the

FIG. 19
Paolo Veronese, *The Family of Darius before Alexander*, 1565–7, oil on canvas, 236.2 × 474.9 cm, National Gallery, London.

exercise of power. Subjects were often drawn from ancient history, classical mythology or the life of Christ. It dealt in archetypes and ideals, addressing weighty issues of state or faith and deriving worthy lessons from them: Paolo Veronese's *The Family of Darius before Alexander* of 1565–7 (fig. 19), for example, was meant to teach Venetian nobles that magnanimity in victory is an attribute of the wise and munificent leader, which is not a daily concern for most people. With the revolutions of the late eighteenth century in America and France, as history itself seemed to speed up and hurl itself into the future, history painters became more intrigued with actual events. In France, Jacques-Louis David was at work on his never-completed *Oath of the Tennis Court* (Musée national du Château de Versailles) and *The Death of Marat* (Royal Museums of Fine Arts, Brussels), when those key events of the French Revolution were very much on every lip. In Britain, J.M.W. Turner, pessimistic about the state of the nation in 1834, painted *The Burning of the Houses of Parliament* (Philadelphia Museum of Art) as Parliament burned. History painters were discovering topicality and with it the potential for a broad new public appeal.

It was in this context that the practice of history painting received an electric jolt of popular enthusiasm in the 1820s and 1830s through the work of the French artist Paul Delaroche (1794–1856). He understood that history was often known and popularly transmitted as anecdote. History painting could capture an audience among the people if it related such anecdotes in an intensely vivid and realistic manner, if it allowed us to experience strong emotion through them rather than merely inculcating abstract lessons. He also understood the importance of time in a painting, of choosing to depict the moment in an unfolding

FIG. 20
Paul Delaroche, *The Princes in the Tower*, 1830, oil on canvas, 181 × 215 cm, Musée du Louvre, Paris.

story most pregnant with meaning. In short, he understood how to invite the viewer into the painting as to a communal experience. An habitué of the theatre, he knew too how to marshal theatrical effects on canvas. He understood finally that an event from the past – in Delaroche's case, often from the distant English past – could powerfully evoke current social and political concerns and perhaps provoke action as well.[18]

The famous *Princes in the Tower* (fig. 20), the sensation of the Paris Salon of 1831, is a case in point. In 1483 the young Edward V and his brother, Richard, Duke of York, were imprisoned in the Tower of London by their uncle, the usurper Richard III. We join them in their bedchamber and wonder why they cower in fear. As we spot the little dog suddenly attentive to the door at left, we realise that he's heard a menacing noise; assassins in thrall to Richard III approach bearing torches. The tiny crack of light at the bottom of the door announces the boys' doom. We empathise with the vulnerable, innocent protagonists; we foresee their fate, indeed are soon to witness it. This riveting sense of immediacy – you are there! – was something new in history painting. Moreover, while this was an event from fifteenth-century London it reverberated in Paris in 1831 as well. France remembered the overthrow and execution of one king, Louis XVI, in 1793; and the overthrow of a second, Charles X, only a year before, in 1830. This was history painting of a powerfully resonant kind, seemingly unrelated to current events but in fact illuminating them. Delaroche would become hugely popular and influential across Europe largely through the distribution of prints after such paintings. This was true not least in Poland. And not least affected was Matejko. He first seems to have seen works by Delaroche in 1859 during his year of study in Munich, where Delaroche was hugely influential, but he remembered them back in Kraków.[19]

Stańczyk of 1862, mentioned above, reveals Delaroche's influence on Matejko. The clown sits in dejection at a ball given by Queen Bona in 1533; Smoleńsk has just been lost to the Russians and he alone amid the frivolity perceives the threat Poland faces from the east, as it would over and again in history. As with Delaroche, we are brought into the room up close to the principal figure; we experience the dissonance between his colourful, slightly comical jester's costume and his melancholic demeanour; our eye drifts to the right and the open door through which courtiers can be seen unheedingly enjoying themselves. (Matejko would use the same device of the half-open door, events only partially seen, in *The Fall of Poland*, fig. 14.) Poland is in danger but the great and powerful fail to recognise the true dimensions of the situation. The nation will soon be partitioned – just as it remained in 1862 – betrayed then as now by its leaders. As the *Princes in the Tower* was for Delaroche, *Stańczyk* became Matejko's first great success, the harbinger of a unique and brilliantly successful career, as much for its powerful emotional charge as for its exemplary clarity of execution and exposition.

History painting was not as moribund in the second half of the nineteenth century as is sometimes assumed. Between 1860 and 1900 exactly 2,997 history paintings were shown at the Paris Salon,[20] which remained the most famous and influential

FIG. 21
Jan Matejko, *The Sermon of Piotr Skarga*, 1864, oil on canvas, 224 × 397 cm, Royal Castle, Warsaw.

forum for the presentation of new art anywhere in the world. It is no surprise that in 1865 an ambitious Matejko chose to send a large-scale history painting to Paris. It was not enough for the Poles to appreciate him; he wanted the approbation of the world. And indeed he won a gold medal there; critics compared him favourably to Delaroche, as he surely intended. *The Sermon of Piotr Skarga* (fig. 21) is a far more densely populated image than *Stańczyk*. It shows a Jesuit priest who served as preacher to the king from 1588. Here, he harangues Poland's elite, including an indifferent King Sigismund III Vasa, shown seated in Spanish court dress. Often, Matejko signals villains, or at least the insufficiently Polish, by giving them foreign costume, tacitly accusing them of neglecting the nation's priorities. He calls on them to abandon petty squabbles and to unite in the national interest. Each of the many men in the room, carefully particularised by Matejko, reacts in his own way. Skarga in full oration at right is a firebrand, a crusader, driven by deep-felt, incantatory fervour. Will he shift the course of events? Matejko was these things himself; Skarga's sharp features in fact resemble his own, prematurely aged; will his own warnings be heeded?

Unlike Skarga, Matejko's message was addressed to ordinary men and women and not to the ruling elite. He was not seeking favour with the powerful but advancing the cause of the people. Like both Skarga and Stańczyk, he sought to assume spiritual leadership in the absence of the political leaders the people needed. He was also an influential teacher to the following generation of Polish painters, ever more so after assuming leadership of the Kraków Academy. He wanted to explain to them how he went about his work. As he told his friend and first biographer, the rector of the Jagiellonian University, Stanisław Tarnowski:

> 'The main aim of works of art of higher standard and significance ... is not the accurate depiction of a fact described in a chronicle ... A history painting ... does, indeed, concern a certain event, but it understands and creates this event independently. It explores the causes of and influences on this particular situation ... This is what I call the independent creative art ... Perhaps it is even for sure that the painting can show only one material moment of some problem, yet it should understand and portray this situation so that it expresses the *entirety* of a historical event ... only then the history painting will be truly independently created ... not ... a slavish imitation to the chronicle, but [an] independent synthesis and reconstruction of what is dispersed and scattered in chronicles ... the painter ... [becomes] a judge of the fact itself ... '[21]

This notion of synthesis, and the related idea that the artist is to come to a judgement about what he depicts, lie at the heart of Matejko's approach. They allow him to bring as many people, as many actions, as many objects into a given picture as he feels he needs to tell a complex story in a way that is far more encompassing than any single image. As with *The Fall of Poland*, the viewer learns to study all the motifs assembled on the canvas before him or her, identify the historical figures and their motivations and in the mind's eye, over time, with concentrated looking, work out not only the specific event depicted but also its deeper meaning and wider implications for Poles. Thus, Matejko slowly leads the viewer to judgement. Conversely, his system allows him, when that will prove more effective, to strip away detail, to focus in with ever greater intensity on a few, or even a single, figure(s) in whose action or emotional state the meaning of the event is encapsulated in its most intense form. Works like *Skarga* and *The Fall of Poland* are sagas, vast canvasses filled with diffuse imagery which none the less cohere; *Stańczyk* and, as we will see, *Copernicus*, are epitomes where the artist brings a laser-like focus to bear on a single, representative figure in order to draw no less monumental conclusions.

Copernicus at 400

As we have seen, the immediate impulse for Matejko to paint *Copernicus: Conversations with God* was the approaching 400th anniversary of the astronomer's birth in 1873. Elsewhere in these pages Andrzej Szczerski has described the specific Polish context including related manifestations by playwrights, scholars, artists, intellectuals and politicians in their efforts to definitively claim Copernicus for his homeland. The celebration of national genius was far from unique to Poland, however. The second half of the nineteenth century saw nations across Europe seek to enshrine geniuses, usually in the context of centennial celebrations, as exemplary embodiments of the race. Nationalism required figureheads other than kings, military heroes and political leaders. The great mind must be honoured as well; in its geniuses the 'genius' of a great nation most fully expresses itself. Inevitably, and again not only in Poland, such manifestations were or quickly became political.

In 1864 the tercentenary of William Shakespeare's birth was celebrated across Britain, but most prominently in Stratford-upon-Avon and London where competing statues went up and competing patriotic orations were delivered. Inside the Crystal Palace, a facsimile of the Bard's birthplace was built for all to tour, showing that he was just a humble English lad like us.[22] It took the French, however, to appreciate the threat implied in all this. In Paris, a production of *Hamlet* and a grand celebratory dinner for the English community were planned but for a time banned by Napoleon III as potentially seditious. *Hamlet*, after all, concerns the murder of a king, and only six years earlier in 1858 Napoleon III had been the target of the *attentat Orsini*, an assassination plot by an Italian backed by English radicals. To add insult to injury, at the banquet a chair was to be left empty at the table for the Emperor's most dangerously articulate enemy, the writer Victor Hugo exiled on Guernsey.[23]

The year 1875 saw Florence in festive mode to celebrate the 400th anniversary of the birth of Copernicus's almost exact contemporary, Michelangelo Buonarroti. Recently unified and seeking affirmation of its collective greatness, Italy needed an artistic exemplar of the Renaissance, then in the exciting process of conceptualisation by historians and art historians as Italy's greatest era of achievement since antiquity. A major exhibition brought Michelangelo's works back together from around the world. Contemporary painters and sculptors depicted scene after scene from the artist's life, every popular and uplifting anecdote from boy genius through Vittoria Colonna's paramour to hoary sage was on display for a fascinated public to peruse.[24] Auguste Rodin could not get to Florence in time for the centenary but arrived soon after, in 1876, when remnants of the celebration remained on view. The personal identification he forged at that time with the *terribilità* of Michelangelo's art subsequently shaped the course of modern sculpture.[25]

Matejko made his first compositional oil sketch for *Copernicus* in 1871 (fig. 22, cat. 2).[26] It already closely anticipates the finished, large-scale painting. Copernicus is at work atop the Tower at Frombork, the Gothic Cathedral where he served as canon rising directly behind him on the left. Just below the balustrade we catch a glimpse of the city and the Vistula. Such details render it irrefutable that we are in Poland. The upper sky is brilliantly clear and filled with stars. Copernicus works by the light of the moon. Publications and scientific instruments are scattered across the rooftop. The angled wooden structure at right is a medieval astronomical instrument, a triquetrum, or parallactic rulers, used to determine the altitudes of heavenly bodies. Copernicus had one such at Frombork. A chest at right, covered in embossed leather, came from Matejko's own collection of historical objects; it remains in his Kraków house to this day. The sketch also includes a telescope but the large-scale painting does not; Matejko subsequently learned that telescopes

had not yet been invented and so in the interests of historical accuracy the anachronism was discarded.

This raises the question of how accurate Matejko intended to be. Very much so as regards location and scholarly apparatus. As for Copernicus himself? We know that one of the models who posed for Matejko as the astronomer was the naturalist Henryk Levittoux (1822–1879) who at not quite 40 would have been more than 15 years younger in 1871 than Copernicus was around the time of his great realisation in about 1530.[27] Even with Levittoux as model, did Matejko also attempt to depict Copernicus's features as known to history? In his essay here, Owen Gingerich identifies three portraits of the astronomer from the sixteenth century, one or all of which Matejko might have seen on his travels. They include Tobias Stimmer's depiction – said to derive from an image (perhaps by Copernicus himself) that was sent from Poland – on the famous astronomical

FIG. 22
Jan Matejko, preliminary study for *Copernicus: Conversations with God*, oil on paper, 41.5 × 52.5 cm, National Museum in Kraków (Jan Matejko House) (cat. 2).

clock at Strasbourg Cathedral completed in 1574, as well as a posthumous woodcut of 1587. The most important, however, is a portrait in the Town Hall at Toruń, Poland, near Frombork on the Vistula, where Copernicus was born. It seems to show him with a broken nose as does, Gingerich points out, the skull of Copernicus himself, recently disinterred in Frombork Cathedral. The aristocratic aquiline nose of the figure in Matejko's painting, more the type of a Romantic poet or matinee idol than a battered cleric, shows no such blemish.

The scene Matejko depicts is imaginary. No contemporary witnessed or recorded Copernicus, alone on the rooftop, in communion with God. Matejko's is an art of synthesis, as he himself said. As so often in his work, the specific moment in the unfolding drama he chooses to depict is vital to the painting's broader meaning. Copernicus has already come to his momentous understanding that the Sun stands at the centre of the cosmos with the planets revolving around it. He has already drawn the famous diagram explaining it, which will appear in *De revolutionibus* published in 1543, the year of his death. There it is, far larger than it will be in the book, pinned to a board behind his raised right arm. The open books and instruments around the astronomer, not least the compasses in his left hand, suggest, however, that the discovery may have occurred only quite recently. It is still fresh, exciting, potentially dangerous.

What this means, first and foremost, is that God has not *revealed* this startling new truth to Copernicus. Events move in the opposite direction. Copernicus has come to the realisation himself and now, in faith, he offers it up to God to whom he turns in rapturous confidence of his findings. What this means further – and here the Polishness of Copernicus and the Catholic faith of Poland are central – is that there is no contradiction between Copernicus's realisation, the result of the unfettered powers of his unique and individual mind, and the workings of God's creation. God and man remain in harmony. Nothing in Copernicus's scientific investigations calls the Supreme Being into question or undermines Polish dedication to the Church of Rome. The recent BBC documentary mentioned above implied that Copernicus as a freethinker must have been working clandestinely and in secret opposition to the Church, but this is not so. Copernicus seemed to recognise no distinction between his scientific and religious work. Nor would his portrait have appeared on the astronomical clock at Strasbourg Cathedral only a few decades later if by that time the Church had taken a firm stand against heliocentrism. That would come later.

The Church did not remain tolerant of scientific innovation for long after *De revolutionibus* was published in 1543 but soon put highly effective instruments of suppression in place to *stop* the Earth from moving. In a bid to stamp out heresy, in 1559 it established the *Index Librorum Prohibitorum* (List of Forbidden Books). *De revolutionibus* was added to it in 1616; had Joshua (10:13) not asked God to stop the Sun in the sky? Therefore, the Sun moves. In 1633 the aged astronomer Galileo Galilei was forced on his knees to recant Copernican heliocentrism before the Roman Inquisition. *De revolutionibus* remained on the *Index* until 1758, 31 years after the death of Newton, and the *Index*

FIG. 23
Eugène Delacroix, *Portrait of Frédéric Chopin*, 1838, oil on canvas, 45 × 38 cm, Musée du Louvre, Paris.

survived until 1966. Perhaps the most that can be said is that Copernicus was fortunate to evade the censure of the Church militant during his lifetime.

As Matejko had learned from Delaroche, a painting could depict a historical event while addressing contemporary realities. Matejko's painting was set in the 1530s but his audience was modern-day Poland, still under foreign domination in the 1870s. To achieve his aim, Matejko set himself the difficult task of depicting the unique mind of a genius at work while in harmony with God. How to capture that inner flame fully illuminated? Delacroix senses the unique energy of Chopin (fig. 23), Paganini or George Sand and captures it with a few deft strokes in the tilt of a head or the angle of a body in inspired performance. But Delacroix was a friend of such geniuses; he observed them at close quarters, engaged with them. Matejko had no such access to Copernicus. Nor was he creating an art of private intimacy; his painting was to be a public statement. He seems instead to have relied on the more distancing and artificial strategies and conventions of the theatre.

The rooftop at Frombork is like a stage on which a youthful, handsome actor 'performs' Copernicus for us; we the viewers seem to float in front of him as audience in a darkened auditorium. (Only the year before, 1872, the cornerstone had been laid for Richard Wagner's theatre at Bayreuth where the audience would experience *Der Ring des Nibelungen* in a new manner meant to intensify the drama, seated in the dark.) And from there the work is done by the light. A strong, theatrical illumination falls on the astronomer's face from above as he lifts it towards the firmament. Another light falls in a curve across the heliocentric diagram, in such a way as to imply a spinning motion. The astronomer's outstretched hands also catch the light, casting strong shadows behind them, the right hand in particular opening in astonishment as the astronomer perceives that he is in direct communication with God. Anna Jasińska says the painting depicts 'profound ecstasy.'[28] She is surely right. As religious mystics have long testified, in the fervour of ecstasy we draw closest to God. Matejko portrays his greatest countryman and at the same time vouchsafes his fellow Poles an image of that precious state of grace.

Notes

1 These remarks on Nietzsche and Polish culture are indebted throughout to Duncan Large, 'Nietzsche and the Figure of Copernicus: Grande Fantaisie on Polish Airs.' *New Readings 2* (1996), pp. 65–87; Nietzsche's letter 'To the Illustrious Pole' is quoted p. 67.

2 Large op. cit. p. 67.

3 Quoted by Large op. cit. p. 75.

4 The Kraków critic Lucjan Siemieński is quoted in *Gallery of 19th-Century Polish Art in the Sukiennice*, Kraków 2011, p. 105.

5 The late nineteenth-century phenomenon of the prince-painter is explored in *Malerfürsten*, exh. cat., Bonn Bundeskunsthalle, 2018.

6 Marta Klak-Ambroziewicz, *The Jan Matejko House: Guide*, Kraków 2010, p. 21.

7 Letter of 10 April 1888 to Georg Brandes, quoted in Large, op. cit, p. 77.

8 According to Ronald Hayman, *Nietzsche: A Critical Life*, London 1980, p. 273, Resa von Schirnhofer, visiting Nietzsche in Nice in 1884, told the philosopher 'that the shape of his head and the growth of his moustache' reminded her of a Matejko painting seen in Vienna; cited Large, op. cit., p.87, note 26.

9 Quoted by Large, op. cit., p. 81.

10 Quoted by Large, op. cit, p. 75.

11 In 1881 Nietzsche wrote of Copernicus that he '... has been the greatest and most triumphant opponent of appearance hitherto.' Quoted by Large, op. cit., p. 73.

12 Nietzsche quoted by Large, op. cit., pp. 69 and 72.

13 Large, op. cit., p. 81.

14 Danuta Batorska, 'The Political Censorship of Jan Matejko.' *Art Journal*, Spring 1992 (vol. 51, no. 1), p. 58.

15 Goethe is quoted in Large, op. cit., 70. Nietzsche, who admired much that Goethe said about Copernicus, would not necessarily have disagreed with his assessment of the astronomer's importance in comparison to the Bible.

16 Anna Jasińska and Aleksander B. Skotnicki, *The Paintings in the Collegium Novum Assembly Hall*, Kraków 2018.

17 Korzeniowski's funeral is described in Maya Jasanoff, *The Dawn Watch: Joseph Conrad in a Global World*, London 2017, p. 43.

18 On Delaroche see Stephen Bann, *Paul Delaroche: History Painted*, London 1997; and Stephen Bann, et al., *Painting History: Delaroche and Lady Jane Grey*, exh. cat., National Gallery, London 2010.

19 Marta Klak-Ambroziewicz, op. cit. p. 6.

20 On late history painting, see Pierre Sérié, *La peinture d'histoire en France 1860–1900: La lyre ou le poignard*, Paris 2014.

21 Tarnowski's précis of Matejko's artistic philosophy is quoted in Barbara Ciciori, 'The Siemiradzki Room : Around the Academy' in *Gallery of 19th-Century Polish Art in the Sukiennice*. Kraków 2011, p. 106.

22 On the Shakespeare tercentenary see Robert Howe, '1864 – Monument or Bust!' https://www.shakespeare.org.uk/explore-shakespeare/blogs/1864-monument-or-bust/

23 On the Shakespeare tercentenary events in Paris see the report in the *New York Times* for 8 May 1864 https://www.nytimes.com/1864/05/08/archives/the-shakespeare-tercentenary.html

24 See Stefano Corsi, *Michelangelo nell'Ottocento: Il Centenario del 1875*, Milan 1994.

25 Christopher Riopelle, 'Rodin confronts Michelangelo,' in Flavio Fergonzi, et al., *Rodin and Michelangelo: A Study in Artistic Inspiration*. exh. cat., Philadelphia Museum of Art 1997, pp. 35–49.

26 The oil sketch is discussed in relation to the finished painting by Anna Jasińska in her exemplary catalogue entry on the latter in Jasińska and Skotnicki, op. cit., pp. 28–31. A second oil sketch, most recently in the collection of the late Barbara Piasecka Johnson, followed in 1872.

27 Jasińska and Skotnicki, p. 30.

28 Jasińska and Skotnicki, ibid.

COPERNICUS AND JAN MATEJKO: DEBATING POLISH HERITAGE

ANDRZEJ SZCZERSKI

On 29 October 1878 in the Wielopolski Palace in Kraków, the seat of the city authority, its president presented Jan Matejko (fig. 24) with a symbolic sceptre in acknowledgement of his exceptional contribution to art (fig. 25). The ceremony took place during the first public display of Matejko's recently finished painting, *The Battle of Grunwald*, the largest he ever created, representing the victory of the Polish-Lithuanian Commonwealth army over the Teutonic Knights in 1410. Contemporary artists all over Europe had been glorified with similar events, but this one had particular significance. The Poles lost their independent state when the country was partitioned between Russia, Prussia and Austria at the end of the eighteenth century. The process of dismemberment of the Polish-Lithuanian Commonwealth began in 1772 and ended in 1795. Russia took two thirds of the land, largely in the east and north including the territories of present-day Belarus, Latvia, Lithuania and Ukraine. Prussia took the western provinces and also the capital, Warsaw, as well as ports on the Baltic coast. Austria took the central and south-eastern regions including the cities of Kraków and Lviv. After the Napoleonic wars Russia extended its partition at the expense of Prussia and Austria, occupying Warsaw and central Poland. Until 1918 Poles lived in three different states, subject to their largely hostile policies. But as proved by the national uprisings, they never abandoned hopes of independence.

Polish artists were entrusted with the task of expressing the cultural identity of their defeated nation and sustaining hopes of regaining freedom. Since the Romantic period poetry and

FIG. 24
Photograph of Jan Matejko, 1891, National Museum in Kraków (Jan Matejko House).

literature had played a central role in this process but, largely thanks to Jan Matejko, in the second half of the nineteenth century the visual arts started to be regarded as important carriers of national sentiments and political demands. Indeed, Matejko consciously assumed the role of Polish history painter, reflecting on Poland's glorious moments as well as on those events that had led to the calamity of partitions. His theatrical compositions, carefully staged with attention both to details and the general impact on viewers, proved highly influential. Exhibited not only in Kraków, then part of Austria, but also other Polish cities in all partitions, they aroused great interest among the public and were reproduced and discussed in popular and professional publications, having almost instant appeal to the national imagination.[1]

Due to his successful presence at foreign exhibitions, especially in Paris, and the prestigious awards he received, Matejko also raised awareness and support for the Polish cause abroad. In France he won medals at the World Exhibition in Paris in 1867 and was given the Légion d'Honneur in 1870. The Austrian Emperor Franz Joseph awarded him the medal of Ritterkreuz des Franz Joseph Ordens in 1867. Matejko became a member of art academies in Paris, Vienna and Berlin, received honorary citizenships of cities in the Austrian partition such as Lviv, Przemyśl and his hometown Kraków, and other medals and distinctions were offered on various occasions to celebrate his life and work. The sceptre Matejko received in 1878 not only summarised such achievements, but also let him be seen as the *interrex*, the actual ruler of Polish minds and hearts and the symbolic king of a country which did not exist on the map of Europe (fig. 26). The title *interrex* (Latin for 'in-between kings') referred to the political custom in the Polish-Lithuanian Commonwealth whereby kings were elected by the nobility. After a sovereign's death, the electoral process began, reaching its climax during a special convocation of the Parliament (Sejm). Until the election of the new king the state was governed by the Catholic Primate of the country, known as the *interrex*. During the period of partitions, the title *interrex* began to be used in a metaphorical sense and given to spiritual leaders of the nation, who sustained hopes for independence when a rightful ruler would be elected. This tradition was reawakened after the Second World War during the Communist era, when for many the role was played by the Catholic Primate of Poland, Cardinal Stefan Wyszyński.

Matejko did not only support Polish ambitions with his paintbrush. As a young man, he illegally delivered weapons to the Polish insurgents against Russia during the January Uprising in 1863–4, and his two older brothers actively took part in the fight. As the hopes of military success failed, he chose the artistic path, which paid off. Jan Matejko remains the most popular painter in Poland, his work part of popular culture and seen in exhibitions and history textbooks, while his expressive painterly style represents for many the pinnacle of Polish artistic achievement.

Copernicus: Conversations with God has always been one of his most widely known and appreciated paintings. Painted in his

FIG. 25
Sceptre presented to Jan Matejko as Polish *interrex* in 1878, National Museum in Kraków (Jan Matejko House).

characteristic mature style, with impressive dramaturgy and meticulous rendering of details, it represents the dual character of Matejko's work. On the one hand it refers to an actual historic event and personality, on the other it offers a complex historiosophical reflection on Polish heritage.[2] The artist planned it in 1871, when he began to prepare for the 400th anniversary of Copernicus's birth in 1873. Matejko often produced paintings in conjunction with jubilee celebrations to strengthen their appeal. In the case of *Copernicus* the idea for the painting also coincided with the vehement debate about the astronomer's national identity that accompanied the 1873 celebrations. During Matejko's lifetime Germanic propaganda against Poles intensified, especially after the unification of Germany in 1871. Polish culture was represented as minor and derivative, Germans given the role of 'bearers of culture' in Poland and the whole of Eastern Europe. Such claims were to justify anti-Polish politics in the German partition and effectively exclude any hopes of Polish independence. The axiomatic claims of Copernicus belonging to the Germanic race reached a climax in the years before 1873.[3] In contrast, Poles in all partitions, but also worldwide, without any state support decided to make the case for the Polishness of Copernicus. They organised conferences, publications, plays, concerts, exhibitions and various public events to celebrate Copernicus belonging to Poland and Polish intellectual history. With his painting Matejko joined the Polish side of the dispute.

The picture accomplished the expected results. Its first public display on 20 February 1873 in the Wielopolski Palace in Kraków

FIG. 26
The country of Poland did not exist on the map of Europe in 1871. Polish territory, indicated here by a white outline, was divided between the Russian, German and Austrian Empires.

as part of the anniversary celebrations won instant acclaim, and it was also praised in the Polish press across the three partitions. Revenues from ticket sales went to charity. To boost its impact Matejko himself prepared a print after the painting and distributed it for free among pupils who visited the exhibition. They were also given explanations about Copernicus's discovery, written by the director of the Kraków University observatory. Reproductions of the painting were immediately offered to subscribers of the popular Polish weekly *Tygodnik Illustrowany*, available in all three partitions. In March, thanks to public subscription, the painting was purchased from the artist and donated to the Jagiellonian University of Kraków, Copernicus's alma mater. At the same time, the Kraków photographer Arwid Szubert made a photographic reproduction for wide distribution. In the city of Toruń, Copernicus's birthplace, then in the German partition, the reproduction immediately reached subscribers to the local Polish language newspaper *Gazeta Toruńska*. Matejko declined the offer made by the German citizens of Toruń to sell them the painting, which was planned as the main attraction during Germanic celebrations of Copernicus's anniversary. That summer Matejko presented the painting in the Austrian pavilion at the Universal World Exhibition in Vienna, where he was awarded a gold medal, so his statement about the Polishness of the astronomer also reached an international arena. The Austrian acknowledgement of Matejko resulted from the new internal policies of the Austrian Empire after 1866, which granted various nations living in its confines a certain degree of cultural autonomy in exchange for their loyalty to the Emperor. This autonomy contrasted with the politics of Germanisation of Poles in the German Empire, seen in the celebrations planned for Copernicus's 400th birthday.

The 1870s had very little in common with the late Middle Ages in terms of defining national identity. While Copernicus's parents were both German, he lived in the kingdom of Poland, initially studied at the University of Kraków and was a loyal subject of the Polish king all his life. His major work *De revolutionibus orbium coelestium*, published in Latin in Nuremberg, proved above all that he belonged to an international community of scholars and that his work had universal appeal. Yet in the eyes of Matejko and his contemporaries, the importance of presenting Copernicus as a Pole was an essential counterbalance to Germanic propaganda. He carefully crafted his painting to convey this message through its sophisticated visual qualities and its inherent theoretical consideration about the unique character of Copernicus's discovery, which made it Polish.

The presentation of the astronomer focuses as much on his personality as on the very place where the discovery took place – a cathedral in Frombork, in the region of Warmia then part of the Polish kingdom, on the Vistula Lagoon. In Matejko's time it was located in the German partition. Indirectly, Matejko hints at the river Vistula, visible in the background, known as one of the national symbols of Poland. He surrounds Copernicus with scholarly instruments, copied after specimens from the museum and library of the Jagiellonian University, where the astronomer studied. Although some of them date from the seventeenth and eighteenth centuries, because of their connection with Kraków they emphasise Copernicus's allegiance to Polish education. The astronomer's face is based on historic sources, but Matejko also modelled it on his cousin and on his friend, the physician and naturalist Henryk Levittoux from Warsaw, the brother of the famous anti-Russian insurgent Karol Levittoux.

The choice of Copernicus as a painterly subject reflected the astronomer's importance for Polish national identity, which dated back to the Romantic period. In 1831 the poet and historian Kazimierz Brodziński claimed that the Polish nation throughout its history had been a moral compass for other nations because of its dedication to Christianity, suffering in the name of ethical values for the salvation of humanity. Brodziński compared the significance of this fundamental Polish vocation to Copernicus's discovery and its impact on the world. He called Poland a 'Copernicus in the world of morality': in a world characterised by destructive national egotisms there was a need to unify around basic values, just as in Copernicus's model of the universe planets circle around the common source of fire.[4] The values that the Polish nation promoted were freedom and brotherhood between peoples, as well as the protection of the civilised world against barbarians. Brodziński further explained that Poles proved ready to suffer for these values during the period of partitions, following Christ and the Christian religion. These ideas laid the foundations for Polish messianic ideology, which greatly influenced the national imagination, including the poetry of Romantic bard Adam Mickiewicz, author of the epic *Pan Tadeusz* (1834), widely read by Matejko's generation.

For Matejko himself the national identification of Copernicus to some extent mirrored his own attitude towards Polish national identity. The artist's father Francis was Czech; as a citizen of the Austrian Empire he had moved to Kraków in his youth to work as a music teacher and until the end of his life he never spoke Polish properly. In Kraków he met his wife, Joanna Rossberg, Matejko's mother. She came from a German-Saxon family of saddlers who had settled in Kraków at the end of the eighteenth century. The ardent Catholicism of his father greatly influenced Matejko's dedication to the Catholic religion, yet his mother was Protestant. In fact his parents married twice, in the Catholic parish church and the Protestant temple in Kraków. In those circumstances the artist's choice of Polish identity must have been a considered and conscious one. His life story, however, was not unique in nineteenth-century non-existent Poland. Despite the lack of political independence, Polish culture retained its dynamism and attractiveness for many foreign nationals who had settled in the divided country during the first decades of partition. In Kraków these citizens, mostly from the Austrian Empire, often married into Polish families and became Polish patriots within one generation, assuming leading positions in the local intellectual and political elites. A symbolic figure was Józef Dietl from an Austrian-Polish family, a professor of medicine at Kraków University and a famous mayor of the city during Matejko's lifetime. The attraction of Polishness was not limited to the inhabitants of former Polish lands. In the 1880s Friedrich Nietzsche claimed that he came from a line of Polish nobles, the Niecki family. His rebellious mind, Nietzsche thought, had much in common with the rule of *liberum veto*, the historic right of any Polish noble to disobey the proceedings of parliament at any time, to single-handedly stop the current session and nullify any legislation – a legal solution unknown in the rest of Europe. Nietzsche also praised the famous Pole Copernicus for his courage to question established scholarly clichés and reinvent the world, which he saw as a unique example of *liberum veto*.[5]

The choice of becoming Polish meant embracing various aspects of Polishness from language to everyday customs, and also rights to political freedom. This attitude, based on the realities of the partitions, corresponded with the then influential writings of the French scholar Ernest Renan, who claimed that nations are spiritual entities and that belonging to them is an act of individual free will, largely grounded in culture. Renan himself was well aware of the Polish case. In 1890 as a representative of the Collège de France, he spoke at the ceremony dedicated to the memory of Adam Mickiewicz in Paris and praised the Romantic poet as a national bard. Renan particularly emphasised that Polish admiration for Mickiewicz and his works was a great lesson for the world of national idealism. He also saw it as a proclamation that a nation is a spiritual being, with a soul that cannot be tamed with the same means used to tame the body.[6]

Matejko grew up in a distinctive culture where intense patriotic emotions were often expressed in surprising ways, such as the map of the Polish-Lithuanian Commonwealth embroidered by Filipina Pełczyńska with human hair, probably her own, in 1858 (fig. 27). The map should be seen as a private statement about her love for the non-existent country, hence the use of hair, which in the mid-nineteenth century symbolised sentimental involvement, usually with another person. Instead of keeping the lock of hair of a beloved man, Pełczyńska chose the unusual fabric to memorialise a lost country she probably remembered as a child, embroidering her rivers, lakes, mountain ranges, and also railways and the dense network of cities and towns. She never finished the map because of eyesight problems, yet her work should be seen as a token of the peculiar patriotism of Poles, which enchanted foreigners.[7] In the same year that he finished *Copernicus*, Matejko, due to his Czech roots and well-known pro-Czech sympathies, was offered the post of director of the newly founded Academy of Fine Arts in Prague. He rejected the lucrative proposal, which included the offer of purchasing his works for display in Prague. In the letter he wrote declining it, he explained that while he appreciated the Czech invitation, Poland and Polish history were his love and artistic vocation.

In the midst of the nationalist struggle in the 1870s the figure of Copernicus would have resonated with Matejko's own preference for belonging to Polish culture, regardless of his ethnic origins. Interestingly, Copernicus was not the only astronomer associated with this choice. Between the 1660s and 1680s Jan Heweliusz, the author of renowned descriptions of the Moon, who came from the German-speaking merchant class in Gdańsk, received generous financial support from the Polish king John III Sobieski. Gdańsk was then part of the Polish kingdom, and Heweliusz memorialised his patron by giving Sobieski's name to a constellation he discovered in the 1680s – 'Scutum Sobiescianum' (Sobieski's Shield) (fig. 28). It was to commemorate the Polish king's victory against the Turks at the Battle of Vienna in 1683, and it was published in his posthumous treaty *Firmamentum Sobiescianum* in Gdańsk in 1690. Heweliusz, despite his global fame, still felt loyal to his Polish sovereign. Copernicus could have been regarded as even more Polish, given his service as defender of the Warmian castle of Olsztyn in the name of the Polish king Sigismund the Great against the Germanic Teutonic Order in 1521. For Matejko such stories

z Przesilenia wzroku, niedokończona robota, przez pannę Filipinę Potczyńską z

FIG. 27
Filipina Pełczyńska, Map of the Polish-Lithuanian Commonwealth with the borders from before the partitions, 1858, National Museum in Kraków.

played an important role in defining his own Polishness in cultural terms. His identification with the heritage of the Polish-Lithuanian Commonwealth was so complete that he hoped to re-establish the historic connections between all nations of the non-existent state. Matejko paid special attention to the national ambitions of Ukrainians then living in Russia and Austria, supporting their aspiration for independence, which he saw as analogous to that of the Poles.[8] His painting did not, however, focus on nationalist arguments but, as the title suggested, hinted at the crucial element in Polish cultural identity, which the artist felt strongly attached to – the Catholic religion. As artist and art critic Stanisław Witkiewicz wrote in his 1912 pioneering study of the artist, Matejko declared as a young man that 'without religion, the Catholic one, nothing can be accomplished'.[9] Although the historic Polish-Lithuanian Commonwealth that Matejko praised was a multi-confessional state, Catholicism had always played a dominant role. Its importance as a bulwark of national spirit was strengthened during the period of partitions. The artist was fascinated by Copernicus precisely because the astronomer had managed to combine scientific work with deep Catholic religiosity. Matejko did not paint a rebellious man who allegedly questioned the power of the Catholic Church and replaced God with human beings. Such claims, which were already proliferating in the sixteenth century, enjoyed the wide support of atheist and positivist scholars in Matejko's lifetime, becoming an intellectual cliché. Matejko rejected them and followed the opposite ideas

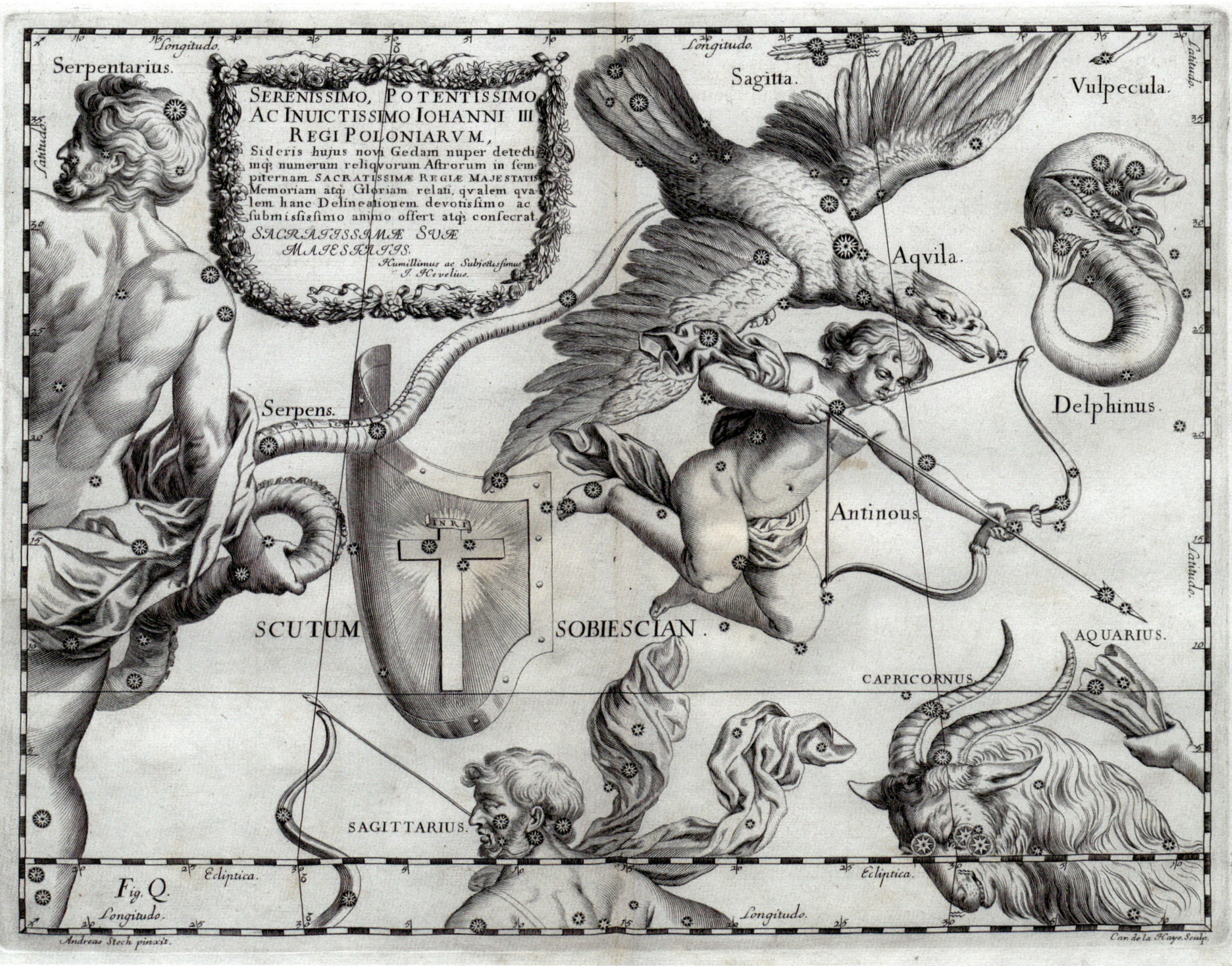

Serpentarius.
Serenissimo, Potentissimo
Ac Inuictissimo Iohanni III
Regi Poloniarum,
Sideris hujus novi Gedani nuper detecti
inq; numerum reliqvorum Astrorum in sempiternam
Sacratissimae Regiae Majestatis
Memoriam atq; Gloriam relati, qvalem qvalem
hanc Delineationem devotissimo ac
submississimo animo offert atq; consecrat
Sacratissimae Suae
Majestatis
Humillimus ac Subjectissimus
J. Hevelius.
Sagitta.
Vulpecula.
Aqvila.
Delphinus.
Serpens.
Antinous.
INRI
SCUTUM
SOBIESCIAN.
AQUARIUS.
CAPRICORNUS.
SAGITTARIUS.
Fig. Q.
Ecliptica.
Longitudo.
Latitudo.
Andreas Stech pinxit.
Car. de la Haye Sculp.

FIG. 28
Jan Heweliusz, *Firmamentum Sobiescianum, sive Urcnographia, totum Coleum Stellarum*, 1690. National Museum in Kraków.

expressed by Józef Szujski, a well-known historian of his own generation in Kraków, who exercised a decisive influence on his interpretation of Polish history. For the 1873 anniversary Szujski, who was also a playwright, wrote a play entitled 'Copernicus', which premiered in the city theatre of Kraków on 19 February, Copernicus's birthday. Most probably Szujski and Matejko worked in parallel and inspired each other, as a scene similar to that in Matejko's painting features in the play.[10] Both hailed Copernicus's Polishness and religiosity. In the play, Copernicus explains that in the middle of the night the Lord's great mystery descended upon him and all his scholarly suppositions became reality. In unique loneliness he and God together faced the truth about the universe, representing what Szujski always praised – the coexistence of humanism and Christianity.

Matejko fully endorsed this interpretation of Copernicus's discovery, emphasising the essential coexistence of human genius and God's revelation. Copernicus himself dedicated his work to Pope Paul III and wrote in the introduction that human greatness is possible only with God's help. In Matejko's painting Copernicus falls on his knees, humbling himself before God, expressing his gratitude and also acknowledging that discovery of the mysteries of the universe happens only through God's intervention and his own faith. This central message of the painting was clear to Matejko's contemporaries, such as the critic Agaton Giller, who compared Copernicus to a saint who, thanks to supreme grace, discovered the truth.[11] Matejko's devotion to Catholicism, expressed through the image of Copernicus, could also be seen as the ultimate proof of the artist's Polishness. Being Polish meant for him a particular understanding of the world where Catholicism played an exceptional role; for him Copernicus's personal contact with God had allowed him to reveal the hidden mysteries of the universe. According to this perspective there was no contradiction between faith and intellect, as often implied by scientists in Matejko's lifetime. Significantly, the idea of the mutual dependence of the 'religious' and the 'rational' continued to persist in Polish intellectual life, and a century later reappeared in the encyclical of the Polish Pope John Paul II 'Fides et Ratio', published in 1998.

Matejko returned to the figure of Copernicus in 1888, while he was working on a series of paintings entitled 'The History of Civilisation in Poland'. The astronomer features in the painting *The Influence of the University on the Country in the fifteenth century – New Tendencies – Hussitism and Humanism*, where he occupies a prominent place among the famous scholars of Kraków University gathered in the courtyard of the historic Collegium Maius (fig. 29). Copernicus holds in his right hand a model of the heliocentric universe, while his left hand points to heaven as the source of his knowledge and of God's providence, which allows the truth to be revealed. Copernicus stands here for Catholic orthodoxy against the Protestant Hussites, who questioned his discovery, representing Polish commitment to Western culture and Roman Catholicism. Matejko remained faithful to the message he had already conveyed in 1873. Copernicus spoke of universal principles, but his universalism and intellectual audacity had roots in particular features of Polish cultural heritage.

FIG. 29
Jan Matejko, *The Influence of the University on the Country in the fifteenth century – New Tendencies – Hussitism and Humanism*, 1888, National Museum, Warsaw.

Notes

1 For a catalogue of Jan Matejko's oil paintings see Katarzyna Sroczyńska (ed.), *Matejko. Obrazy olejne*. Katalog, vols 1–2, Warsaw 1993.

2 See Jarosław Krawczyk, *Matejko i Historia*, Warsaw 1990; Henryk Marek Słoczyński, *Matejko*, Wrocław 2000.

3 For a contemporary account see Jan Jędrzejewicz, *Kosmografia*, Warsaw 1886, pp. 17–20.

4 Kazimierz Brodziński, *O narodowości Polaków*, (reprinted) Warsaw 1917, p. 16.

5 Duncan Large, 'Nietzsche and the figure of Copernicus: Grande Fantaisie on Polish Airs', *New Readings*, vol. 2, 1996, pp. 65–87.

6 Konstanty Górski, 'Głosy prasy zagranicznej o obchodzie 4 lipca', *Przegląd Polski*, 1890, year XXV (July, August, September), vol. 97, pp. 219–22.

7 Joanna R. Kowalska, Map of the Polish-Lithuanian Commonwealth, in: #heritage, ed. Andrzej Szczerski, exh. cat., National Museum in Kraków 2017, p. 142.

8 Adam Świątek, *Lach serdeczny. Jan Matejko a Rusini*, Kraków 2013.

9 Stanisław Witkiewicz, *Matejko*, (II ed.) Warsaw 1912, p. 36.

10 Kazimierz Nowacki, 'W roku 1873', *Rocznik Krakowski*, vol. XLIII, Kraków 1972; pp. 121–30 and Zofia Sołtysowa, '"Kopernik"'Matejko', ibid., pp. 131–42.

11 Agaton Giller, *Polska na wystawie powszechnej w Wiedniu 1873*, Lwów 1873, vol. 2, p. 101. See also Mieczysław Treter, *Matejko: osobowość artysty, twórczość, forma i styl*, Lwów 1939, p. 300–5.

GORGONIS ƒ CASSEPIE
CAVDA·LEONIS
SPICA
PES CORVI
ALA·CORVI
CRATER
CAPVT·HERCVLIS·CORONA
NARES·PEGASI·DELHIN
CAPVT·HIDRE
PROCHION
SIRIVS
LEPVS
PES·CANIS
PRORA·NAVIS
BELLATRIX
GEMINI
CANCER
LEO
VIRGO
LIBRA
SCORPIO
ARIES
PISCES
MARCIVS
FEBRVARIVS
IANVARIVS
AQVARIVS
DECEMBER
RECTE
VERSE
VMBRE
LATVS

EXHIBITED WORKS

CAT. 1

Jan Matejko

Self Portrait, about 1887

Oil on canvas, 24 × 23.7 cm
National Museum in Kraków
(Jan Matejko House)

PROVENANCE

Purchased by the Jan Matejko House in 1962

This intimate image of the aging artist dates to the year *Copernicus: Conversations with God* was installed in the Collegium Novum at the Jagiellonian University, when Matejko was also awarded an honorary doctoral degree by the institution. It was the model for a full-length seated self portrait completed in 1892 (National Museum, Warsaw).

CAT. 2

Jan Matejko

Preliminary study for The Astronomer Copernicus: Conversations with God, 1871

Oil on paper, 41.5 × 52.5 cm
National Museum in Kraków
(Jan Matejko House)

PROVENANCE

Purchased by the Jan Matejko House in 1960

This is the earliest of two preparatory studies for the large painting, freer and more loosely painted than the final work of 1873. The second such study, from 1872, was most recently in the collection of the renowned Polish-born collector Barbara Piasecka Johnson. Such small-scale oils by Matejko are gaining increasing admiration. The first word of the painting's subtitle is variously translated in the singular and the plural. We have opted for 'Conversations'.

CAT. 3

Jan Matejko

The Astronomer Copernicus: Conversations with God, 1873

Oil on canvas, 226 × 315 cm
The Jagiellonian University Museum, Kraków

PROVENANCE

Painting completed in 1873; purchased by the Kraków public for 12,000 Polish zloty in March 1873, and donated to the Jagiellonian University.

This image of the archetypal Polish genius in ecstatic conversation with God has been famous in Poland since first shown in Kraków in 1873. Painted on speculation in anticipation of the 400th anniversary of the great astronomer's birth, it soon found its way by public subscription to the Jagiellonian University where Copernicus himself had been a student in the late fifteenth century.

CAT. 4

Nicolaus Copernicus

De revolutionibus orbium coelestium, 1543

Paper, 28 × 20 × 5 cm
National Maritime Museum, Greenwich

PROVENANCE

Almost certainly bought for the Royal Observatory Greenwich by the Astronomer Royal, George Biddell Airy (1801–1892), in 1838 from Samuel Maynard, bookseller, of 8 Earl's Court, Cranbourn Street, Leicester Square, London; transferred to the National Maritime Museum in 1999.

Published in Nuremberg in the year Copernicus died, its findings only slowly filtered into the wider world, decisively dislocating the earth and humankind from the centre of God's creation. It is open here to its most famous image, the heliocentric model, showing the planets revolving around a stationary Sun, or Sol; the volume is written in Latin, the scientific language of the day.

CAT. 5

Hans Dorn

Astrolabe, Buda, 1486

Brass, partially gilded
58.8 × 45.2 × 3 cm
The Jagiellonian University Museum, Kraków

PROVENANCE

Bequeathed by Professor Marcin Bylica in 1493.

Used for calculating time and the position of the Sun and stars, this astrolabe was one of three exquisite astronomical instruments bequeathed to the Jagiellonian University in 1493 by their owner, the Polish astronomer Marcin Bylica (about 1433–1493). It would have arrived at what was then Kraków University while Copernicus himself was a student there between 1491 and 1495.

CAT. 6

Torquetum

Brass, 71 × 42.3 × 56 cm, 18.8 kg
The Jagiellonian University Museum, Kraków

PROVENANCE

Replica of the torquetum bequeathed by Professor Marcin Bylica in 1493, commissioned by the Jagiellonian University Museum in 2008.

The torquetum measures astronomical coordinates and calculates their relationships. The original of this instrument was also bequeathed by Marcin Bylica and arrived in Kraków in 1493, when the university was emerging as an important European centre for mathematics and astronomy. This replica was commissioned by the Jagiellonian University Museum in 2008 for display purposes.

ACKNOWLEDGEMENTS

The exhibition curator wishes to thank Polish friends and colleagues, beginning with Marta de Zúñiga, Director of the Polish Cultural Institute, London, who wholeheartedly supported the project from the beginning and made so many crucial introductions on behalf of the National Gallery; Professor Krzysztof Stopka, Director, Anna Jasińska, Curator of the Paintings Department, and Jolanta Pollesch, Head of Conservation, Jagiellonian University Museum, Kraków; Andrzej Betlef, former Director of the National Museum in Kraków; Agnieszka Zagrajek, Manager, Jan Matejko House, Kraków; Zofia Machnicka, Adam Mickiewicz Institute, Warsaw; and Natalia Puchalska at the Polish Cultural Institute, London. In London as well the good advice of Sian Prosser, Librarian and Archivist, Royal Astronomical Society, has been invaluable.

PHOTOGRAPHIC CREDITS

KANSAS CITY

Linda Hall Library, Kansas City. Courtesy of The Linda Hall Library of Science, Engineering & Technology: fig. 7.

KRAKÓW

The Jagiellonian University Museum, Kraków. Photo by Grzegorz Zygier: figs 3, 4, 10, 15.
Jan Matejko House, National Museum in Kraków. Laboratory Stock National Museum in Kraków: figs 12, 17, 22, 24, 25.
National Museum in Kraków. Laboratory Stock National Museum in Kraków: figs 27, 28.

LONDON

© akg-images: fig. 1. © akg-images / WHA / World History Archive: fig. 16.
Bridgeman Art Library, London © Granger / Bridgeman Images: fig. 5.
© Bridgeman Images: figs 6, 11.
Martin Lubikowski: fig. 26.
© The National Gallery, London: fig. 19.

MUNICH

Munich, Bayerische Staatsbibliothek Clm 27003 fol. 33v: fig. 2.

PARIS

Musée du Louvre, Paris © RMN-Grand Palais (musée du Louvre) / René-Gabriel Ojéda: fig. 20. Photo © RMN-Grand Palais (musée du Louvre) / Michel Urtado: fig. 23.

STRASBOURG

Fondation de l'œuvre Notre-Dame, Strasbourg © Photo Scala Florence/ Heritage Images: fig. 8.

TORUŃ

Toruń Town Hall © Photo Josse/Scala, Florence: fig. 9.

WARSAW

The Royal Castle, Warsaw / Photo Andrzej Ring, Lech Sandzewicz. (inv. no. ZKW/1048): fig. 14. (inv. no. ZKW/2048): fig. 21.
Collection of National Museum, Warsaw. Krzysztof Wilczyński/NMW: figs 13, 18. Piotr Ligier/NMW: fig. 29.